Byron, Shelley, Hunt,
and *The Liberal*

BYRON, SHELLEY, HUNT, AND *THE LIBERAL*

by

William H. Marshall

UNIVERSITY OF PENNSYLVANIA PRESS
Philadelphia

135486

Printed in Great Britain by
Strangeways Press, Ltd., London
One of the Billing Group of Companies

For Shirl

Preface

THE MATERIALS WHICH TELL THE STORY OF *THE LIBERAL* HAVE not previously been brought together. Some of them are to be found among the manuscripts in certain of the libraries in this country and in Great Britain; others are in the numerous periodicals current in 1822 and 1823; many are scattered through various published works, particularly those editions of letters and journals which have appeared during the last sixty years. There have been two attempts to treat the subject. Leslie Pickering left much to be desired in his brief, undated book, *Lord Byron, Leigh Hunt and the "Liberal."* In 1882, James Ashcroft Noble was clearly restricted by the limited scope of available materials when he wrote "Leigh Hunt, Lord Byron and 'The Liberal,' " an article which has remained unpublished.

Many writers have made reference to *The Liberal*. Certainly all who have written about Byron, Shelley, or Leigh Hunt during this period have been obliged to do so. Some have written in a perfunctory manner, dismissing as insignificant the periodical and even the association of literary figures which its existence brought about. Others have attempted to explore the episode somewhat more thoroughly, though without giving it sufficiently extensive treatment. In all too many of these cases, the writers have reflected the conflict which began in 1828 when Leigh Hunt published his *Lord Byron and Some of His*

Contemporaries; each has become an apologist for either Byron or Hunt, and, as such, has tended to lose perspective. When I began my study of *The Liberal*, I tried to approach my materials with objectivity, particularly in regard to this conflict, whether Byron or Hunt should be given blame for the outcome of the episode, for it seemed, even then, that here lay most of the pitfalls. My study has confirmed my vague suspicion that the shortcomings of one of the literary partners simply stimulated the faults of the other, and those writers who have tried to place blame directly on Byron or on Hunt have failed to understand properly the human and therefore complicated situation which existed at Pisa and Genoa in 1822 and 1823.

I have also tried to avoid the dangers which sometimes result from an indiscriminate mixture of history and criticism. The following is primarily a history, written upon the firm assumption that the episode studied is of fundamental significance in understanding those participating in it, who were themselves major literary figures of the early nineteenth century. I have attempted to give brief summaries of the articles in *The Liberal*, with seemingly essential observations, but I have consistently recognized that no amount of comment in this direction can substitute for the work itself.

I wish to express my very deep gratitude to Professor Frederick L. Jones of the University of Pennsylvania, who has always been extremely helpful and encouraging in the face of all problems. The members of the Reference Department and Mrs. D. O. Richardson, Interlibrary Loan Librarian, of the University of Pennsylvania Library have constantly been cheerful and resourceful in handling my many requests. Mr. Ralph Brown and his staff at B. F. Stevens and Brown of London have gone to great lengths to procure scarce items in various parts of Great Britain. There are those who have made it possible for me to use the facilities or materials of certain libraries in this country and in England—the Library of

Congress, the New York Public Library, the New York Historical Society, the Pierpont Morgan Library, the Library Company of Philadelphia, the Libraries of the State University of Iowa, the Duke University Library, the University of Texas Library, Yale University Library, Columbia University Library, the British Museum, the Bodleian Library, and the Manchester Public Library.

Finally, there are my wife and our daughters, whose assistance has been inestimable.

W. H. M.

Cynwyd, Pennsylvania
August 1959

Contents

Byron, Shelley, Hunt,
and *The Liberal*

I

Byron, Shelley, and Hunt:

1813-21

§ *i*

ON AUGUST 26, 1821, PERCY BYSSHE SHELLEY WROTE FROM
Pisa to Leigh Hunt in London. Since his last letter, Shelley
reported, he had been to Ravenna to visit Lord Byron. One
result of his journey was Byron's decision to come to Pisa to
live. More important than this, however, was Byron's proposal,
which Shelley was to convey to Hunt, "that you should come
out and go shares with him and me in a periodical work, to be
conducted here; in which each of the contracting parties
should publish all their original compositions, and share the
profits."[1] The idea was not new with Byron, for, on December
25, 1820, he had first made a similar suggestion to Thomas Moore
"in case we both get to London again."[2] A literary alliance with
Moore was impractical then, but the idea remained with Byron
at the time of Shelley's visit. Leigh Hunt seemed suitable as a
participant in the venture, and the proposal was made which
was to find reality in the four issues of *The Liberal, Verse and
Prose from the South*, appearing from October, 1822, to July, 1823.

---

[1] *The Complete Works of Percy Bysshe Shelley*, ed. Roger Ingpen and Walter E.
Peck (10 vols.; London, 1926-30), X, 318—hereafter referred to as *Works*.
[2] *The Works of Lord Byron: Letters and Journals*, ed. Rowland E. Prothero (6 vols.;
London, 1898-1901), V, 143, 214, 215, 309, 319, 336—hereafter referred to as *L.
& J.* The other series of this edition, *The Works of Lord Byron: Poetry*, ed. E. H.
Coleridge (7 vols.; London, 1898-1903), will be referred to hereafter as *Poetry*.

Leigh Hunt first saw Lord Byron in 1809 while Byron was swimming in the Thames "under the auspices of Mr. Jackson, the prize-fighter." Since Byron impressed Hunt merely as "a young man who, like myself, had written a bad volume of poems," Hunt felt no desire to become acquainted and left the scene unobserved.[3] Actual acquaintance began four years later, on May 20, 1813, under the sponsorship of Thomas Moore, who had known Hunt, primarily as a fellow literary man, since 1811. Leigh Hunt and his brother John, as editor and publisher of *The Examiner*, were serving their two-year sentences for the supposed libel of the Prince Regent, which had appeared in their newspaper on March 22, 1812.[4] Byron shared Moore's sympathy with the Hunts and became particularly interested by Moore's description of Leigh Hunt's life and surroundings in prison—"his trellised flower-garden without, and his books, busts, pictures, and pianoforte within"— and asked that Moore arrange a meeting.[5] When Moore carried Byron's request to Hunt, he mentioned Byron's admiration for "The Feast of the Poets,"[6] and shortly thereafter he

---

[3] *The Autobiography of Leigh Hunt*, ed. J. E. Morpurgo (London, 1949), pp. 313-14.

[4] *The Examiner*, No. 221 (March 22, 1812), p. 179. On December 9, 1812, the Hunts were convicted, and on February 3, 1813, they were sentenced to pay fines of £500 each and "to be each imprisoned for the space of two years,—the defendant John Hunt in Coldbath-fields prison, and the defendant Leigh Hunt in his Majesty's gaol for the county of Surrey, situate in Horsemonger-lane, Southwark" (*The Times*, No. 8,827 [February 4, 1813], p. 3).

[5] Thomas Moore, *The Letters and Journals of Lord Byron* (2 vols.; Philadelphia, 1840), I, 313—hereafter referred to as Moore, *Byron*.

[6] Hunt, *Autobiography*, p. 314. In a letter to Hunt, dated February 9, 1814, Byron wrote that Hunt's "The Feast of the Poets" was "the best 'Session' we have, and with a more difficult subject, for we are neither so good nor so bad (taking the best and worst) as the wits of the olden time" (*L. & J.*, III, 28). "The Feast of the Poets" was first published in *The Reflector*, No. 4 (1811), pp. 400-404. It was reprinted twice during Byron's life, in 1814 and 1815. In 1814, there was only a note devoted to Byron, in which he was described as a poet of great promise, but in the edition of 1815, a passage (11. 224-58) was given to him, in which Apollo praised Byron but at the same time suggested that he should not always indulge his "misanthropy."

wrote to Byron that they were expected by Leigh Hunt on May 20.[7] The meeting was probably brief, but on Sunday, May 23, Byron came alone to visit Hunt, and the impression he made was extremely favorable. His manner was "very frank, unceremonious," and when he gave Hunt a book of Italian travels, needed at this time for *Rimini*, he displayed "the air of one who did not seem to think himself conferring the least obligation." Hunt decided that not only friendship but a strong similarity existed between himself and Byron. "I think we were cut out of the same piece, only a different wear may have altered our respective naps a little."[8] Byron's "wear" had been somewhat detrimental to the underlying good impulses, but this was the greater reason to encourage friendship. "Perhaps a friend, if we grow intimate, of a taste like his own and full of quite as much excitability, but luckily induced to more philosophic habits by the nature of circumstances," Hunt wrote to his wife Marianne, who remained somewhat skeptical, "may be able to render his heart and his understanding a service, and help to lead him off into enjoyments more congenial with both."[9]

In late May or early June, Hunt invited Byron and Moore to a dinner party which was to take place on June 11.[10] Although Moore recalled fifteen years later that the event had been "if

---

[7] Inferred from Byron's reply of May 19, 1813 (*L. & J.*, II, 204-5):

> But now to my letter—to *yours* 'tis an answer—
> To-morrow be with me, as soon as you can, sir,
> All ready and dress'd for proceeding to spunge on
> (According to compact) the wit in the dungeon.

[8] Leigh Hunt to Marianne Hunt, May 25, 1813 (*The Correspondence of Leigh Hunt*, ed. Thornton Hunt [2 vols.; London, 1862], I, 88—hereafter referred to as Hunt, *Corr.*). Hunt also recalled of Byron's visits: "He used to bring books for the *Story of Rimini*, which I was then writing. He would not let the footman bring them in. He would enter with a couple of quartos under his arm; and give you to understand that he was prouder of being a friend and a man of letters, than a lord" (*Autobiography*, p. 314).

[9] Leigh Hunt to Marianne Hunt, May 28, 1813 (Louis Landré, *Leigh Hunt* [2 vols.; Paris, 1935-36], I, 77).

[10] Leigh Hunt to Marianne Hunt, June 5, 1813 (Hunt, *Corr.*, I, 90).

not agreeable, at least novel and odd,"[11] there is no evidence that Byron found the day unpleasant. It is true that this was probably Byron's last contact with Hunt for some months, but in December, 1813, Byron was placing blame for the interruption on "the rapid succession of adventure, since last summer, added to some serious uneasiness and business." He resolved to see Hunt again, for "he is a man worth knowing; and though, for his own sake, I wish him out of prison, I like to study character in such situations." The character in this case seemed to be particularly interesting, "not exactly of the present age. He reminds me more of Pym and Hampden times—much talent, great independence of spirit, and an austere, yet not repulsive, aspect." Though "the bigot of virtue," Hunt was "a valuable man, and less vain than success and even the consciousness of preferring 'the right to the expedient' might excuse."[12] On December 2, Byron wrote to Hunt that he intended to visit him in two days. "It is my wish that our acquaintance or, if you please to accept it, friendship, may be permanent. I have been lucky enough to preserve some friends from a very early period, and I hope, as I do not (at least now) select them lightly, I shall not lose them capriciously." Hunt replied the same day with an invitation to luncheon on the approaching Saturday.[13]

The letters between Byron and Hunt in the year 1814 reveal little of their relationship except its cordiality. Hunt for the first time omitted Byron's title in the salutation—"My dear Byron, (to fall in with your very kind and acceptable mode of addressing me)."[14] He was to do this in the dedicatory letter to *Rimini*, by which he was unknowingly to cause an unfortunate reaction that was to be felt most acutely years later at the time of *The Liberal*. But for the moment, there was no irritation.

---

[11] Moore, *Byron*, II, 313.
[12] Byron's journal, December 1, 1813 (*L. & J.*, II, 357-58).
[13] *Ibid.*, II, 296-97.
[14] Hunt to Byron, April 2, 1814 (*Ibid.*, III, 416).

In 1815, the correspondence between Byron and Hunt appears to have become more frequent. Although the letters primarily reveal the interests in literature and criticism which the two men shared, they are at times rather personal. *The Examiner* began to devote more space to Byron than it had previously done. On January 1, 1815, there appeared an announcement that Byron had left London to be married.[15] During the year, three of Byron's poems were published in the newspaper's pages.[16] And on August 20, there was a brief but favorable mention of an edition of Byron's *Works* just published.[17]

Much of this can be attributed to the fact that the Hunt brothers were released from their respective prisons on February 3, 1815. Leigh, in a rather bad state of health, went to live temporarily with his brother John on Edgeware Road, where Byron now came rather frequently to visit him. He played with the children, sometimes riding Thornton Hunt's rocking horse "with a childish glee becoming a poet." Yet the visits did not come to include the families. Lady Byron would remain in the carriage, frequently going on an errand while her husband visited with Hunt, but on one occasion, at least, Byron remained "so long that Lady Byron sent up twice to let him know she was waiting."[18] Presumably, discussions of literature and drama formed the core of these visits, as of their relationship itself. Byron frequently invited Hunt to join him at the theater, but Hunt felt that he could not accept, because of his health primarily, but also because he might compromise his "critical independence," since Byron was at this time a member of the Sub-Committee of Management of the Drury Lane Theater.[19]

---

[15] *The Examiner*, No. 366 (January 1, 1815), p. 8.
[16] "Oh! Snatched Away in Beauty's Bloom!" *Ibid.*, No. 382 (April 23, 1815), p. 269; "Bright Be the Place of Thy Soul!" No. 389 (June 11, 1815), p. 381; "Farewell to the Land," No. 396 (July 30, 1815), p. 491.
[17] *Ibid.*, No. 399 (August 20, 1815), pp. 538-39.
[18] Hunt, *Autobiography*, pp. 252-53.
[19] *Ibid.*, p. 252. There were at least two occasions on which Byron sent tickets to Hunt, June 1, 1815 and March 14, 1816 (*L. & J.*, III, 199, and VI, 457).

On October 15, 1815, Byron sent Hunt what would appear to be a rather special gift, his own copy of the now suppressed poem, *English Bards and Scotch Reviewers*, explaining somewhat casually that it was "a thing whose greatest value is its present rarity."[20]

The most significant event in their literary association in 1815 was Byron's intervention with his publisher, John Murray, for the publication of Hunt's *Rimini*. Hunt sent Byron the poem for criticism, which Byron readily gave. The poem was excellent and original, he wrote, but he would suggest that Hunt attempt to avoid the "occasional quaintness and obscurity" found in the work, "a kind of a harsh and yet colloquial compounding of epithets."[21] Hunt agreed to make certain changes, but he argued that in some instances he must retain the original form "in vindication of a theory which I have got on the subject, and by which it appears to me that the original part of my style . . . must stand or fall."[22] Byron, feeling that such discussion was an impasse, offered no further comment to Hunt on matters of style,[23] and directed his attention to Hunt's request that he speak to Murray about the poem. He apparently discussed it with Murray almost at once, for within several days he was writing to Murray that he had already informed Hunt of Murray's "willingness to treat with him." Byron was not concerned with the financial arrangements, of course, but, "as a man of business," he believed that *Rimini* was "the *safest* thing" Murray had ever planned to publish. "Were I to talk to you as a reader or a critic," he continued, "I should say it was a very wonderful and beautiful performance, with just

---

[20] *L. & J.*, III, 225.

[21] Byron to Hunt, October 22, 1815 (*Ibid.*, III, 226).

[22] Hunt to Byron, October 30, 1815 (*Ibid.*, III, 418).

[23] Byron wrote Thomas Moore on June 1, 1818: "When I saw *Rimini* in MS., I told him that I deemed it good poetry at bottom, disfigured only by a strange style. His answer was, that his style was a system, or *upon system*, or some such cant; and, when a man talks of system, his case is hopeless: so I said no more to him" (*Ibid.*, IV, 237).

enough of fault to make its beauties more remarked and remarkable."[24] Hunt thanked Byron for acting "so quickly respecting Murray,"[25] and on December 18, presumably after revising and copying the poem, Leigh Hunt offered *Rimini* to John Murray for £450. Murray refused, for the price would presuppose the sale "of at least 10,000 copies," but at this time he was willing to "print an edition of 500 to 750 copies as a trial at my own risk," of which Hunt was to receive half the profits and the copyright after this edition.[26] Hunt accepted the offer, and *Rimini* appeared early in 1816. By March 29, Hunt's profits were approximately £45, but Murray was not impressed with the financial possibilities of the work, for when Hunt proposed somewhat later that Murray buy all rights to *Rimini*, Murray refused to deal and suggested that Hunt try to dispose of these elsewhere.[27] Hunt eventually did this,[28] but the breach which the affair of *Rimini* had opened between Murray and himself—an effect which was quite contrary to Byron's intentions[29]—never closed.

Hunt was undoubtedly grateful to Byron, and in his gratitude he wrote and published the dedication of *Rimini*: "My dear Byron,—You see what you have brought yourself to by liking my verses." There is no evidence of any malevolence in his decision to omit Byron's title;[30] nor does it seem probable that Byron was the least annoyed at the time. "Your prefatory

---

[24] Byron to Murray, November 4, 1815 (*Ibid.*, III, 246).

[25] Hunt to Byron, November 7, 1815 (*Ibid.*, III, 421).

[26] Samuel Smiles, *A Publisher and His Friends: Memoir and Correspondence of the Late John Murray* (2 vols.; London, 1891), I, 308-9.

[27] *Ibid.*, I, 310-12.

[28] The second edition was printed by Bensley and Son for Taylor and Hessey, R. Triphook, and C. and J. Ollier, 1817.

[29] Byron to Murray, April 9, 1813 (*L. & J.*, IV, 99).

[30] "I dedicated the 'Story of Rimini' to Lord Byron, and the dedication was a foolish one. I addressed him, as at the beginning of a letter, and as custom allows in private between friends, without his title; and I proceeded to show how much I thought of his rank, by pretending to think nothing about it" (Leigh Hunt, *Lord Byron and Some of His Contemporaries* [London, 1828], p. 32).

letter to *Rimini*, I accepted as it was meant," he wrote, "as a public compliment and a private kindness."[31]

Approximately at this time, in early 1816, Leigh Hunt, feeling sufficiently recovered, repaid the visits which Byron had made him in prison and on Edgeware Road. "His wife's separation from him had just taken place, and he had become ill himself; his face was jaundiced with bile; he felt the attacks of the public severely; and, to crown all, he had an execution in his house."[32] If Hunt offered friendship, Byron would accept it. Hunt had asked about the allusions to Byron's domestic troubles, and Byron answered him candidly. "Of the 'fifty reports,' it follows that forty-nine must have more or less error and exaggeration," Byron wrote, "but I am sorry to say, that on the main and essential point of an intended, and, it may be, an inevitable separation, I can contradict none." He asked from Hunt only "a suspension of opinion."[33] It is rather improbable that Hunt gave him merely this, although there is no record of a public statement until four days before Byron's departure from England when *The Examiner* carried Leigh Hunt's "Distressing Circumstances in High Life." The purpose of the article was to crush rumors about Byron which had arisen from "the base passions of the scandalizers," and the heart of the article was an unqualified assertion of confidence:

We have the honour of knowing the Noble Poet; and as friendship is the first of principles in our theory, involving as it does the final purposes of all virtue itself, we do not scruple to confess, that whatever silence we may have thought ourselves bound to keep with regard to qualities which he could not have possessed, had he been such as the scandalmongers represented him, we should nevertheless, if we thought our arm worth his using, have stood by him and his misfortunes to the last. But knowing him as we do, one

---

[31] Byron to Hunt, February 26, 1816 (*L. & J.*, III, 265).
[32] Hunt, *Autobiography*, p. 260.
[33] Byron to Hunt, February 26, 1816 (*L. & J.*, III, 265).

fact at least we are acquainted with; and that is, that these reckless calumniators know nothing about the matter;—and we know further, that there have been the vilest exaggerations about it;—and that our Noble Friend with all his faults, which he is the last man upon earth to deny, possesses qualities which ought to crumble the consciousness of these men into dust.

The article closed optimistically: "A woman, who wishes to be a model to her sex, and a man, who never yet lost a manly friend, cannot but re-unite." Following this, "Fare Thee Well" was reprinted, as evidence of the absurdity of the charges against Byron, together with a fragment of "A Sketch from Domestic Life."[34] The following week, Leigh Hunt announced in *The Examiner* "the poor though angry retreat" of the scandalizers and Byron's departure for the Continent. Hunt himself retained his "perfect conviction that the separation will not be lasting." His comments were followed by his own signed poem, "To the Right Honourable Lord Byron, on His Departure for Italy and Greece."[35]

After Byron's departure, Hunt "did not see him again, or hear from him, scarcely of him," until Byron proposed that Hunt come to Italy.[36] The closeness of their friendship had contained more of promise than of reality. There was great difference in background between them and in their social and artistic purposes. Byron's humor was not Hunt's humor, and it is extremely difficult to imagine a successful correspondence apart from matters of literature and criticism. Yet despite all this, it is possible that several more years of association in England, where neither would have been dependent upon the other, would have brought about a friendship that could endure beyond the limits of momentary enthusiasm.

Byron departed with Leigh Hunt's defense of him fresh in his mind. Remembrance of this was to stimulate part of his

---

[34] *The Examiner*, No. 434 (April 21, 1816), pp. 247-50.
[35] *Ibid.*, No. 435 (April 28, 1816), pp. 266-67.   [36] Hunt, *Autobiography*, p. 261.

ambiguous attitude toward Hunt. "When party feeling ran
highest against me, Hunt was the only editor of a paper, the
only literary man, who dared say a word in my justification,"
Byron supposedly told Thomas Medwin years later in Italy.
"I shall always be grateful to him for the part he took on that
occasion."[37] The other side of Byron's feelings toward Hunt was
not at first apparent, as when he wrote to John Cam Hobhouse,
"my remembrances to Kinnaird—and Mrs. Kinnaird—to all
and everybody, and Hunt in particular."[38] But time, distance,
and perhaps the literary and political comments of Byron's
somewhat more fashionable friends developed in Byron a kind
of contempt for Leigh Hunt, which in the ensuing years found
more frequent expression in his letters than did the earlier
sympathy. "He is a good man, with some poetical elements in
his chaos," Byron wrote of Hunt in 1818, "but spoilt by the
Christ-Church Hospital and a Sunday newspaper,—to say
nothing of the Surrey gaol, which conceited him into a martyr."
He was "an honest charlatan, who has persuaded himself into
a belief of his own impostures." Yet despite this, he added
contemptuously, "Leigh Hunt is a good man, and a good
father—see his Odes to all the Masters Hunt;—a good husband
—see his Sonnet to Mrs. Hunt;—a good friend—see his
Epistles to different people;—and a great coxcomb and a very
vulgar person in every thing about him."[39] With such directly

---

[37] Thomas Medwin, *Conversations of Lord Byron* (2nd ed.; London, 1824), pp.
402-3. John Cam Hobhouse ("Dallas's *Recollections* and Medwin's *Conversations*,"
Westminster Review, V [1825], 6) denied that *The Examiner* had stood alone in
defense of Byron: "*The Morning Chronical* was a zealous advocate of his lordship;
and Mr. Perry, the editor, had a personal altercation with Sir R[alph] Noel on the
subject."

[38] Byron to John Cam Hobhouse, June 23, 1816 (*Lord Byron's Correspondence*, ed.
John Murray [2 vols.; London, 1922], II, 12—hereafter referred to as Byron,
Corr.).

[39] Byron to Moore, June 1, 1818 (*L. & J.*, IV, 237-39). The extremely contemptuous references with political significance to "Hunt" in Byron's letters have
to do with Henry ("Orator") Hunt, whose incitement of the mob resulted in the
"Peterloo Massacre." Byron's use of the surname has caused some confusion.
See *L. & J.*, IV, 245 and 410; *Corr.*, II, 134, 138, 143, 146, and 148.

opposed attitudes toward Leigh Hunt, Byron passed the years
until Shelley's visit to Ravenna in August, 1821.

§ *ii*

Leigh Hunt's relationship with Percy Bysshe Shelley was of
a different nature. Although there was little or nothing parallel
in their backgrounds, they possessed much in common in their
social, political, and artistic purposes. Like the Hunt-Byron
association, the friendship between Hunt and Shelley had a
false start, but after it had achieved firm beginnings, it developed
without inner opposition or ambiguity.

The earliest letters relating Shelley and Leigh Hunt are
from the year 1811. Shelley first wrote to Hunt from University
College, Oxford, congratulating him on his place in the fight
for liberty and proposing that a society of enlightened people
be formed to discuss and direct policies toward the preservation
of liberty.[40] Two months later, after Shelley and Thomas
Jefferson Hogg had been expelled from Oxford, Shelley told
Hogg that within the past several days he "had a polite note
from a man of letters, to whom I had been named, to invite me
to breakfast." The "man of letters" was Leigh Hunt, whom
Shelley met for the first time on Sunday, May 5, 1811. Shelley
was clearly impressed with his new acquaintance. "He is a
man of cultivated mind, and certainly exalted notions," he
wrote.[41] However, at this time, nothing developed from this
meeting or from any of the "few short visits" which Leigh Hunt
later recorded.[42] After the Hunts were sentenced in 1813 for
the libel against the Regent, Shelley was so sympathetic with
their situation that he wrote to Thomas Hookham, the book-

---

[40] Percy Bysshe Shelley to Leigh Hunt, March 2, 1811 (Shelley, *Works*, VIII, 55-56).

[41] Shelley to Hogg, May 8, 1811 (*Ibid.*, VIII, 81).

[42] Hunt, *Autobiography*, p. 261.

seller of Old Bond Street, to propose that a subscription be raised to pay the Hunts' fines. He himself contributed £20, with an apology that he could not give more.[43] The Hunts wished to pay their fines themselves, but they were greatly moved. "To evils I have owed some of my greatest blessings," Leigh Hunt remarked years later. "It was imprisonment that brought me acquainted with my friend of friends, Shelley."[44] This is not entirely accurate, for in spite of Shelley's willingness to help and Hunt's gratitude for it, the friendship between the two men did not actually begin until December, 1816.

Leigh Hunt's article "Young Poets" appeared in *The Examiner* on December 1 of that year. Its purpose was to bring before the educated public the names of Shelley, John Hamilton Reynolds, and John Keats. Hunt admittedly had seen little of Shelley's work, but "if the rest answer to what we have seen, we shall have no hesitation in announcing him for a very striking and original thinker."[45] On the day that this appeared, Mary recorded in her journal, "Letter from Leigh Hunt."[46] Shelley answered Hunt's letter before he saw the article in *The Examiner*,[47] and enclosed a sum of money.[48] On December 8, Shelley was writing again to Hunt, on this occasion, of his own ostracism and, partly because of that, of his deep gratitude for Hunt's friendship.[49] Four days later, Mary remarked that she

---

[43] Shelley to Hookham, February 19, 1813 (*Works*, IX, 46-48).

[44] Hunt, *Autobiography*, p. 247.

[45] *The Examiner*, No. 466 (December 1, 1816), p. 761.

[46] *Mary Shelley's Journal*, ed. Frederick L. Jones (Norman, Oklahoma, 1947), p. 70.

[47] Even somewhat later, on December 8, Shelley had not seen the article (*Works*, IX, 208).

[48] Mary wrote to Shelley on December 5, 1816: "Leigh Hunt has not written. I would advise [a] letter ad[d]ressed to him at the Examiner office if there is no answer tomorrow—he may not be at the Vale of Health for it is odd that he does not acknowledge the receipt of so large a sum" (*The Letters of Mary W. Shelley*, ed. Frederick L. Jones [2 vols.; Norman, Oklahoma, 1946], I, 15—hereafter referred to as Mary Shelley, *Letters*).

[49] Shelley, *Works*, IX, 208-9.

had received a letter from Shelley, who had gone from Marlow to London "to visit Leigh Hunt." On December 15, news arrived that Harriet, Shelley's estranged wife, had committed suicide. Shelley, who had returned from London only the day before, left for the city again after supper.[50] The following day, he was writing to Mary of the comfort which Leigh Hunt gave him in his present situation.[51]

Shelley assumed that his claim to custody of his children by Harriet would be honored. "My friend Mr. Leigh Hunt will take charge of my children and prepare them for their residence with me," he wrote to Eliza Westbrook, Harriet's older sister.[52] But he was optimistic, for on January 10, 1817, John Westbrook, Harriet's father, filed a bill in Chancery to deprive Shelley of guardianship and to have himself and Eliza, or other suitable persons, appointed guardians.[53] Hunt was Shelley's mainstay at this time. "He was so kind as to listen to the story of persecution which I am now enduring from a libidinous and vindictive woman, and to stand by me as yet by his counsel, and by his personal attention to me," Shelley wrote to Byron.[54] On January 18, Shelley filed his reply to the Westbrook bill.[55]

The case came before the Chancellor, Lord Eldon, on January 24. Two days later, *The Examiner* carried an objective account of the proceedings.[56] This was followed by a factual correction on February 2.[57] On March 27, 1817, Lord Eldon decided to deprive Shelley of the guardianship of his children,

---

[50] *Mary Shelley's Journal*, p. 71.
[51] Shelley to Mary, December 16, 1816 (*Works*, IX, 211-13).
[52] Shelley to Eliza Westbrook, December 18, 1816 (Leslie Hotson, "Shelley's Lost Letters to Harriet," *Atlantic Monthly*, CXLV [1930], 175).
[53] Newman Ivey White, *Shelley* (2 vols.; London, 1947), I, 489; II, 508-17.
[54] Shelley to Byron, January 17, 1817 (*Works*, IX, 219).
[55] White, I, 492.
[56] *The Examiner*, No. 474 (January 26, 1817), p. 60.
[57] *Ibid.*, No. 475 (February 2, 1817), p. 75. The account of the previous week had mentioned "Sir A. Piggott" as the counsel for the defense, whereas Basil Montagu was actually Shelley's counsel.

but nothing appeared in *The Examiner* until August 31, when
Leigh Hunt defended Shelley against two charges made by a
reporter in one of the morning papers:

We are not about to enter into the particulars of the case ourselves,
though we conceive that if statements that appear to tell for one
side are allowed to transpire, the very greatest and most awful
hints on the part of the Noble and Learned Arbiter cannot reason-
ably act as a check to the publication of the others:—but we happen
to know a good deal of this remarkable and important question, as
we shall hereafter shew, if it is found necessary to bring it before
the public; and we here notice it in order to contradict two erroneous
impressions, to which the report alluded to might give rise;—first,
that a book written, though not published, by Mr. Shelley, at the
age of 18 [*Queen Mab*], and certainly "singular" both for its ability
as well as bold theories, promulgates opinions against marriage
with no better *fors* for its arguments and *principles* than the report
seems to insinuate; and second, that the Lady with whom he
lives, and who inherits an intellect equally striking and premature,
from celebrated parents, is not his wife.—The book is full of the
strongest evidences both of talent and principle, whether its
opinions are right or wrong; and the Lady *is* his wife.[58]

Hunt and Shelley's association was not, of course, to be
exclusively concerned with the Westbrook suit. Nor was it to
be restricted to the men themselves, apart from their families,
as Hunt and Byron's relationship had been; Mary Shelley, as
her journal indicates, was a frequent participant. A picture of
Shelley relaxing at Hampstead was to be recalled later by
Hunt:

Shelley often came there to see me, sometimes to stop for several
days. He delighted in the natural broken ground, and in the fresh
air of the place, especially when the wind set in from the north-
west, which used to give him an intoxication of animal spirits. Here
also he swam his paper boats on the ponds, and delighted to play

---

[58] *Ibid.*, No. 505 (August 31, 1817), p. 552.

with my children, particularly with my eldest boy, the seriousness of whose imagination, and his susceptibility of a "grim" impression (a favourite epithet of Shelley's), highly interested him. He would play at "frightful creatures" with him, from which the other would snatch "a fearful joy," only begging him occasionally "not to do the horn," which was a way that Shelley had of screwing up his hair in front, to imitate a weapon of that sort.[59]

An immediate effect of these visits was an increasingly stronger literary association. Shelley had previously sent his "Hymn to Intellectual Beauty" to Hunt for *The Examiner*, over the signature "Elfin-Knight," one of Mary's pet names for him.[60] *The Examiner* of October 6, 1816, carried a simple notice, "The Elfin-Knight, the first opportunity."[61] The sequel appeared in *The Examiner* of January 18, 1817, after Shelley and Hunt had become good friends:

The following Ode, originally announced under the signature of the Elfin Knight, we have since found to be from the pen of the author, whose name was mentioned among others a week or two back in an article entitled "Young Poets." The readers will think with us, that it is also sufficient to justify what was there observed.

The poem was signed "Percy B. Shelley."[62] During the next five years, *The Examiner* paid frequent attention to Shelley's poetry, publishing "Ozymandias" for the first time[63] and carrying reviews of his other work. In all instances, Leigh Hunt remained firm, defending Shelley's intellectual integrity and moral principles as well as his poetic ability. Hunt himself included two sonnets to Shelley in *Foliage*, published in 1818,[64] and Shelley, for his part, dedicated *The Cenci* to Hunt, in a

---

[59] Hunt, *Autobiography*, p. 270. [60] White, I, 475.
[61] *The Examiner*, No. 458 (October 6, 1816), p. 631.
[62] *Ibid.*, No. 473 (January 19, 1817), p. 41.
[63] *Ibid.*, No. 524 (January 11, 1818), p. 24.
[64] *The Poetical Works of Leigh Hunt*, ed. H. S. Milford (London, 1923), p. 242.

letter dated May 29, 1819, with a clear expression of his feelings of friendship.[65]

Shelley left England on March 12, 1818, and Hunt was to see him next in Italy in 1822. But Shelley was unlike Byron, for Hunt was to hear from him and of him, and by correspondence to share what Hunt called their "common stock in trouble as well as joy."[66] The letters of 1818 were infrequent though regular, but in 1819 Leigh Hunt, hoping to help alleviate the Shelleys' grief at the loss of their children,[67] became their principal correspondent, for a while following his own proposal to write every Monday.[68] His letters were at times painfully cheerful, but in 1820 and 1821 both Leigh and Marianne Hunt were concerned in their letters, with increasing frequency, with the problems of health and finance which they faced. Shelley then repeatedly suggested that they come to Italy, where health might be improved and living was cheaper, but for many months there seemed to be no practical means for this.

§ *iii*

It is significant that the beginning of Hunt's friendship with Shelley followed by eight months the termination of his direct association with Byron. In May, 1816, Byron and Shelley met at Geneva and began that uneven relationship which was to last until Shelley's death. Shelley returned to England, where he came to know Hunt, and then in 1818 he came back once more to the Continent and, in time, fell into rather close association with Byron. At no time, therefore, before the

---

[65] Shelley, *Works*, X, 51. *The Cenci* was published by Ollier in March, 1820. It was favorably reviewed in *The Examiner* (No. 638 [March 19, 1820], pp. 190-91) and more extensively in *The Indicator* (No. 41 [July 19, 1820], pp. 320-28; No. 42 [July 26, 1820], pp. 329-36).

[66] Hunt to Percy and Mary Shelley, July 10, 1821 (*Corr.*, I, 164).

[67] Clara Shelley died on September 24, 1818, and William Shelley on June 6, 1819.

[68] Hunt to Percy and Mary Shelley, August, 1819 (*Corr.*, I, 135).

extremely brief period in 1822 preceding Shelley's death were
the three poets actually together, so that the potential success
of their union could not be determined. Shelley obviously became the link, writing both to Byron and to Hunt. The letters
to Byron consistently gave a favorable picture of Hunt. "Hunt
has been with me here, and we have often spoken of you,"
he wrote at one point, then emphasized, "Hunt is an excellent
man, and has a great regard for you."[69] In his letters to Hunt,
Shelley was generally positive regarding Byron though occasionally critical of situations such as that which existed at Venice.
In some instances, Byron's generosity became the theme of his
remarks, particularly as it might affect Hunt. "I cannot doubt
that he would hesitate in contributing at least £100 towards
extricating one whom he regards so highly from a state of
embarrassment," he wrote in December, 1816, when he and
Hunt had been friends only a short time.[70] In Italy, Shelley
persisted in his suggestions that Hunt try to find some means of
joining him, and on December 22, 1818, the suggestion was
coupled with the report of an offer by Byron to lend Hunt four
or five hundred pounds because Byron, too, wished that Leigh
Hunt would come out. " 'Twas very frankly made," Shelley
remarked, "and it would not only give him great pleasure, but
might do him great service, to have your society." There was,
however, still the question of practical needs, of which Shelley
was aware. "Pray could you not make it in some way even
profitable to visit this astonishing country?"[71]

Shelley followed this letter by one to Thomas Love Peacock,
urging him to try to determine Hunt's attitude.[72] Peacock saw
Hunt twice, then replied to Shelley that a trip to Italy would
ruin Hunt, "for what in the interval would become of his

---

[69] Shelley to Byron, July 9, 1817 (*Works*, IX, 233).
[70] Shelley to Hunt, December 8, 1816 (*Ibid.*, IX, 210).
[71] *Ibid.*, X, 10-11.
[72] Shelley to Peacock, December, 1818 (*Ibid.*, X, 19).

paper?"[73] In March, 1819, Hunt himself replied, protesting that "doubt and difficulties" had prevented a more prompt response. " 'But what, Hunt, of Italy?' Oh, you see, I delay speaking of Italy. I cannot come; I wish to God I could." He confirmed what Peacock had said. John Hunt had retired to the country, leaving his son Henry to take over the management of the publishing affairs, including *The Examiner*; despite Henry's excellence, it would be necessary for Leigh to be at *The Examiner* office every Saturday when the paper was put together.[74]

It was now obvious that in order to make successful any trip abroad Leigh Hunt must meet certain needs. The journey must be economically self-sustaining, and it should in some way be related to *The Examiner* so that he might fulfil his clear responsibilities to the newspaper. At the moment, there seemed to be no answer. Shelley was persistent in his invitation,[75] suggesting in September, 1819, that Hunt meet the Shelleys in Florence, "and we would try to muster up a 'lièta brigata,' which, leaving behind them the pestilence of remembered misfortunes, might act over again the pleasures of the Interlocutors in Boccaccio."[76] Hunt was constant in his wish to accept the invitation, although it now seemed impossible, for aside from health and cheaper living which Italy had come to represent in his mind, there was also abundant literary associa-

---

[73] Peacock to Shelley, January 13, 1819 (*Thomas Love Peacock Letters to Edward Hookham and Percy B. Shelley*, ed. Richard Garnett [Boston, 1910], pp. 86-87).

[74] Hunt to Mary Shelley, March 9, 1819 (*Corr.*, I, 127).

[75] Although in Shelley's mind, Hunt was a particular case because of health and financial difficulties, Shelley wished to see other friends also for their company. In May, 1820, he wrote to Peacock, "I wish you, and Hogg, and Hunt, and—I know not who besides—would come and spend some months with me together in this wonderful land" (*Works*, X, 169). He consistently tried to prevail upon Horace Smith, the banker and literary man, to come to Italy, until he received Smith's letter of August 30, 1821, stating that because of his wife's health, Smith could not travel but had rented a house at Versailles (*Shelley and Mary* [3 vols.; London: For private circulation only, 1882], II, 690—hereafter referred to as *S. & M.*).

[76] Shelley to Hunt, September 27, 1819 (*Works*, X, 86).

tion. "But Chaucer, as well as Milton, paid a visit to Italy," he wrote, "so did Gray, so did Drummond, Donne, and the Earl of Surrey."[77]

With the passage of time, however, the practical considerations became more significant than the literary. In the winter of 1820-21, Leigh Hunt was seriously ill. He required constant attention from Marianne, who wrote to Mary that his illness left him "irritable beyond anything you ever saw in him, and nervous to a most fearful extent." Migration to Italy seemed to be the only solution, and since Hunt hesitated because of practical considerations, Marianne suggested that Mary "ask Mr. Shelley, my dear Mr. Shelley, to *urge it to him.*" Sale of their furniture would not be difficult for the Hunts, so that the principal question remaining in Marianne's mind concerned the cost of passage on a ship and the weekly expenses in Italy.[78] In March, 1821, Hunt himself wrote, "I have indeed had a hard bout of it this time; and if the portrait you have with you sympathised with my appearance, like those magic glasses in romance, the patience you found in it ought at least to look twice as great, and the cheeks twice as small."[79]

Added to Leigh Hunt's other difficulties, there was John Hunt's conviction for libel of the House of Commons, which had supposedly occurred in *The Examiner* of July 23, 1820.[80] On May 28, 1821, John was sentenced to imprisonment for one year in Coldbath-fields Prison and "to give securities at the end of that period for his good behaviour during three years:—himself in 500 *l.*, and two other persons in 250 *l.* each."[81] John suggested to Leigh early in 1821 that he withdraw from ownership of the paper and thereby protect himself against prosecution. "I consented at last with the less scruple,"

---

[77] Hunt to the Shelleys, September 20, 1819 (Hunt, *Corr.*, I, 148).
[78] Marianne Hunt to Mary Shelley, January 24-26, 1821 (*S. & M.*, II, 578-79).
[79] Hunt to Shelley, March 1, 1821 (*Corr.*, I, 161).
[80] *The Examiner*, No. 656 (July 23, 1820), pp. 465-66.
[81] *The Times*, No. 11,258 (May 29, 1821), p. 3.

Leigh Hunt wrote to Shelley, "not only because my health was the more precarious, but because my brother's name is obliged to be at the bottom of the paper as printer, and printers, though not editors, are indictable, like proprietors."[82] Leigh had not been writing for *The Examiner* during the months of his illness, and the sales of the newspaper had seriously declined, but in the summer he began writing again, and the circulation gradually rose.[83] This gave him hope, not for the present but perhaps for the not very distant future, of making contributions to *The Examiner* from Italy, as a means of satisfying his needs and fulfilling his responsibilities. Hunt suggested this possibility to Shelley in a letter dated August 28, 1821,[84] some days after Shelley's return from his visit to Byron at Ravenna. In the mail, this would have crossed Shelley's letter of August 26, in which he passed along Byron's proposal concerning the periodical work. Yet if this letter had reached Shelley much earlier, it would not have added greatly to his knowledge and feelings concerning Hunt, for when Shelley left Mary at the Baths of Pisa on August 3, 1821,[85] he was thoroughly inundated with accounts of Hunt's difficulties, and he obviously would have been totally susceptible to any suggestion that seemed to hold reasonable promise of alleviating them, particularly if it would bring Hunt to Italy.

In this instance, Shelley's calculation of reasonable promise would be largely based upon his estimate of Byron and the course of Byron's living. Shelley had no illusions concerning Byron, "this spirit of an angel in the mortal paradise of a decaying body."[86] He placed Byron's genius far above his own,[87]

---

[82] Hunt to Shelley, March 1, 1821 (*Corr.*, I, 162).
[83] Hunt to the Shelleys, July 10, 1821 (*Ibid.*, I, 163).   [84] *Ibid.*, I, 168.
[85] *Mary Shelley's Journal*, pp. 154 n., 159. White (II, 315, 616) estimated on the basis of Shelley's letter to Mary dated August 7, and a letter to Thomas Medwin, dated August 22, that the visit lasted "from August 6 to about August 22."
[86] Shelley to John Gisborne, January 12, 1822 (*Works*, X, 345).
[87] Shelley to Mary, August 10, 1821 (*Ibid.*, X, 304).

and yet was frequently disgusted with Byron's behavior, particularly during the Venetian period of Byron's life in Italy.[88] Another source of annoyance for Shelley was Byron's treatment of Claire Clairmont, Mary's step-sister, in the matter of their child, Allegra.

Presumably, then, at the time of his departure for Ravenna, Shelley had grave doubts about the nature of Byron's life. He arrived on August 6 and sat up until five on the morning of August 7, talking with Byron. The impression was favorable. Later that day, Shelley wrote to Mary that Byron "has in fact completely recovered his health, and lives a life totally the reverse of that which he led at Venice."[89] Three days later, he returned to the subject. Byron had "greatly improved in every respect—in genius, in temper, in moral views, in health, in happiness." Much of this could be attributed to the connection with the Countess Guiccioli, which had existed since 1819. Byron "has had mischievous passions," Shelley concluded, "but these he seems to have subdued, and he is becoming what he should be, a virtuous man."[90] The proposal for a periodical, in which Byron would participate as well as Hunt and Shelley, would seem, then, to hold reasonable promise of success.[91]

---

[88] "Our poor friend Lord Byron is quite corrupted by living among these people," Shelley had written to Hunt on December 22, 1818, "and, in fact, is going on in a way not very worthy of him" (*Ibid.*, X, 10).

[89] Shelley to Mary, August 7, 1821 (*Ibid.*, X, 296).

[90] Shelley to Mary, August 10, 1821 (*Ibid.*, X, 302-3). Shelley was obviously impressed. He wrote to Peacock at approximately the same time, "Lord Byron is in excellent cue both of health and spirits. He has got rid of all those melancholy and degrading habits which he indulged [in] at Venice" (*Ibid.*, X, 306). In the letter of invitation to Hunt, Shelley made a point of the fact that "Lord Byron is reformed, as far as gallantry goes" (*Ibid.*, X, 319). And to Horace Smith, he wrote on September 14, "He is now quite reformed, and is leading a most sober and decent life, as cavaliere servente to a very pretty Italian woman" (*Ibid.*, X, 324).

[91] Thornton Hunt ("Shelley, By One Who Knew Him," *Atlantic Monthly*, XI [1863], 190), who did not have the advantage of Shelley's collected correspondence, was correct, with the exception of his broad use of the date, when he wrote, "I am sure that before 1821 Byron had risen in his friend's estimation, or the 'Liberal' scheme would never have been contemplated."

The question of the exact authorship of the proposal has been constantly troublesome. On August 26, Shelley was to write of Byron to Hunt, "He proposes that you should come out. . . ." This, it would seem, should suffice, certainly with the corroborating statement by Mary Shelley: "When Shelley visited Lord Byron at Ravenna, the latter had suggested his [Hunt's] coming out, together with the plan of a periodical work, in which they should all join."[92] However, there have been serious doubts that Byron was sufficiently motivated to make such a proposal. Leigh Hunt himself at first maintained a suspicion that the idea was Shelley's. "I was not sure whether it was not a generous artifice of his [Shelley's] own," Hunt wrote to Byron, "and though I knew no reason why he should not be as plain with me on this as on all other occasions, I was additionally mystified by his giving me no answer to this question,—perhaps an oversight in the hurry of some important business."[93] Thomas Medwin believed that Shelley's influence over Byron "was proved in nothing more than his being persuaded to join in that review, the first idea of which was suggested by Shelley for the benefit of Mr. Hunt."[94] Certainly Shelley's motivation was strong, appearing quite clearly when he told Mary of Thomas Moore's sale of the manuscript of Byron's memoirs to John Murray. "I wish I had been in time to have interceded for a part of it for poor Hunt," he wrote. He had mentioned Hunt to Byron, "but not with a direct view of demanding a contribution."[95] Yet all this proves no more than Shelley's susceptibility to suggestion or situation. There is possibly some further evidence for Shelley's author-

---

[92] Mary Shelley, "Notes on the Poems of 1821," *The Poetical Works of Percy Bysshe Shelley* (4 vols., London, 1839), IV, 154.

[93] Unpublished letter from Leigh Hunt to Lord Byron, January 27, 1822 (courtesy of the Henry W. and Albert A. Berg Collection of the New York Public Library).

[94] Thomas Medwin, *The Shelley Papers. Memoir of Percy Bysshe Shelley* (London, 1833), p. 82.

[95] Shelley to Mary, August 10, 1821 (*Works*, X, 304).

ship of the proposal in the fact that Shelley has been suspected
of having at one time edited a periodical, *The Theological
Inquirer; or Polemical Magazine*, existing from March to September, 1815.[96] These suspicions can be no more than hypothetical,
and, aside from them, there remains only Shelley's proposal
to Peacock early in 1819, that Peacock organize a review to
oppose the powerful *Quarterly*. Such a periodical could have
great power "if a band of staunch reformers, resolute yet
skilful infidels, were united in so close and constant a league as
that in which interest and fanaticism have bound the members
of that [*Quarterly Review*'s] literary coalition!"[97] The suggestion
never materialized, but it is important that Shelley made it.

There were reasons why Byron would be interested in such
a scheme as the periodical, but there has been much disagreement concerning them. He himself maintained, in conversation
with Dr. Kennedy several years later in Greece, that his "connexion with these people [the Hunts] originated from humanity."[98] Leigh Hunt came to hold another opinion, that "his
Lordship undoubtedly looked for considerable returns from
the work ultimately, & was not a little disappointed that the
first number made him lower his expectations."[99] There have
been partisans of both sides,[100] but in all probability the truth

---

[96] Bertram Dobell ("Shelleyana," *Athenæum*, No. 2,993 [March 7, 1885], p. 313)
advanced this hypothesis on the grounds that the work "contained a good deal
of matter relating to Shelley, although his name is not once mentioned in the
volume." One of the strong points is the fact that Shelley's "Refutation of Deism,"
first printed but not published in 1814, follows the Editor's Address.

[97] Shelley to Peacock, February 25, 1819 (*Works*, X, 34).

[98] James Kennedy, *Conversations on Religion with Lord Byron and Others* (Philadelphia, 1833), p. 135. In a letter dated May 17, 1823, and written to an unidenti-
fied lady, Byron described *The Liberal* as "a publication set up for the advantage
of a persecuted author and a very worthy man" (*L. & J.*, VI, 213).

[99] Payson G. Gates, "Leigh Hunt's Review of Shelley's *Posthumous Poems*," *The
Papers of the Bibliographical Society of America*, XLII (1948), 18.

[100] John Gibson Lockhart ("*Lord Byron and Some of His Contemporaries*," *The
Quarterly Review*, XXXVII [1828], 418-19) took Byron's side, asserting that since
Byron knew that "the world had utterly condemned the [Hunt] school of poetry
and criticism," he could expect neither profit nor advantage from his association

lies at some point between extremes. If Byron's motives were
humane, they were not spontaneously so, for he had not been
in direct contact with Leigh Hunt for more than five years;
he was moved, then, by Shelley's remarks concerning Hunt.
Nor is it likely that Byron's motives were exclusively humane,
for there were possible practical advantages to such a union
that must have appeared to him at the time of the proposal.
These can be detected in his correspondence with John Murray,
who had published Byron's writings since 1811 but now hesitated
to continue with *Don Juan* and to bring forth certain of Byron's
other works. Byron was annoyed, and he would be ready to
accept an idea that would seem to relieve the annoyance at
its cause. Since at this time, Byron apparently did not consider
turning entirely to a new publisher, a periodical would be the
remedy that might most readily occur to him. He had proposed
it to Thomas Moore the previous Christmas, as "a *newspaper*—
nothing more nor less—weekly, or so," in which there should
always be "a piece of poesy from one or other of us *two*,
leaving room, however, for such dilettanti rhymers as may be
deemed worthy of appearing in the same column." His intention with such a work would be to "give the age some new
lights upon policy, poesy, biography, criticism, morality,
theology, and all other *ism, ality*, and *ology* whatsoever."[101] The
scheme was not clearly worked out in Byron's mind, but it was
more persistent than most of his ideas, for on August 2, 1821,
only four days before Shelley's arrival at Ravenna, Byron
wrote to Moore, "Is there no chance of your returning to
England, and of our Journal?"[102]

---

with the Hunts. Edward J. Trelawny (*Recollections of the Last Days of Shelley and
Byron* [London, 1923], p. 103), who was always critical of Byron, took the other
side, arguing that Byron hoped, through his connection with the Hunts, to acquire
the use and support of *The Examiner*. Thomas Moore (*Byron*, II, 395) attributed
to Byron both the humane and the practical motives, placing the humane foremost.

[101] Byron to Moore, December 25, 1820 (*L. & J.*, V, 143).

[102] *Ibid.*, V, 336.

None of this is proof, of course, but, in the case of Byron, there is at least direct statement in favor of his authorship of the proposal for a journal, and, unless overwhelming evidence appears for the view that Shelley actually made the proposal, it must be accepted that in some way it was Byron's. In 1863, Thornton Hunt wrote, "I believe it would be nearly impossible for any one of the three men interested in that venture [*The Liberal*] to ascertain exactly who was its author."[103] What was then improbable is now impossible. Both Shelley and Byron would be susceptible, and as they sat talking through most of each night, what began as the merest germ of an idea might have developed into a proposal. Byron—moved by Shelley's talk of Hunt, by his own recollections of Hunt's loyalty in 1816, and by awareness of his own publishing needs—might well have made the proposal, which Shelley seized upon.[104]

The time of the proposal can be approximately determined by the nature of the remarks in Shelley's letters to Mary during his stay at Ravenna. On August 11, he wrote of Byron's plans to come to Pisa to live, but there is no suggestion of any further proposals or intentions. "I don't think this circumstance ought to make any difference in our plans with respect to this winter in Florence," he continued, "because we could easily resume our station with the spring at Pugnano or the baths in order to enjoy the society of the noble lord."[105] Four days later, Shelley passed along Byron's request that Mary begin to look "for the best unfurnished palace in Pisa."[106] On the following day, he continued this letter, with concern about their plans for the winter. He was now urging Pisa rather than Florence as their location, and it would appear that he had probably

---

[103] Thornton Hunt, "Shelley, By One Who Knew Him," p. 190.

[104] Harold Nicolson (*Byron: The Last Journey, April* 1823—*April* 1824 [London, 1948], p. 23) rejected the notion that a "proposal" was ever made: "it *wasn't* a proposal, it was only an idea; on second thoughts it was a devilish bad idea," but Shelley "could never see the difference between an idea and a proposal."

[105] Shelley, *Works*, X, 308.   [106] *Ibid.*, X, 310.

mentioned Hunt to Byron, for he suggested to Mary that the Williamses might remain near them, and "Hunt would certainly stay at least this winter near us, should he emigrate at all."[107] But there was not the barest suggestion of the need for permanence and concentration, such as the management of a periodical would require. It would seem then that the definite proposal was not made until some time during the last six days of Shelley's visit.[108]

The development of the proposal was undoubtedly Shelley's; in fact, it is probably a safe assumption that, if he had not acted at this time, nothing further would have happened. He returned to Mary on approximately August 26, and four days later, he wrote to Leigh Hunt:

Since I last wrote to you, I have been on a visit to Lord Byron at Ravenna. The result of this visit was a determination, on his part to come and live at Pisa; and I have taken the finest palace on the Lung'Arno [the Palazzo Lanfranchi] for him. But the material part of my visit consists in a message which he desires me to give you, and which I think, ought to add to your determination —for such a one I hope you have formed—of restoring your shattered health and spirits by a migration to these "regions mild of calm and serene air."

He proposes that you should come out and go shares with him and me in a periodical work, to be conducted here; in which each of the contracting parties should publish all their original compositions, and share the profits. He proposed it to Moore, but for some reason or other it was never brought to bear. There can be no doubt that the profits of any scheme in which you and Lord Byron engage, must from various, yet co-operating reasons, be very great. As for myself, I am, for the present, only a sort of link between you and him, until you can know each other, and effectuate the

---

[107] *Ibid.*, X, 314.
[108] Harold Nicolson (p. 23) has suggested that Byron expressed his "idea" on the night that Shelley arrived, August 6-7, but he has offered no evidence for this specific date.

arrangements; since (to entrust you with a secret which, for your sake, I withhold from Lord Byron) nothing would induce me to share in the profits, and still less, in the borrowed splendour of such a partnership. You and he, in different manners, would be equal, and would bring, in a different manner, but in the same proportion, equal stock of reputation and success. Do not let my frankness with you, nor my belief that you deserve it more than Lord Byron, have the effect of deterring you from assuming a station in modern literature, which the universal voice of my contemporaries forbids me either to stoop to or to aspire to. I am, and I desire to be, nothing.[109]

At first Hunt hesitated. "That ever the time should come, when I had such an offer to visit the country of Petrarch and Boccaccio, and think of refusing it," he wrote Mary on September 7, presumably right after he had received Shelley's letter.[110] But it appears that he quickly changed his mind. The proposal actually removed all obstacles facing him in his desire to join Shelley in Italy. John Hunt agreed "that while a struggle was made in England to reanimate the *Examiner*, a simultaneous endeavour should be made in Italy to secure new aid to our prospects, and new friends to the cause of liberty."[111] Leigh Hunt, therefore, wrote to the Shelleys, accepting the invitation which he had previously been forced to refuse:

We are coming. I feel the autumn so differently from the summer, and the accounts of the cheapness of living and education at Pisa are so inviting, that what with your kind persuasions, the proposal of Lord Byron, and last, to be sure not least, the hope of seeing you again and trying to get my health back in your society, my brother as well as myself think I had better go. We hope to set off in a month from the date of this letter, not liking to delay our preparation till we hear from you again, on account of the approach of winter; so about the 21st of October we shall all set off, myself, Marianne, and the six children. With regard to the proposed publication of Lord

---

[109] Shelley, *Works*, X, 318-19.   [110] *S. & M.*, II, 692-93.
[111] Hunt, *Autobiography*, p. 289.

B., about which you talk so modestly, he has it in his power, I believe, to set up not only myself and family in our finances again, but one of the best-hearted men in the world, my brother and his. I allude, of course, to the work in which he proposes me to join him. . . . I agree to this proposal with the less scruple, because I have had a good deal of experience in periodical writing, and know what the getting up of the *machine* requires, as well as the soul of it. You see I am not so modest as you are by a great deal, and do not mean to let you be so either. What? Are there not three of us? And ought we not to have as much strength and variety as possible? We will divide the world between us, like the Triumvirate, and you shall be the sleeping partner, if you will; only it shall be with a Cleopatra, and your dreams shall be worth the giving of kingdoms.[112]

The Hunts then launched into preparations for their departure "with strange new thoughts and feelings,"[113] while Shelley awaited their reply and looked toward Byron's move to Pisa.

---

[112] Hunt to the Shelleys, September 21, 1821 (Hunt, *Corr.*, I, 172-73).
[113] Hunt, *Autobiography*, p. 289.

II

Anticipation

§ *i*

DURING THE PREPARATION FOR BYRON AND THE HUNTS, THE Shelleys remained at the Baths of Pisa, not moving until October 25 to Pisa,[1] where they occupied an apartment "at the top of the Tre Palazzi di Chiesa."[2] In August, Teresa Guiccioli arrived,[3] accompanied by her father and two brothers, Pietro and Vincenzo Gamba.[4] Early in September, Shelley, on behalf of Byron, made arrangements with the physician, André Berlinghieri Vaccà, for the rental of the Palazzo Lanfranchi on the Lung'Arno across from the Tre Palazzi.[5] Somewhat later, at Byron's request, Shelley sent wagons to Ravenna for Byron's effects.[6]

Byron, however, felt no hurry. "He left Ravenna with great regret," Teresa Guiccioli later recalled, "and with a presentiment that his departure would be the forerunner of a thousand

---

[1] *Mary Shelley's Journal*, p. 160 n. Edward Williams' journal for October 25, 1821 (*Maria Gisborne and Edward E. Williams, Shelley's Friends: Their Journals and Letters*, ed. Frederick L. Jones [Norman, Oklahoma, 1951], p. 105—hereafter referred to as *Gisborne and Williams*).

[2] Mary Shelley to Maria Gisborne, November 30, 1821 (Mary Shelley, *Letters*, I, 150).

[3] *Mary Shelley's Journal*, p. 159.

[4] C. L. Cline, *Byron, Shelley and Their Pisan Circle* (Cambridge, Massachusetts, 1952), p. 44. Teresa and her brothers first occupied Casa Finocchietti, then moved to Casa Parra on the Lung'Arno.

[5] Shelley to Byron, undated (*Works*, X, 320-21).

[6] Shelley to Byron, September 14, 1821 (*Ibid.*, X, 321).

evils to us."[7] On September 3, he was "packing for Pisa,"[8] but at this time he himself intended merely to leave "in a few weeks."[9] By September 20, he apparently felt that the time for departure was approaching,[10] but, by October 1, "a slight incipient intermittent fever" posed a threat.[11] Otherwise, he was occupied writing "The Vision of Judgment." His "furniture, horses, carriages, and live stock" were removed in early October, but Byron remained, using "some *jury* chairs, and tables, and a mattrass [*sic*]."[12] On October 28, he had been "sitting up all night to be sure of rising," for he intended to depart within several hours. "I have just made them take off my bed-clothes—blankets inclusive—in case of temptation from the apparel of sheets to my eyelids."[13] Temptation or something else intervened, for, two days later, he was still in Ravenna, "just setting off for Pisa."[14] He arrived on the first of November.[15]

Shelley believed that the Hunts would leave England in late October, according to their intentions, and arrive in Pisa in November.[16] He suggested that they come by sea, rather than attempt the overland route.[17] Leigh Hunt, with his usual faith in Shelley's judgment, accepted the suggestion. "And, I believe, if he had recommended a balloon," Hunt recalled later, "I should have been inclined to try it."[18] The Hunts were expected during all of November, and the Shelleys were keenly disap-

---

[7] Moore, *Byron*, II, 334.

[8] Byron to Moore, September 3, 1821 (*L. & J.*, V, 357).

[9] Byron to Murray, September 4, 1821 (*Ibid.*, V, 358).

[10] On September 20, Byron wrote to both Moore and Murray, asking them to address him at Pisa (*Ibid.*, V, 369, 373).

[11] Byron to Moore, October 1, 1821 (*Ibid.*, V, 384).

[12] Byron to Samuel Rogers, October 21, 1821 (*Ibid.*, V, 395).

[13] Byron to Moore, October 28, 1821 (*Ibid.*, V, 397-98).

[14] Byron to Murray, October 30, 1821 (*Ibid.*, V, 401).

[15] *Mary Shelley's Journal*, p. 160.

[16] Shelley to Byron, October 21, 1821 (*Works*, X, 331).

[17] Shelley to Hunt, October 6, 1821 (*Ibid.*, X, 329).

[18] Hunt, *Autobiography*, p. 289.

pointed at their failure to arrive by the end of the month.[19] Early in December, the Shelleys bought furniture for the Hunts, who were to occupy the first floor of Byron's Palazzo Lanfranchi,[20] and toward the end of the month they were expecting the Hunts "anxiously and daily."[21] But they were to wait for many months.

Before Leigh Hunt could leave England, he was obviously faced with certain preliminary arrangements, primarily with regard to his own connection with *The Examiner* and to the funds necessary for the journey. Although he certainly made a very general agreement by which John Hunt would be the publisher of the proposed journal,[22] it is unlikely that he felt any need to treat with the question of ownership of *The Examiner* until it was far too late. Actually, the matter would be of little importance regarding *The Liberal* itself were it not for John Cordy Jeaffreson's assertion that Leigh Hunt consciously deceived Shelley and Byron by his "crafty silence respecting his disconnexion from 'The Examiner.' "[23] Leigh Hunt's account to Shelley, on March 1, 1821, that he had given up proprietorship of *The Examiner*[24] furnishes some basis for refuting this accusation. It is likely that Shelley, considering the legal reasons for Hunt's move, believed that the surrender of ownership had been more apparent than real, for early in 1822 he inquired of Hunt concerning the "arrangement you have made about the receipt of a regular income from the profits of the

[19] Mary Shelley to Maria Gisborne, November 30, 1821 (Mary Shelley, *Letters*, I, 151).

[20] *Mary Shelley's Journal*, p. 162. Although the Shelleys selected the furniture, Byron paid for it; the cost was £50, Byron wrote Kinnaird on February 23, 1822 (Byron, *Corr.*, II, 216-17).

[21] Mary Shelley to Maria Gisborne, December 21, 1821 (Mary Shelley, *Letters*, I, 153).

[22] In the matter of a publisher for the proposed periodical, any arrangements could hardly have been specific at this time, for Leigh Hunt's notions about the periodical, as they appear in his subsequent correspondence, were far too vague.

[23] John Cordy Jeaffreson, *The Real Lord Byron* (2 vols.; London, 1883), II, 196.

[24] *Corr.*, I, 162.

Examiner."[25] Shelley was asking a question, which Hunt rather characteristically neglected to answer, rather than stating conditions under which Hunt could join the literary alliance in Pisa; nor does such a statement ever appear in Shelley's correspondence. Byron ignored the subject in his letters, so that it can be safely assumed, especially since Byron was later to emphasize Hunt's failings and mistakes, that Byron did not believe that Hunt had deceived him with regard to *The Examiner*. Hunt's own candid assertion that through the association with Byron he hoped to re-establish his fortunes would seem to be further testimony against the charge of duplicity. The worst that can be sustained against Leigh Hunt in this situation is a charge of indefiniteness and inability in handling matters vital to his own well-being.

The question of the financial aspect of his journey is more difficult. "He had no grasp of things material," Thornton Hunt wrote of his father after Leigh Hunt's death, "but exaggerating his own defects, he so hesitated at any arithmetical effort, that he could scarcely count."[26] This fact alone has rendered it improbable that a correct estimate of the Hunt finances during the Italian period can be reached.[27]

In Shelley's letter of invitation to Leigh Hunt, he remarked that he had not asked Byron "to assist me in sending a remittance for your journey," for he did not wish to incur an obligation. He would instead "ask Horace Smith to add to the many obligations he has conferred on me."[28] It appears that for some reason Shelley did not ask Smith.[29] In any event, Leigh Hunt

---

[25] Shelley to Hunt, January 25, 1822 (*Works*, X, 351).

[26] Thornton Hunt, "A Man of Letters of the Last Generation," *Cornhill Magazine*, I (1860), 90.

[27] Nearly all those who have dealt with this phase in the lives of those involved have made estimates of Hunt's obligations, particularly to Byron; there has been very little agreement.

[28] Shelley to Hunt, August 26, 1821 (*Works*, X, 319).

[29] Thomas Medwin (*The Life of Percy Bysshe Shelley*, ed. H. B. Forman [London, 1913], p. 325) believed that Shelley applied to Horace Smith, who provided funds

was not very hopeful in this regard and had other intentions. "I shall do my best, with my brother's help, to raise the money," he told Shelley, adding significantly, "and have an impudent certainty that you will help me out with the return of it."[30] The amount that Leigh borrowed from John Hunt at this time, specifically for his passage and other needs related to the proposed journey, is not known, but by the end of 1821 Leigh owed his brother £1868.6.5.[31] Shelley felt himself unable to contribute extensively. By January, he no longer refused to apply to Byron, but he wished Byron to be certain that Shelley himself could not assist Hunt. On January 25, Shelley sent Hunt £150, "within 30 or 40 of what I had contrived to scrape together,"[32] in the form of an order on Brookes and Company of London, Shelley's bankers.[33] Meanwhile, Leigh Hunt was writing to Byron, with the admitted intention of borrowing £250.[34] He apparently asked Shelley to intercede for him with Byron, and Shelley, with some annoyance at Hunt, forwarded the letter to Byron. He commented on his own reluctance to approach Byron. "As it has come to this in spite of my exertions, I will not conceal from you the low ebb of my money-affairs in the present moment." He suggested to Byron that since he doubted that "poor Hunt's promise to pay in a given time is worth very much," Shelley himself would be responsible for Hunt's debt.[35] Byron consented "with *tolerable willingness*,"

for Hunt's passage and the clearance of Hunt's debts in England. However, Shelley's letters to Smith do not substantiate this. On September 14, 1821, he mentioned Hunt; on January 25, 1822, he mentioned the proposed journey; in his letter of April 11 there is nothing about Hunt; and during May, he asked Smith for a loan of £400, but this was specifically for William Godwin, who had recently lost a lawsuit (Shelley, *Works*, X, 323-25, 347, 377-78, 392-93).

[30] Hunt to P. B. and M. W. Shelley, September 21, 1821 (*Corr.*, I, 173).

[31] Unpublished letter from John Hunt to Leigh Hunt, June 6, 1824 (British Museum MS. ADD. 38108, f. 324).

[32] Shelley, *Works*, X, 349.   [33] *Ibid.*, X, 348.

[34] Unpublished letter from Hunt to Byron, January 27, 1822 (the Berg Collection of the New York Public Library).

[35] Shelley to Byron, February 15, 1822 (*Works*, X, 357).

Shelley informed Hunt, "with a tacit agreement that he is not to call on me for it before my father's death."[36] Byron gave Shelley "£250 in Italian bills,"[37] so that on February 20 Shelley was able to write an order for Brookes and Company to pay Leigh Hunt £220.[38] He was, he later explained to Hunt, retaining "£30 to dispose of at your orders."[39]

It is likely that Shelley enclosed the order for Brookes and Company in the letter he had written on February 17, for both appear to have been mislaid. In 1828, Leigh Hunt wrote that only later did he learn "that his Lordship had had a bond for the money from Mr. Shelley."[40] By April 10, Shelley had not received acknowledgment of the money from Hunt,[41] who denied years later that he had received money at this time.[42] On April 12, Shelley wrote another order on Brookes and Company for £220, which, like the preceding order, was payable on Lady Day, which had now passed.[43] The money apparently reached Leigh Hunt this time and was the "two hundred pounds" which he remembered in 1828.[44] Shelley probably sent the additional £30 to Hunt after he had arrived in Italy,[45]

---

[36] Shelley to Hunt, February 17, 1822 (*Ibid.*, X, 357).

[37] Shelley to Hunt, March 2, 1822 (*Ibid.*, X, 361).   [38] *Ibid.*, X, 359.

[39] Shelley to Hunt, March 2, 1822 (*Ibid.*, X, 361).

[40] Hunt, *Lord Byron*, p. 15.

[41] On this date, Shelley wrote to Hunt that he hoped Hunt would have received the order on Brookes, "which I *think* I sent to you" (*Works*, X, 369).

[42] In a letter to an unknown correspondent, dated April 26, 1858, Hunt denied that Shelley could have written the letter to him of March 2, 1822, for Hunt had not asked Shelley to apply to Byron for money, and he had received none, as the letter of March 2 asserted (Hunt, *Corr.*, II, 180). Hunt might well have forgotten by 1858 that he had written to Byron on January 27, 1822 (n. 34, above); according to Richard Garnett (*Relics of Shelley* [London, 1862], p. 107 n.), before his death in 1859 Hunt found Shelley's letter of March 2 among his papers, but he persisted in denying that he had received the money to which Shelley referred. That Brookes and Company obviously would not have honored identical orders on the same quarter of Shelley's income vindicates Hunt.

[43] Shelley, *Works*, X, 379. The amount due Shelley from his quarterly income was £220.

[44] Hunt, *Lord Byron*, p. 15.

[45] Shelley wrote Hunt on June 24, 1822, "The other £30 you shall have when we meet or within a few days afterwards" (*Works*, X, 408).

so that the total remittance between January and July, when Shelley met Hunt at Leghorn, was £400.[46] Of this, at least £250 came from Byron, though it is likely that the money remitted in January was Shelley's.[47] Aside from the money already spent for furniture and the later traveling expenses, Byron probably contributed a total of £150 later in 1822,[48] bringing the total from Byron to approximately £400 and from both Shelley and Byron to £550.

On November 14, 1821, Leigh Hunt, with his wife and six children, left Hampstead.[49] Marianne Hunt appeared to be in the dangerous stages of consumption, but the doctor had recommended a voyage as "the best thing in the world for her."[50] In the Thames, they boarded the *Jane*, "a small brig of a hundred and twenty tons burden," which sailed on November 16.[51] The voyage was short-lived. The *Jane* managed to clear the Thames, but on November 21 was forced by a storm into Ramsgate. The Hunts disembarked and "took a quiet lodging at the other end of the town" while they awaited better weather.[52] On December 11, the *Jane* set forth again, but the good weather did not hold, and after an unsuccessful attempt to come into Falmouth, the ship docked at Dartmouth on December 22.[53] On January 4, the captain considered the weather promising, but "Marianne fell so ill, that it was quite impossible to move her," and the *Jane* departed without the Hunts.[54] The money for the passage was forfeit.[55] The Hunts

---

[46] Shelley reported to Mary on July 4, 1822, that Hunt "arrived with no other remnant of his £4[00] than a debt of 60 crowns" (*Ibid.*, X, 413). In a copy of this letter made by Mary Shelley, now in the Berg Collection of the New York Public Library, "£400" occurs.

[47] Byron to Douglas Kinnaird, February 23, 1822 (*Corr.*, II, 216-17; Cline, p. 82).

[48] Byron to Kinnaird, December 23, 1822 (*Corr.*, II, 239).

[49] Charles Armitage Brown to Thomas Richards, November 15, 1821 (*Some Letters and Miscellanea of Charles Brown*, ed. M. B. Forman [London, 1937], p. 7).

[50] Hunt to Shelley, November 16, 1821 (*Corr.*, I, 174).

[51] Hunt, *Autobiography*, p. 290.   [52] *Ibid.*, 293.   [53] *Ibid.*, 294-98.

[54] Hunt to the Shelleys, January 6, 1822 (*Corr.*, I, 175-76).

[55] Thomas Jefferson Hogg to Shelley, January 29, 1822 (*S. & M.*, II, 735).

moved to Plymouth, where Leigh Hunt arranged with the master of a ship bound for Genoa that the Hunts pay £30 at once and the remainder of their passage money on arrival; but after he had boarded the vessel with his family, Hunt became uncertain that he could obtain the rest of the money as soon as they arrived, and the family disembarked.[56] They settled at Stonehouse for the winter.

Marianne was confined to her bed much of the time, while Leigh was at work with his six "Letters to the Readers of the Examiner"[57] and active making new acquaintances at Plymouth.[58] He kept in touch with his London friends, who occasionally passed along reports and comments upon Hunt's progress in his journey. Thomas Jefferson Hogg wrote to Shelley:

I would have written by Hunt, but I was unable to muster up sufficient gravity to address a grey-headed, deaf, double, tottering, spectacled old man, for such I was persuaded you would be before he reached Pisa, if he is ever to reach it, and I was unwilling to interrupt, by any recollection of "poor Hogg, who has been dead these fifty years," the meeting of Old Shelley and Old Hunt, which might possibly take place about the close of the nineteenth century.[59]

This would obviously not help to ease the anxiety for the

---

[56] Unpublished letter from Hunt to Byron, January 27, 1822 (the Berg Collection of the New York Public Library). This was possibly the ship of which the mate frightened Marianne with tales about the captain and the ship, so that the Hunts disembarked (Hunt, *Autobiography*, p. 298).

[57] "Letters to the Readers of the Examiner, No. 1," *The Examiner*, No. 748 (May 26, 1822), pp. 329-30; "No. 2—Lord Byron's 'Cain,'" No. 749 (June 2, 1822), pp. 338-41; "No. 3—On the Quarterly Review," No. 750 (June 9, 1822), pp. 355-57; "No. 4—'Prometheus Unbound,'" No. 751 (June 16, 1822), pp. 370-71; "No. 5—'Prometheus Unbound' (Concluded)," No. 752 (June 23, 1822), pp. 389-90; "No. 6—On Mr. Shelley's New Poem, Entitled 'Adonais,'" No. 754 (July 7, 1822), pp. 419-21.

[58] Hunt, *Autobiography*, pp. 298-99.

[59] Hogg to Shelley, January 29, 1822 (*S. & M.*, II, 735). Another source of information was Maria Gisborne in her letters to Mary Shelley, February 9, April 28, May 17, 1822 (*Gisborne and Williams*, pp. 76, 84, 85).

Hunts' safety[60] or the impatience for their arrival at Pisa. The apartment in Byron's Lanfranchi Palace was ready for them, most of those who would form the group about Shelley and Byron had already come to Pisa, and now only Leigh Hunt was needed for work to begin on the periodical which would constitute part of the activities of many of the group. Byron was never actually enthusiastic about the literary project, as was Shelley,[61] but Hunt's delay served to diminish much of the interest that Byron did have.

There were other sources of distraction for Byron. In February, Francis Jeffrey published in *The Edinburgh Review* "a little cruel medicine" for Byron concerning his three plays, *Sardanapalus*, *The Two Foscari*, and *Cain*.[62] Although Byron could not forget that Jeffrey had supported him "for ten good years, without any motive to do so but his own good will,"[63] he was bothered by John Murray's discouraging reports.[64] On March 24, the fight took place between members of Byron's party and that of the Italian dragoon, Sergeant-Major Stephani Masi. Since Masi was critically wounded, the police became quite concerned with the affair, and the position of Byron and the Gambas with regard to the Tuscan authorities became more

---

[60] The storms during the winter of 1821-22 were severe and destructive, and this worried Mary, as she reported to Maria Gisborne on January 18, 1822 (Frederick L. Jones, "Mary Shelley to Maria Gisborne: New Letters, 1818-1822," *Studies in Philology*, LII [1955], 73).

[61] Some have denied that Byron had any interest. "It was probably not until it became necessary to take practical steps for transforming a vagrant fancy into a stable fact that Byron began to realise the possibility of his having made a mistake, but the very weakness which was the root of his vacillation of purpose prevented him from making a courageous admission of it" (J. Ashcroft Noble, "Leigh Hunt, Lord Byron, and 'The Liberal'" [an unpublished article dated 1882, used by permission of the Committee of the Manchester Public Libraries], pp. 16-17).

[62] Francis Jeffrey to Charles Wilkes, April 13, 1822 (Henry, Lord Cockburn, *Life of Lord Jeffrey* [2 vols.; Philadelphia, 1856], II, 161). See "Lord Byron's Tragedies," *The Edinburgh Review*, XXXVI (1822), 413-52.

[63] Byron to Murray, May 17, 1822 (*L. & J.*, VI, 64).

[64] Byron to Shelley, May 20, 1822 (*Ibid.*, VI, 67).

difficult.[65] In the spring, plans were made for summer residence.
In late April, the Shelleys, with the Williamses as their guests,
moved to the Villa Magni near Lerici.[66] Byron leased a furnished house with outbuildings and gardens near Monte Nero
from Francesco Dupuy, a banker, for a period from May 1 to
October 31, but, not long after he moved into the house in
May, Byron discovered that the water supply was impure, and
he decided to return to his more permanent residence at the
Palazzo Lanfranchi. In his attempts to break the lease, he
became involved with litigation which was to last until July,
1823.[67] Finally, there was the death of Allegra, daughter of
Byron and Claire Clairmont, on April 19 in the Convent of
Bagnacavallo, where Byron had insisted upon placing her
despite Claire's objections and Shelley's obvious disapproval.[68]
This, of course, removed the necessity that Shelley continue to
act as Claire's advocate with Byron in matters concerning the
child, but this would hardly have eliminated tensions between
Byron and Shelley on that score, and it obviously served to
bring new emotional disturbances to Byron.

Shelley's attitude toward Byron, on which much of the
success of the proposed journal would seem to depend, deteriorated during the first six months of 1822. "Lord Byron is
established now, and we are constant companions," Shelley
wrote to John Gisborne in January,[69] but in another letter,
written in June, he remarked, "I detest all society—almost all,
at least—and Lord Byron is the nucleus of all that is hateful
and tiresome in it."[70] Some of the cause lay in specific incidents,
such as Byron's having the name *Don Juan* painted across the

---

[65] Cline (pp. 91-154) examines this episode with extreme thoroughness.

[66] Shelley to Mary, April 28, 1822 (*Works*, X, 383-84).

[67] Byron, *L. & J.*, VI, 413-15. Byron was at length ordered to pay 300 france-
sconi, three months' rent with interest.

[68] Shelley to Mary, August 15, 1821 (*Works*, X, 310-16).

[69] Shelley to John Gisborne, January 11, 1822 (*Ibid.*, X, 342).

[70] Shelley to Gisborne, June 18, 1822 (*Ibid.*, X, 402).

mainsail of the Shelleys' boat.[71] But much resulted from Byron's vacillation toward the project. Shelley could write to Leigh Hunt, "He expresses himself *again* warmly about this literary scheme and I am sure you would do well to engage with him,"[72] but Shelley's position was at best difficult, and was gradually becoming worse. "He dreaded failure, and resolved that he would do his best to prevent it," Thornton Hunt commented more than forty years later, "and yet again he scarcely anticipated success."[73] In June, after Hunt's arrival at Genoa, Shelley wrote that since Hunt had "the faculty of eliciting from any given person the greatest possible quantity of good they are capable of yielding," including Byron, "all will go well."[74] He wished, above all else perhaps, to spare Leigh Hunt the pain of unnecessary discouragement, but he could be more candid with Horace Smith: "Between ourselves, I greatly fear that this alliance will not succeed; for I, who could never have been regarded as more than the link of the two thunderbolts, cannot now consent to be even that,—and how long the alliance between the wren and the eagle may continue, I will not prophesy."[75]

§ *ii*

During the early months of 1822, it became quite apparent that Byron's close friends in England were strongly opposed to the possible literary association of Byron with Hunt and Shelley. They were Thomas Moore, John Cam Hobhouse, John Murray, and Douglas Kinnaird. Their avowed intention

---

[71] See Frederick L. Jones, "Shelley's Boat," *Times Literary Supplement*, January 18, 1936, p. 55. After the piece of the mainsail on which the name had been painted was removed, Mary wrote to Maria Gisborne on June 2, 1822, "I do not know what Lord Bryon will say, but Lord and Poet as he is, he could not be allowed to make a coal barge of our boat" (Mary Shelley, *Letters*, I, 171).

[72] Shelley to Hunt, February 17, 1822 (*Works*, X, 358).

[73] Thornton Hunt, "Shelley, By One Who Knew Him," p. 190.

[74] Shelley to Hunt, June 24, 1822 (*Works*, X, 408).

[75] Shelley to Smith, June 29, 1822 (*Ibid.*, X, 410).

was to save Byron from the serious results of such a public
association. Other motives, certainly less commendable, have
been attributed to all but Kinnaird. Although by 1850 Leigh
Hunt had come to believe that Thomas Moore was sincere in
his desire to help Byron,[76] he suggested in 1828 that Moore was
resentful of criticism of his work which had appeared in *The
Examiner* during 1819.[77] In 1826, William Hazlitt accused
Moore of an underlying fear for his own reputation: "Mr.
Moore had lived so long among the Great that he fancied
himself one of them, and regarded the indignity as done to
himself."[78] And more recently, George Dumas Stout has made
the suggestion that since Moore had been led to expect that
he himself might join Byron in producing a periodical, he
naturally would resent Byron's association with Hunt for the
purpose.[79] John Cam Hobhouse acted in opposition to the

---

[76] Hunt, *Autobiography*, p. 315.

[77] Hunt, *Lord Byron*, p. 57. Although Hunt wrote here that Moore resented
Hunt's comments on "Lalla Rookh," he was confused and had in mind "A
Selection of Irish Melodies" (*The Examiner*, No. 575 [January 3, 1819], p. 11;
No. 577 [January 17, 1819], pp. 43-44). Moore, in fact, did resent these notices,
but it hardly seems probable that this would be significant as part of his motivation
in 1822. Moore wrote in his diary for January 19, 1819, "A review of my political
character in the '*Examiner*;' good-naturedly meant, but I had much rather Hunt
would *let me alone.*" He turned again to the subject on January 21, "Wrote to
Hunt, and gave him a little hint to keep his theories upon religion and morality
somewhat more to himself, as they shock and alienate many of his best intentioned
readers" (*Memoirs, Journals, and Correspondence of Thomas Moore*, ed. Lord John
Russell [8 vols.; London, 1853-56], II, 255-56—hereafter referred to as Russell,
Moore).

[78] "On Jealousy and Spleen of Party," *The Complete Works of William Hazlitt*,
ed. P. P. Howe (21 vols.; London, 1930-34), XII, 378. Hazlitt was not alone in
recognizing the irony of Moore's position regarding Byron's association with the
Hunts. In the Preface to the satire on William Gifford, *Ultra-Crepidarius* (1823),
Leigh Hunt recalled, "It has been my fortune of late . . . to see a party of men,
who have risen into what is called 'good company' out of the families of grocers
and linen-drapers . . . doing their best to obstruct the fortunes of a family, which
had suffered in their own cause, and which had the misfortune of being neither
'high' nor 'low' " (*Poetical Works*, ed. Milford, p. 712). Moore's father was a
grocer and wine merchant.

[79] George Dumas Stout, "Studies Toward a Biography of Leigh Hunt" (Doctoral
dissertation, Harvard University, 1928), p. 102 n.

proposed periodical, according to Hazlitt, because, after his
brief imprisonment in Newgate for a breach of privilege of the
House of Commons, he felt "particularly sore and tenacious
on the score of public opinion."[80] Hunt argued that Hobhouse
was annoyed at *The Examiner*'s criticism of certain of his statements during the campaign for Westminster in 1820.[81] John
Murray was, of course, widely accused of resentment of the
fact that Byron had made another connection for publication
of his works. Murray had been thrown with Hunt at least in
connection with *Rimini*. His acquaintance with Shelley had
been slight, but certainly no more fortunate in its results than
that with Hunt.[82] How much this influenced Murray in his
opposition to the proposed literary alliance cannot, of course,
be known, just as the accusations against Moore and Hobhouse
can never be clearly proved or refuted. The results were more
important with respect to the new periodical than were the
causes, for each of these four friends of Byron was able in his
own way to strike at the project.

Thomas Moore represented the early opposition. His activity
was, as Hazlitt described it, almost frenzied:

Mr. Moore darted backwards and forwards from Cold-Bath-Fields'
Prison [where John Hunt remained until May, 1822] to the
Examiner-Office, from Mr. Longman's to Mr. Murray's shop, in

---

[80] Hazlitt, *Works*, XII, 379. Hobhouse was imprisoned from December, 1819,
to February, 1820, for writing the pamphlet *A Trifling Mistake in Thomas Lord
Erskine's Recent Preface*, which was voted by the House a breach of privilege. See
Byron, *L. & J.*, IV, 395, 410, 418, 423, 498.

[81] Hunt, *Lord Byron*, pp. 54-57. *The Examiner* supported Hobhouse from nomina-
tion to election (*The Examiner*, No. 633 [February 13, 1820] to No. 639 [March 26,
1820]). Hunt perhaps referred to comments in *The Examiner*, No. 637 (March 12,
1820), p. 170.

[82] On January 16, 1816, Shelley applied unsuccessfully to have Murray publish
Alastor (*Works*, IX, 125-26). In September, 1816, he brought to England the
manuscript of the Third Canto of *Childe Harold*, for which Murray paid 2,000
guineas although he had believed he was to pay 1,200 (*Ibid.*, IX, 198-99). Murray
then refused to let Shelley proofread the work, as Byron had requested. Murray
was angry, Shelley suspected, over the part Shelley played in the transaction
(*Ibid.*, IX, 205).

a state of ridiculous trepidation, to see what was to be done to prevent this degradation of the aristocracy of letters, this indecent encroachment of plebeian pretensions, this undue extension of patronage and compromise of privilege.[83]

Moore first understood that Byron, Shelley, and Hunt were "to *conspire* together in the Examiner," and he wrote to Byron in late January or early February to "deprecate such a plan with all my might." Byron must stand alone, especially since he had chosen a "bankrupt" partnership, for "partnerships in fame, like those in trade, make the strongest party answerable for the deficiencies or delinquencies of the rest." Both of Byron's proposed associates, Moore continued, were "clever fellows," Shelley himself "a man of real genius," but Byron could not serve his enemies better "than by forming such an unequal and unholy alliance." Byron replied simply, on February 19, 1822, "Be assured that there is no such coalition as you apprehend."[84] Moore was persistent, concentrating his opposition upon Shelley, who—despite his fancy "sufficient for a whole generation of poets"—was extremely immature in his political and philosophic thoughts; these, like Shelley's poetry itself, were "distilled through the same over-refining and unrealising alembic."[85] Nevertheless, such ideas were dangerous, particularly those dealing with religious teachings. Moore wrote to Byron, warning that if he must fill his works with political materials, he should at least avoid religious comments. "You will easily guess that, in all this, I am thinking not so much of you, as of a friend and, at present, companion of yours, whose influence over your mind . . . I own I dread and deprecate most earnestly."[86] As Moore had anticipated,[87] Byron showed this

---

[83] Hazlitt, "On Jealousy and Spleen of Party," *Works*, XII, 378.

[84] Byron, *L. & J.*, VI, 22-23.

[85] Moore, *Byron*, I, 550. White (I, 745-46) believed that Moore and Shelley never met; the slight correspondence between them appears to have been pleasant.

[86] Moore to Byron, February 19, 1822 (Moore, *Byron*, II, 362.)

[87] *Ibid.*, II, 397.

letter to Shelley, who became concerned over what appeared to be Moore's misconception of the situation. Shelley, clearly underestimating his own capacities, wrote to Horace Smith asking him to assure Moore "that I have not the smallest influence over Lord Byron, in this particular."[88] Smith in turn wrote to Moore,[89] who sent back an "obliging message" for Shelley.[90] In this particular instance, the matter ended, but opposition from Byron's fashionable friends was to continue.

§ *iii*

The Tory press was as upset as Byron's friends—and with as much reason—at the thought of the new alliance. There were of course moderate and radical organs which might have been expected to support the Pisan group, but actually many of these remained, during the period of *The Liberal*, disappointingly noncommittal. The more moderate journals were probably disturbed by what appeared to be the extremism of the new coalition, while the radical were often concerned primarily with politics and looked upon *The Liberal* as largely literary. Whatever was the cause, the only consistent source of support for *The Liberal* was to be *The Examiner* itself.

Leigh Hunt had long been the target of the Tory periodicals, especially *Blackwood's Edinburgh Magazine*.[91] Although in many instances Shelley's talents were recognized, he was damned in

[88] Shelley to Smith, April 11, 1822 (*Works*, X, 377-78).

[89] Moore recorded in his diary for May 14, 1822, "Shelley too has written anxiously to Smith to say how sorry he should be to stand ill in my opinion, and making some explanation of his opinions which Smith is to show me" (Russell, *Moore*, III, 353).

[90] Shelley's reply to Smith, acknowledging the message from Moore, was dated June 29, 1822 (*Works*, X, 409-10).

[91] Six articles, each entitled "On the Cockney School of Poetry," appeared between October, 1817, and October, 1819 (*Blackwood's Edinburgh Magazine*, II [1817], 38-41, 194-201; III [1818], 453-56, 519-24; V [1819], 97-100; VI [1819], 70-75).

that quarter for his religious and political ideas.[92] Byron was not frequently disturbed, because of his rank, his association with John Murray of *The Quarterly Review*,[93] and the fact that he was not actually one of the reformers. Yet, as one of Byron's earliest biographers recognized, the new literary association with the Hunts "was the signal for the bloodhounds to shake themselves clear and pursue, with the utmost speed, their victim."[94]

In the first of the "Letters to the Readers of the Examiner," written in the winter of 1822, Leigh Hunt promised that after his arrival in Italy he would tell his readers about the "work in which I am about to be engaged, and respecting which there have been the idlest misrepresentations."[95] In *The New Monthly Magazine*, there was literally a "misrepresentation," an account of an imaginary flood in London and "of some of the heart-breaking particulars," including the following:

Messrs. Leigh Hunt and Bysshe Shelly [*sic*] were driven with their respective establishments from Messrs. Longman's down Ave Maria-lane, and before they could utter a single paternoster, found themselves hurled with considerable violence against Vauxhall-bridge. The ladies were received in a Penitentiary, but the gentlemen sailed in a felucca for Pisa.[96]

---

[92] See Newman Ivey White, *The Unextinguished Hearth: Shelley and His Contemporary Critics* (Durham, North Carolina, 1938).

[93] John Murray was one of the founders of *The Quarterly Review* in 1809. William Gifford was editor from 1809 to 1824.

[94] [Alexander Kilgour] *Anecdotes of Lord Byron from Authentic Sources, with Remarks Illustrative of his Connection with the Principal Literary Characters of the Present Day* (London, 1825), p. 47.

[95] *The Examiner*, No. 748 (May 26, 1822), pp. 329-30.

[96] "Grimm's Ghost. Letter VII," *The New Monthly Magazine and Literary Journal*, IV [*Original Papers*], 1822), 161. Founded in protest against the "Jacobinism" of *The Monthly Magazine* in 1814, this work, published by Henry Colburn, was first called *The New Monthly Magazine and Universal Register*. In 1820, the emphasis shifted from politics to literary criticism, the title was changed to that given above, and Thomas Campbell was made editor. The *Original Papers* were issued separately each year, in a bound volume, so that it is impossible to assign a specific time to their publication. See Walter Graham, *English Literary Periodicals* (New York, 1930), pp. 284-85.

More to the point was the comment in *The European Magazine and London Review* for January, 1822: "Leigh Hunt and Bysche [*sic*] Shelley are . . . understood to be his Lordship's colleagues at Pisa, where they are engaged in the production of some periodical work, for transmission to England, to console their native country for their absence."[97] In March, *The Gazette of Fashion* carried a simple announcement that Byron, Shelley, and Hunt were preparing a magazine "which will be published quarterly, and superintended in this country by the present Editor of the Examiner, Mr. John Hunt."[98] And in September, *The Imperial Magazine* compared Byron to Voltaire with his group of followers at Ferney: "so, according to accounts, Lord Byron in his retreat at Pisa, is engaged in forming a school of sceptics, who, it seems, are to club their wits in a journal, for the dissemination of what they are pleased to term liberal opinions."[99]

Aside from these early comments, *Blackwood's Edinburgh*

---

[97] "Literary Intelligence," *The European Magazine and London Review: Illustrative of the Literature, History, Biography, Politics, Arts, Manners and Amusements of the Age*, LXXXI (1822), 71. This work, founded by James Perry in 1782, was a monthly periodical intended to be nonpartisan. It existed until 1825. An announcement of the proposed periodical appearing in the January 12 issue of *The Windsor and Eton Express and General Advertiser* (p. 3), which W. G. Bebbington recently brought to light ("The Most Remarkable Man of His Age," *Keats-Shelley Memorial Bulletin*, VII [1956], 28), shows similarities: "Lord Byron has got a new literary coadjutor in Mr. Leigh Hunt, whom he has invited to reside with him at Pisa: it is stated that the 'Tria juncta in uno,' Byron, Shelley and Hunt, are to write some sort of periodical work, and send it to console their native land for their own absence." Charles Knight edited this paper from 1812 to 1826. In a new "Prospectus" (1816), he declared his intention "to advocate the good old cause of national liberty, constitutional authority, and sound morality" (Bebbington, "Charles Knight and Shelley," *Keats-Shelley Journal*, VI [1957], 84).

[98] "Literary Notices," *The Gazette of Fashion, and Magazine of Literature, the Fine Arts, and Belles Lettres*, No. 5 (March 2, 1822), p. 83. This journal, "Dedicated to His Royal Highness the Duke of York," lasted for only thirteen numbers, from February 2 to July 27, 1822. On April 3, it gave Shelley adverse mention (No. 7, p. 177). Had it survived, it would have opposed *The Liberal*.

[99] "Memoirs of the Living Poets of Great Britain (Byron)," *The Imperial Magazine; or, Compendium of Religious, Moral, and Philosophical Knowledge*, IV (1822), 825. This magazine, conservative and orthodox, appeared monthly from 1819 to 1834.

...*ugazine* had the field to itself. Although William Hazlitt insisted that at the time of the alliance between Byron and Hunt *Blackwood's* "overflowed, as might be expected, with tenfold gall and bitterness,"[100] in reality the writers of *Blackwood's* usually gave the appearance of detachment so that they were able to bring to their comments the humor and irony that rendered these comments much more effective than those of others. The opening of the *Blackwood's* attack, a "Letter from London" addressed to "Christopher North" and appearing in the February number, was characteristic:

You must be careful how you wreak your disdain on the principles of Lord Byron's later poetry, as he will soon have it in his power to make fierce reprisals on you and other *dissenters*. You have perhaps heard of the Journal which is to be written by him at Pisa, and sent over here for publication, in order that the balance of critical power may be restored, which has preponderated lately too much on the Tory side. In this great undertaking he has called to himself two allies, namely, Mr Bysshe Shelly [*sic*] and Mr Leigh Hunt, the latter of whom has abandoned his suburban villa, (No. 13, Lisson Grove North,) to brave, with his wife and "Little Johnnys," a perilous voyage on the un-cockney ocean. The sphere of this poet's experience will now be nobly enlarged. No one must twist [*sic*] him any more about "poplar rows" and "back gardens."[101]

In March, "Maga" carried two items concerning the proposed journal. One reported, erroneously enough, that Byron was soon to make a visit to England. "This will be awkward for the beginning of the Pisan Journal," continued the writer, "which, by the bye, is to be edited in London by Mr John Hunt of the Examiner."[102] In the other item, part of the first number of the "Noctes Ambrosianæ," the "holy alliance of Pisa" was discussed by "Morgan Odoherty" and "The Editor."

---

[100] Hazlitt, "On Jealousy and Spleen of Party," *Works*, XII, 378.
[101] "Letter from London," *Blackwood's Edinburgh Magazine*, XI (1822), 237.
[102] "London Chit-Chat," *Ibid.*, XI (1822), 331.

The prospect of Leigh Hunt abroad seemed to them ridiculous: "The pictures and statues will drive him clean out of his wits. He'll fall in love with some of them." But then, the entire scheme seemed absurd. "Imagine Shelly [*sic*], with his spavin, and Hunt, with his staingalt, going in the same harness with such a caperer as Byron, three a-breast," commented The Editor. "He'll knock the wind out of them both the first canter."[103] In April, there appeared a verse, "Critique on Lord Byron"—of which the theme was the supposed boredom of the public with Byron's work—containing the warning, " 'Twould be wrong, noble Bard, Oh! permit me to tell ye,/ To establish a league with Leigh Hunt and Byshe [*sic*] Shelley."[104] "Letter from Paddy," an article in the same number of *Blackwood's*, introduced an idea which was to appear frequently in subsequent comment upon *The Liberal*—Byron's susceptibility to Leigh Hunt's literary influence. "Since Shelley has been with him, he has written 'Cain,' " remarked Paddy. "And now Leigh Hunt is about to join him, I'll lay a guinea to an apple-paring, that his Lordship sets up an Examiner, or writes a Cockney poem, commencing,

> Lack-a-day! but I've grown wiser,
> Since Mister Hunt has come to Pisa*r*."[105]

In June, *Blackwood's* commented favorably upon Jeffrey's review of Byron's plays in *The Edinburgh Review*: "it has probably crushed out, with the last trample of its heel, the whole breed of 'Cains' which were threatened from Pisa!" In fact, the Pisan alliance itself would probably disintegrate. "Shelley will henceforth rave only to the moon. Hunt will sonneteer himself,

---

[103] "Noctes Ambrosianæ, No. 1," *Ibid.*, XI (1822), 363. Named for Ambrose's, a public house, this feature continued until 1835. John Wilson wrote forty-one of the seventy-one numbers, in which he appeared as "Christopher North," William Maginn as "Odoherty," and John Gibson Lockhart as "The Editor." Other persons, real and imaginary, were also frequently introduced.

[104] "Critique on Lord Byron," *Ibid.*, XI (1822), 460.

[105] "Letter from Paddy," *Ibid.*, XI (1822), 463.

and 'urge tear on tear,' in memory of Hampstead butter and
Chelsea buns; and Byron, sick of his companions, and
ashamed of his career, will at length ask his dæmon, how it is
that he has cast himself out of all the advantages that life
lavished on him?" The idea that Byron's life had become
meaningless and futile, and that in his isolation he recognized
this, was to become a recurrent theme of later comments.
"Is an English nobleman to have no correspondent but his
bookseller? No friends but a vulgar group, already shaken out
of English society? No objects but the paltry praises of tem-
porizing reviews? And no studies but the shame and scorn of
honourable literature?"[106]

Obviously, contempt was a dominant attitude of the *Blackwood's* writers when they regarded the Pisan group, but the
frequency of their comment gives rise to the suspicion that their
contempt was not unmixed with apprehension. Nevertheless,
there was rarely a suggestion of the self-righteousness and
distorted fear with which others were to regard the new journal.
William Wordsworth, for example, reported that he had heard
"that Byron, Shelley, Moore, Leigh Hunt . . . are to lay their
heads together in some Town of Italy, for the purpose of
conducting a Journal to be directed against everything in
religion, in morals and probably in government and literature,
which our Forefathers have been accustomed to reverence."
He believed that "the notion seems very extravagant," but
added, "perhaps the more likely to be realized on that account."[107] John Watkins affords a further illustration in his
biography of Byron, which was published in May, 1822. Byron
had called together a "set of writers for the purpose of com-
piling a literary journal at Pisa," including "the proprietor and

---

[106] "Cambridge Pamphlets," *Ibid.*, XI (1822), 740-41.
[107] William Wordsworth to Walter Savage Landor, April 20, 1822 (*The Letters
of William and Dorothy Wordsworth. The Later Years,* ed. Ernest de Selincourt
[3 vols.; London, 1939], I, 69).

editor of the most seditious paper in England." They were to form an "academy of blasphemy" and a "poetical school of immorality and profaneness," which would, Watkins believed, "make a considerable noise in the world." There was, however, the probability "that mankind, after having so recently witnessed the practical effects resulting from a combination of talents, employed in overturning religion, will contentedly suffer a repetition of the experiment."[108]

The adverse comment written in anticipation or in review of *The Liberal* during the following months was in general to show either the indifference and amusement assumed by *Blackwood's* or the fear and sober condemnation illustrated by Wordsworth. Much of the reaction was doubtless expressive of attitudes toward the participants in the Pisan association and toward their other writings as it was expressive of critical judgments of *The Liberal* itself.[109] Few individual comments were extraordinary, but the extent of them reveals clearly with what concern the conservative forces looked toward Pisa;[110] and the direction which the criticism took, particularly regarding Byron, did much to cause *The Liberal* to terminate as it did.

---

[108] [John Watkins] *Memoirs, Historical and Critical, of the Life and Writings of the Right Honourable Lord Byron, with Anecdotes of Some of His Contemporaries* (London, 1822), pp. 408-14. Isaac Disraeli described John Watkins, LL.D., to Byron as "a dead hand at a Life" (*L. & J.*, VI, 86 n.).

[109] White, *The Unextinguished Hearth*, p. 373.

[110] See Appendix IV.

III

The First Number

§ *i*

THE HUNTS SAILED FROM PLYMOUTH ABOARD THE *DAVID WALTER* ON May 13, 1822.[1] They arrived at Genoa one month later, and Leigh Hunt wrote to inform Shelley.[2] On June 28, they proceeded toward Leghorn,[3] having "a long passage" and arriving on July 1.[4] Leaving his wife and children in the town, Leigh set forth to visit Byron at Monte Nero. Here he encountered the rather absurd situation in which an enraged servant, who had already slightly wounded Pietro Gamba with the knife he wielded, was besieging the house, with Byron, Teresa, and Pietro caught inside; the scene ended when the servant suddenly threw himself upon Byron's mercy and was forgiven though dismissed from Byron's service.[5] Leigh Hunt returned to Leghorn, where he and his family moved from quarters on board ship to a hotel; here they awaited Shelley.[6]

---

[1] Hunt, *Autobiography*, p. 299.

[2] Hunt gave June 13 as the date of the arrival (*Autobiography*, p. 311), but in the letter to Shelley dated June 15, he wrote, "We have just arrived here" (*Corr.*, I, 181); and in "Letters from Abroad. Letter II.—Genoa," he reported, "It was at two o'clock on the 15th of June that our vessel entered the harbour" (*The Liberal*, I [1822-23], 270).

[3] Hunt, *Autobiography*, p. 312.

[4] Leigh Hunt to Elizabeth Kent, his sister-in-law, July 2, 1822 (*Corr.*, I, 185-86). For further discussion of the exact time of Hunt's arrival at Monte Nero, see Cline, p. 244, n. 57.

[5] The accounts of this incident are numerous and marked with variation. For a comparison of many of them, see Cline, pp. 172-75.

[6] Hunt, *Autobiography*, p. 324.

On July 1, Shelley and Edward Williams sailed on the *Don Juan* from Lerici to Leghorn. They arrived in the evening and spent the night on board the boat. In the morning, when they came ashore, they heard that the Counts Ruggero and Pietro Gamba, father and brother of Teresa Guiccioli, had just been ordered to leave Tuscany and that Byron was planning to accompany them.[7] Shelley met the Hunts, and on July 3 he took them to Pisa, where they began to move into their quarters in Byron's Palazzo Lanfranchi. They were joined by Byron, who now openly brought Teresa with him, for the Gambas were moving on to Lucca, and Byron had changed his plans for an immediate departure.[8] Shelley returned to Leghorn on July 7 to set out with Williams the next day for Lerici, and Leigh Hunt settled down in his new home and thought hopefully of the future.

From the beginning, however, there were indications of trouble. Although Byron might have welcomed Hunt "with the most marked cordiality,"[9] his reception of Mrs. Hunt was, according to Shelley's account to Williams, "most shameful."[10] This is hardly surprising, since the personalities of Byron and

---

[7] Williams' journal for July 1 and 2 (*Gisborne and Williams*, p. 156). On the basis of chronology, Cline (pp. 244-45) has successfully denied what many had previously asserted, that the exile resulted from this latest affray, which had been witnessed by Hunt.

[8] At approximately this time, Luigi Torelli, a police spy observing the Byron-Gamba activities, recorded in his diary the somewhat garbled but nevertheless alarming account of Byron's intentions:

> "Byron no longer talks of leaving. On the contrary, he is expecting another English poet, a certain Smith, and they intend to start a newspaper against the Italian Government, which is to be printed in England, and bring them in much money. This will be something far worse than Lady Morgan's book—a weekly satire directed chiefly against Austria, whom they call the usurper of Italian freedom" (Janet Ross, "Byron at Pisa," *The Nineteenth Century*, XXX [1891], 763).

[9] Hunt to Elizabeth Kent, July 2, 1822 (*Corr.*, I, 186).

[10] Edward Williams to Jane Williams, July 6, 1822 (*Gisborne and Williams*, p. 163).

5

Marianne Hunt showed marked contrast,[11] and from the beginning she had doubted the sincerity of what her husband considered the "single-hearted and agreeable qualities in Lord Byron."[12] Certainly the tension was increased by the fact that the physician Vaccà, who came to the Palazzo Lanfranchi shortly after the Hunts' arrival, predicted that Marianne would not outlive the year.[13]

The situation regarding the journal itself was at the moment no more promising. Although Shelley had informed Hunt in the letter of invitation that the project was to be "a periodical work" filled with the writings of each of the participants, Hunt had either forgotten this or hoped to draw forth Byron's views. "Shelley has not told me what sort of writing is proposed," he wrote from Plymouth in January, "but I conclude something in a periodical shape." He himself had ideas, which in part at least resemble a description of what *The Liberal* was to come to be. "Suppose, for instance, we made a monthly or two-monthly publication, entirely of Pisan origin, that is to say, written by ourselves & friends there . . . we might have essays, stories, poetry, poetical translation, especially from the Italian,—in short, any thing we chose to blurt out or to be inspired with."[14] In the ensuing months, no further arrangements were made. At the time of Leigh Hunt's arrival, Shelley apparently revealed his pessimism and made some effort to warn Hunt about false hopes.[15] Byron showed no inclination to be specific about the new periodical, so that Shelley resolved to remain at Pisa,

---

[11] The Marchesa Iris Origo (*The Last Attachment* [London, 1949], p. 320) has described Marianne Hunt as "one of the most uncompromisingly British matrons who ever set foot upon the Continent . . . as intransigent in her middle-class independence as in her moral outlook."

[12] Hunt, *Lord Byron*, p. 2.

[13] Hunt, *Autobiography*, p. 325. As many writers on the subject who have a sense of the ironic have observed, Marianne Hunt lived until 1857, while Vacca was dead in 1826.

[14] Unpublished letter from Hunt to Byron, January 27, 1822 (the Berg Collection of the New York Public Library).

[15] Hunt, *Lord Byron*, pp. 13-14.

despite his own wish to return home, until specific arrangements were made.[16] Hunt was, by Williams' account, "shuffled off from day to day," and Williams himself grew impatient at Leghorn, "kept day after day waiting for Shelley's definitive arrangements with Lord B." At one time, Byron insisted on remaining an anonymous participant, it seems,[17] and when he offered "The Vision of Judgment" for the first issue of the periodical, he acted with reluctance, which he apparently explained as the result of fears that the "*actionable* passages" would cause legal difficulties for the publisher.[18] Yet, in all probability, Byron was, as Leigh Hunt later remarked, "delighted to have the opportunity of printing it,"[19] for despite his recognition that the poem might be judged libellous or even blasphemous, Byron had persisted in his efforts to have it published after he finished it and sent a copy to Murray in October, 1821.[20] Since there was not a copy at Pisa at the time

---

[16] Shelley to Mary, July 4, 1822 (*Works*, X, 412-13).

[17] Edward Williams to Jane Williams, July 6, 1822 (*Gisborne and Williams*, pp. 162-63).

[18] Byron to Kinnaird, December 23, 1822 (*Corr.*, II, 239-40).

[19] [Leigh Hunt] "Lord Byron and Leigh Hunt," *The Examiner*, No. 1,043 (January 27, 1828), p. 52.

[20] Byron to Murray, October 4, 1821 (*L. & J.*, V, 386-87). Byron began the poem in May, 1821, a month after the publication of Southey's official poem on the death of George III, "A Vision of Judgment." He laid it aside until late September. His intention was to ridicule Southey, with whom he had maintained a quarrel since 1817 (see Appendix I, "Quarrel Between Byron and Southey," *L. & J.*, VI, 377-99), but he fully realized that many might consider George III as the object of his satire. When he sent the poem to Murray, he suggested that Murray might prefer to have another publish the work. He sent a copy to Kinnaird in November, and on November 28 Byron wrote Kinnaird that Murray or another must publish the poem (*Corr.*, II, 207). The existence and nature of the poem were apparently an open secret, for in January, 1822, *The European Magazine* (LXXXI [1822], 71) described the poem as "*unfit for publication.*" On February 6, Byron ordered Kinnaird to "*print* fifty copies (at *my expense*), distribute them amongst my acquaintances, and you will soon see that the booksellers *will* publish them, even if we opposed them" (*Corr.*, II, 210). On March 15, he suggested that Murray publish the poem "anonymously and *secretly*," and on April 9, he proposed further, "with some other bookseller's name, or as a *foreign* edition; and in such a *cheap* form that the pirates cannot undersell you" (*L. & J.*, VI, 40, 47-48).

of the Hunts' arrival,[21] it was necessary for Byron to request Murray to give John Hunt the one which he had on hand. On July 3, Byron wrote an order for Murray to do so, specifying "the corrected copy of the proofs," which Murray had printed,[22] as well as the Preface to the poem, in which Byron attempted to make it clear that he was aiming at Robert Southey rather than at the memory of George III.[23] It was Byron's intention to send this order to John Hunt, but he had not done so by the following day, when Shelley wrote to Mary that Byron's "offer if sincere is *more* than enough to set up the journal."[24] Possibly, the order was enclosed in a letter from Leigh to John Hunt dated July 6.[25] There certainly appears

---

[21] According to Edward Williams' journal, there had been a copy of "The Vision of Judgment" at Pisa on November 9, 1821, when Shelley read the poem aloud (*Gisborne and Williams*, p. 111). By early 1822, however, Byron was without a copy. "The only one I have is in London," he told Medwin (*Conversations of Lord Byron*, p. 223), probably referring to that which he had sent to Douglas Kinnaird in November.

[22] These might have been the result of Byron's order that Kinnaird have fifty copies printed. On April 9, 1822, Byron requested Murray to apply to Kinnaird for a corrected proof of the poem (*L. & J.*, VI, 48). It was this which he later asked Murray to give to John Hunt.

[23] Byron to Murray, July 3, 1822 (*L. & J.*, VI, 92-93).

[24] Shelley to Mary, July 4, 1822 (*Works*, X, 413). Regarding Byron's sincerity in this matter, it is necessary to point to a letter in the *Correspondence* (II, 225-27) addressed to John Cam Hobhouse and dated in the edition July 18, 1822, roughly two weeks after Byron ordered that John Hunt publish "The Vision of Judgment." Referring to Kinnaird, Byron wrote, "Douglas has not got the 'Vision' publicated, will you axe [*sic*] him *why*? as he seemed to like it, and to wish it 'stampata.' " If the date were correct, then Byron would clearly be guilty of duplicity, but in another part of the letter he mentioned that he was at work on the fifth act of *Werner*. Since Byron sent the manuscript of *Werner* to Thomas Moore on January 29, 1822 (*L. & J.*, VI, 28), it is clear that the date of the letter in the *Correspondence* has been misread, written possibly "Jy" for January—one of Byron's practices—and Byron is, in this instance, exonerated. See my note, "The Misdating of a Letter: An Exoneration of Byron," *Notes and Queries*, N.S. IV (1957), 122-23.

[25] Luther A. Brewer, *My Leigh Hunt Library* (2 vols.; Cedar Rapids and Iowa City, 1932-38), II, 154—hereafter referred to as Brewer, *Library*. The first volume is entitled *The First Editions*, the second *Holograph Letters*. The materials printed in these volumes are now part of the Leigh Hunt Collection of the State University of Iowa Library, which has given permission for their use here.

to have been such a letter.[26] In any event, Byron covered
the situation by writing to Murray the same day. He had,
he reported, given "The Vision of Judgment" to John Hunt,
who "must publish it at his *own* risk, as it is at his own desire."
He repeated that Murray was to give Hunt "the *corrected* copy
which Mr. Kd. had, as it is mitigated partly, and also the
preface."[27] This apparently satisfied Shelley, who soon departed
for Leghorn and Lerici.

Leigh Hunt's letter of July 6 contained something "for *The
Examiner*" rather than for the new periodical. Byron had not
signed the work although he had "no objection to being
mentioned in private as the author:—in other words, he does
not at all mind being *known* as the author, but thinks perhaps
the verses too trivial to put his name to them publicly." John
was given a free hand with the work, especially in pruning
what might seem to be libellous passages. "Some things, which
I have marked can be left out in common prudence," Leigh
suggested. "Besides the very omissions can be turned to account,
as you can see."[28] The work which he enclosed in this letter
was probably "The Blues,"[29] the short dramatic satire that

---

[26] On July 8, Byron wrote to Murray, "I have consigned a letter to Mr. John
Hunt for the *Vision of Judgement* [*sic*], which you will hand over to him" (*L. & J.*,
VI, 94). It would seem, then, that Byron wrote a letter to John, or to Douglas
Kinnaird for John, but John's subsequent publication of "The Vision of Judg-
ment" without the Preface indicates that he did not receive a specifically worded
order from Byron.

[27] Byron to Murray, July 6, 1822 (*L. & J.*, VI, 94).

[28] Brewer, *Library*, II, 154.

[29] Triviality and possible libellousness of the verse would be attributes of "The
Blues." The only other work which could in any way answer the description would
be "The Vision of Judgment," which R. E. Prothero indeed believed this passage
concerned (*L. & J.*, VI, 123 n.). However, Leigh Hunt had both seen and marked
the copy of the work enclosed in the letter to John, but by his own testimony he
did not see "The Vision of Judgment" prior to his receiving a copy of the first
number of *The Liberal* (Payson G. Gates, "A Leigh Hunt-Byron Letter," *Keats-
Shelley Journal*, II [1953], 14), and there is nothing of Byron's to appear in *The
Examiner* in this period. Probably John Hunt decided to withhold it from the
newspaper for possible use in the periodical. Leigh Hunt described the work as
"the only thing connected with 'The Liberal' that I gave myself occasion to regret"
(*Lord Byron*, p. 62).

Byron had written on the basis of his recollections of Regency England,[30] sending it to John Murray in August, 1820, with some doubts as to the advisability of publication.[31] On July 8, Byron requested Murray to transfer still other materials to John Hunt, "the *Pulci*, original and Italian, and any *prose* tracts of mine . . . all things in your care, except the volume now in the press [*Heaven and Earth* and *Werner*], and the MSS. purchased of Mr. Moore [Byron's memoirs]." Byron obviously intended to exclude his translation from Dante, "Francesca of Rimini," and his "Stanzas to the Po," for in this same letter he suggested that these should not be published "in the same volume."[32] It is, therefore, difficult to determine what were Byron's positive intentions. They apparently included his "Letter to the Editor of 'My Grandmother's Review' " and obviously his translation of the first canto of Luigi Pulci's *Il Morgante Maggiore*. The first, a prose piece aimed at William Roberts, editor of *The British Review* from 1811 to 1822, Byron had sent to Murray in August, 1819.[33] The canto from Pulci,

---

[30] For a hypothetical identification of the models for characters in "The Blues," see Byron, *Poetry*, IV, 570.

[31] Byron to Murray, August 7, 1821 (*L. & J.*, V, 338). If the work were published, Byron wrote, "it must be *anonymously:* but it is too short for a separate publication; and *you* have no miscellany, that I know of for the reception of such things." By September 20, 1821, Byron had changed his mind, describing "The Blues" to Murray as "a mere buffoonery, never meant for publication" (*Ibid.*, V, 369).

[32] Byron to Murray, July 8, 1822 (*Ibid.*, VI, 94-95).

[33] Byron to Murray, August 23, 1819 (*Ibid.*, IV, 346-47). The following day, Byron wrote Murray again, "Keep the *anonymous*, in every case" (*Ibid.*, IV, 348). Murray soon had Thomas Davison, the printer, run off about six copies (see Thomas J. Wise, *Bibliography of Byron* [2 vols.; London, 1932-33], II, 214; and G. H. Deane, "Byron's Letter to the Editor of My Grandmother's Review," *Bibliographical Notes and Queries*, I [1935], 8). Byron was apparently returning one of these copies with corrections on September 27, 1819 (*L. & J.*, IV, 354-55). Murray hesitated to publish the work, so that Byron decided that since the prose piece was extremely topical it should not appear. He ordered its suppression on October 12 and 25, 1820 (*Ibid.*, V, 96, 107), but by November 12, 1821, he was once more concerned with its publication (V, 473). The "Letter" is reprinted (*L. & J.*, IV, 465-70) as Byron wrote it rather than as it appears in *The Liberal*. It is dated "*Sept.* 4th, 1819" rather than merely "Sept. —, ——." The editorial

which Byron considered "the best thing I ever did in my life,"[34] "my grand performance,"[35] had been in Murray's hand since March, 1820.[36]

Byron had not stated clearly in his letters to Murray whether he expected John Hunt to publish "The Vision of Judgment" separately or in the new periodical. Leigh was of the impression that the work was to appear by itself, but, since he believed that Byron had made an outright gift of the poem,[37] he felt that he could suggest that John put the work in the first number of the periodical. This and the other pieces contributed by Byron convinced Leigh that Byron had come into the new project "with great ardour."[38]

§ ii

On July 9, Hunt wrote Shelley a letter, "terrible in its uninformed cheerfulness," in which he reported, "Things go on remarkably well."[39] But soon Hunt, like the others at Pisa, was to learn that Shelley and Williams had gone down in the *Don Juan*. "From that time," Hunt was to recall, "Italy was a black place to me."[40] The "link of the two thunderbolts" was no longer there, and "the wren and the eagle" stood face to

changes, probably John Murray's, though somewhat concerned with mechanical matters, include correction of Byron's impression that William Roberts was a clergyman and deletion of direct references to John Atkins, Lord Mayor of London, and to William Sotheby's poem *Saul*.

[34] Byron to Murray, September 28, 1820 (*L. & J.*, V, 83).

[35] Byron to Murray, January 19, 1821 (*Ibid.*, V, 225). Byron's admiration for this work was apparently deep and consistent, but few shared the feeling with him.

[36] Byron finished the translation on February 21, 1820, and sent it to Murray on February 28 (*Ibid.*, IV, 407, 412-13).

[37] Byron himself was not clear as to what he understood to be the conditions of his donation of "The Vision of Judgment." He would not ask for an account of the profits from the journal until profits had made the Hunts comfortable, he said consistently; but he did reserve all copyrights, he told Kinnaird in a letter of December 30, 1822 (*Corr.*, II, 245). It is doubtful that he made this reservation openly at the time he gave "The Vision of Judgment."

[38] Hunt to Elizabeth Kent, July 8, 1822 (*Corr.*, I, 189).

[39] *S. & M.*, II, 838.   [40] Hunt, *Lord Byron*, p. 18.

face. Byron at once asked Hunt "to look upon him as standing
in Mr. Shelley's place."[41] But Hunt, though aware of what at
this time he considered Byron's kindness, could only ask, "what
can fill up the place that such a man as S[helley] occupied in
my heart?"[42]

Hunt believed that Byron's offer had particular reference to
Hunt's financial needs but "doubted whether even in that,
the most trivial part of friendship, he could resemble Mr.
Shelley if he would."[43] Shelley's death increased Hunt's
dependence on Byron, but it also rendered such dependence
far more objectionable than it had been. "Bitter indeed, for
the first time in my life," Hunt remarked, "was the taste I then
had of obligation."[44] Byron appeared to lose respect for Hunt
as soon as he had discovered his need,[45] and this became one of
the chief factors in the disintegration of their relationship.[46]
The Hunts now tried to live in what they believed was "the
most economical Italian manner," so that they might apply to
Byron for very little, but, Hunt recalled, Byron "put me under
the necessity of asking even for that in driblets, and for these
he sent me every time to his steward."[47] Marianne complained
that "the good actions of *noblemen* are not done in a *noble
manner!*"[48] The fault seemed to lie with Byron's lack of
generosity, Hunt believed, and indeed the accounts of financial

---

[41] *Ibid.*, p. 18.

[42] Hunt to Vincent and Mary Novello, September 9, 1822 (Charles and Mary
Cowden Clarke, *Recollections of Writers* [New York, 1878], p. 217).

[43] Hunt, *Lord Byron*, p. 18.

[44] "Lord Byron and Leigh Hunt," *The Examiner*, No. 1,043 (January 27, 1828),
p. 52. Byron wrote to Kinnaird on September 26, 1822, "I could not help assisting
Hunt—who is a good man—and is left taken all aback by Shelley's demise"
(Cline, p. 189).

[45] Hunt, *Lord Byron*, vi.

[46] "Lord Byron—Mr. Moore—and Mr. Leigh Hunt," *The Tatler*, No. 114
(January 14, 1831), p. 453.

[47] *The Examiner*, No. 1,043 (January 27, 1828), p. 52.

[48] Marianne Hunt, September 19, 1822 ("Unpublished Diary, Pisa, September
18, 1822—Genoa, October 24, 1822, Mrs. Leigh Hunt," *Bulletin and Review of the
Keats-Shelley Memorial Association*, II [1910], 72).

arrangements between the two men would seem to bear this out; yet, these are derived largely from Hunt himself and must be accepted with some qualifications. Some of the fault lay in the manner of Hunt's application for money. "I must trouble you for another 'cool hundred' of your crowns," he cheerfully wrote Byron at one time.[49] The situation was clearly cyclic, for Hunt's manner was doubtless influenced in part at least by his uneasiness in his position, but in turn it caused Byron further irritation. Obviously, the financial situation was basic, but it did not exist in isolation and would not have taken the course it did if other aspects of the situation had not so directed it.

In 1850, Leigh Hunt recognized that he himself should assume some of the blame for the failure of his association with Byron. "I did not mend the matter by my own inability to fall in cordially with his ways," he remarked.[50] These were many and varied. Byron's pride in rank, for example, which had probably been sharpened by comments from his friends, caused him now to resent Hunt's form of address, "My dear Byron."[51] This became "Dear Lord Byron" in late 1822, to which Byron countered with humorous intention, "Dear Lord Hunt." But Leigh Hunt was too sensitive for this, and Byron quickly dropped it.[52] However, sensitivity was also one of Byron's "ways." He was more easily annoyed than pacified, Hunt recalled. "Sympathy would probably have drawn upon you a discussion of matters too petty for your respect; and gaiety would have been treated as an assumption, necessary to be put down by sarcasms."[53] And undoubtedly, during all their association, there was much "mystifying" of Hunt on the part of

---

[49] Nicolson, p. 29. The letter is given without a date.

[50] Hunt, *Autobiography*, p. 350.

[51] The probability that Byron's resentment showed the influence of his friends was first pointed out by Edmund Blunden (*Leigh Hunt and His Circle* [New York, 1930], p. 80).

[52] Nicolson, p. 30.   [53] Hunt, *Lord Byron*, p. 82.

Byron, for the temptation would prove irresistible.[54] This obviously would not assist Hunt in understanding Byron's intentions. Added to the developing tension between the two men, it might easily cause Hunt to read only the worst in Byron's actions. "If Lord Byron appeared to be in good spirits, Hunt called him heartless; if he took a bath, a sybarite," Teresa Guiccioli wrote later, with as much bias as Leigh Hunt revealed in his accounts. "If he tried to joke with him, he was guilty of the insufferable liberties that a great nobleman will allow himself with a poor man. If he presented Hunt with numerous copyrights, with the sole intention of helping him, it could only be because he lacked an editor. If he was charitable, it was out of ostentation."[55]

Misunderstanding should have been expected.[56] In background, Byron and Hunt had little in common, and in temperament and daily habits perhaps even less. This becomes clear from Hunt's account of their routine at Pisa:

Our manner of life was this. Lord Byron, who used to sit up at

---

[54] John Gibson Lockhart ("Lord Byron and Some of His Contemporaries," *The Quarterly Review*, XXXVII [1828], 412) suggested that the difficulty arose not from the fact that Byron would find Hunt one he would enjoy mystifying, but that Hunt would take literally all that Byron might say. John Cam Hobhouse wrote in his diary for May 27, 1824, "Mrs. Leigh and I talking over Lord Byron agreed that his principal failing was a wish to mystify those persons with whom he lived, especially if they were in an inferior condition and of inferior intellect to himself" (*Recollections of a Long Life* [6 vols.; London, 1910-11], III, 44).

[55] Guiccoioli, "Vie de Byron," p. 1532 (Origo, p. 322).

[56] It was expected in some quarters. Jonathan H. Christie wrote to John Gibson Lockhart on January 24, 1823, "Leigh Hunt and he must make a strange couple, Byron as proud as H——, Hunt as vain as a peacock: Byron perpetually doing or saying something to wound Leigh Hunt's self-love" (Andrew Lang, *The Life and Letters of John Gibson Lockhart* [2 vols.; London, 1897], I, 311). Many years later, Cyrus Redding, at this time the actual though not the titular editor of *The New Monthly Magazine*, recalled, "The moment I heard Hunt and his family were in the same house as Lord Byron, I remarked that it could never last long. Domestic habits, manners, familiar modes of expression, dissimilarity of feeling, between persons so differently educated, when in immediate contact and in social conduct so diverse, could never be brought to harmonise" (Cyrus Redding, *Yesterday and Today* [3 vols.; London, 1863], III, 109).

night writing *Don Juan* (which he did under the influence of gin and water), rose late in the morning. He breakfasted; read; lounged about, singing an air, generally out of Rossini; then took a bath, and was dressed; and coming downstairs, was heard, still singing, in the courtyard, out of which the garden ascended, by a few steps, at the back of the house. The servants, at the same time, brought out two or three chairs. My study, a little room in a corner, with an orange tree at the window, looked upon this courtyard. I was generally at my writing when he came down, and either acknowledged his presence by getting up and saying something from the window, or he called out "Leontius!" (a name into which Shelley had pleasantly converted that of "Leigh Hunt") and came up to the window with some jest or other challenge to conversation. His dress, as at Monte Nero, was a nankin jacket, with white waistcoat and trousers, and a cap, either velvet or linen, with a shade to it. In his hand was a tobacco box, from which he helped himself occasionally to what he thought a preservative from getting too fat. Perhaps, also, he supposed it good for the teeth. We then lounged about, or sat and talked, Madame Guiccioli, with her sleek tresses, descending after her toilet to join us.[57]

The differences between Teresa Guiccioli and Marianne Hunt were potentially even greater, but these were given no opportunity for development, since neither spoke the language of the other, and after their introduction there was no gesture on either side. Teresa supposedly objected to Byron's expenditures for the Hunts,[58] and the Hunts for their part objected to Byron's attachment to Teresa. It was not love, Hunt believed, for he doubted that Byron "ever had the good-fortune of knowing what real love is."[59] Marianne disapproved because

---

[57] Hunt, *Autobiography*, p. 331. The picture given in this account is similar to those of Medwin (*Conversations*, pp. 20-22) and Trelawny (*Recollections*, p. 23). It is only fair to point out that it contrasts with that of William Parry (*The Last Days of Lord Byron* [Philadelphia, 1825], pp. 57-59), who described Byron's life under very different circumstances in Greece.

[58] Landré, *Leigh Hunt*, I, 147. No source is given for this statement.

[59] Hunt, *Lord Byron*, p. 7. One reviewer of Leigh Hunt's book ("Lord Byron and Some of His Contemporaries," *The Monthly Review*, VII [1828], 306-7) pointed

she regarded the relation of the Cavalier Servente to his lady with the eyes of an English matron with rather precise moral attitudes and, of course, because she disliked Byron. The attitudes which she and Byron maintained towards each other have been described as "armed neutrality,"[60] which on occasion dangerously weakened. "He said to her one day, 'What do you think, Mrs. Hunt? Trelawney [*sic*] has been speaking against my morals! What do you think of that?'—'It is the first time,' said Mrs. Hunt, 'I ever heard of them.' "[61]

A further cause for tension was the six Hunt children, to whom their father was obviously devoted. Byron clearly did not share Hunt's feelings,[62] and he was distinctly unsympathetic with the view that complete freedom for the children would permit them to develop according to the designs of nature. "They are dirtier and more mischievous than Yahoos," Byron complained. "What they can't destroy with their filth they will with their fingers."[63] But Marianne Hunt saw the matter quite differently:

Mr. Hunt was much annoyed by Lord Byron behaving so meanly about the Children disfiguring his house which his nobleship chose to be very severe upon. How much I wish I could esteem him more! It is so painful, to be under any obligation to a person you cannot esteem! Can anything be more absurd than a peer of the realm—and a *poet* making such a fuss about three or four children disfiguring the walls of a few rooms—The very children would blush for him, fye Lord B.—fye.[64]

---

out that Hunt had no right to complain of the situation at this time, for he had been well aware of the nature of it before he brought his family into it.

[60] Noble, "Leigh Hunt, Lord Byron, and 'The Liberal,' " p. 28.

[61] Hunt, *Lord Byron*, p. 27.

[62] "Hunt expected that all others should see with his eyes, and be moved with similar motives in regard to his family. He loved his family, and expected others to enter into his feelings regarding it" (Redding, *Yesterday and Today*, III, 111).

[63] Byron to Mary Shelley, October 6, 1822 (*L. & J.*, VI, 119).

[64] Marianne Hunt's diary for September 23, 1822 (*Bulletin and Review of the Keats-Shelley Memorial Association*, II [1910], 72-73).

Byron attempted to assure the privacy of his own quarters—whether from the children or from the entire Hunt family is uncertain—by chaining his bulldog across the stairs. On at least one occasion, he dramatized his intentions, and Trelawny, who was a witness, recorded the scene: "When I took my leave he followed me into the passage, and patting the bulldog on the head, he said, 'Don't let any Cockneys pass this way.' "[65]

In matters of literary taste, there was hardly more chance for agreement. "When Leigh Hunt comes we shall have battles enough about those old *ruffiani*, the old dramatists, with their tiresome conceits, their jingling rhymes, and endless play upon words," Byron had told Medwin.[66] But the reality was not so pleasant as the anticipation. "Our tastes are so opposite, that we are totally unsuited to each other," Byron told Lady Blessington. "He admires the Lakers, I abhor them; in short, we are more formed to be friends at a distance, than near."[67] There was but slight respect for the works of each other, and this presumably decreased as critical judgments became involved with personal feelings. "Hunt would have made a fine writer, for he has a great deal of fancy and feeling, if he had not been spoiled by circumstances," Byron remarked. "He was brought up at the Blue-coat foundation, and had never till lately been ten miles from St. Paul's. What poetry is to be expected from such a course of education?"[68] And for his part, Hunt showed rather clearly that Byron's works interested him less than others' writings. The "unpardonable offence" in Byron's eyes, Hunt believed, lay in his "thinking Mr. Wordsworth the first poet of the day, and of being the first to hail the rise of the

---

[65] Edward J. Trelawny, *Records of Shelley, Byron, and the Author* (2 vols.; London, 1878), I, 174.

[66] Medwin, *Conversations*, p. 130.

[67] The Countess of Blessington, *A Journal of Conversations with Lord Byron* (Boston, 1859), p. 100.

[68] Medwin, *Conversations*, pp. 404-5.

younger poet, Mr. Keats, who promised, he thought, to rival Mr. Wordsworth."[69]

Despite the intensity of Thomas Moore's earlier warnings against Byron's association with Shelley and Hunt, Moore apparently was not worried about the proposed journal in the summer and autumn of 1822. By August, the news of Shelley's death had reached England, and Moore perhaps felt that this fact and his own efforts had done much to weaken the chances for success of the new periodical. Obviously, Byron was wavering. Hunt seemed "sanguine about the matter," he wrote Moore, "but (*entre nous*) I am not."[70] He was thinking of going to South America, he told Moore in another letter, "fluctuating between it and Greece," and would have left long before "but for my liaison with the Countess G^i."[71] Aside from such reports as these in Byron's letters to Moore, the knowledge which Moore had of Byron's activities appears to have been surprisingly restricted.[72]

In the late summer, John Cam Hobhouse took a turn as representative of the opposition to the periodical. During a

---

[69] "Lord Byron—Mr. Moore—and Mr. Leigh Hunt," *The Tatler*, No. 114 (January 14, 1831), p. 453. The "English Gentleman in the Greek Military Service" gave an untrue but nevertheless interesting account of the breakdown of the Byron-Hunt relationship, according to which Hunt criticised "Parisina" in the press of Leghorn and Lucca; since this work "was considered by Lord Byron as the best of all his minor poems," he became angry and "never saw or spoke to Mr. Leigh Hunt, or any of his connexions" (*Life, Writings, Opinions, and Times of the Right Hon. George Gordon Noel Byron, Lord Byron* [3 vols.; London, 1825], II, 145-46).

[70] Byron to Moore, July 12, 1822 (*L. & J.*, VI, 97).

[71] Byron to Moore, August 27, 1822 (*Ibid.*, VI, 110).

[72] Moore wrote in his diary on November 15, 1822, that he had met "a Capt. Medwin, a friend of Lord Byron's, who passed a great part of last year at Pisa. . . . Tells me Hunt's whole family is living in the same house with B., and he believes Mrs. Shelley also and her children [*sic*]" (Russell, *Moore*, IV, 20). Although this account was obviously erroneous and confusing, it would have disturbed Moore's feelings of security concerning the supposed end of the Pisan coalition. Yet Moore's diary for the period of *The Liberal* contains surprisingly slight mention of Byron and apparently no comment upon Byron's connection with Hunt or upon the periodical itself.

trip on the Continent, he came to Pisa, arriving on September 15 for six days.[73] "Mr. Hobhouse rushed over the Alps," Hunt recalled in 1828, "not knowing which was more awful, the mountains, or the Magazine."[74] He and Hunt had not seen each other since the elections of 1820,[75] but they now met in the Palazzo Lanfranchi. Hobhouse seemed to Hunt "very polite and complimentary; and then, if his noble friend was to be believed, did all he could to destroy the connexion between us."[76] Byron was to be believed. "Leigh Hunt induced Lord Byron to agree to set up a journal with him," Hobhouse wrote in his diary, "but I endeavoured to persuade Lord Byron that he had better not engage in any such partnership, and it appears Lord Byron has managed to give up the scheme."[77] It would seem likely that, as Hazlitt believed, Hobhouse offered a substitute scheme, that Byron "should write once a week, *in his own name*, in the *Examiner*."[78] Leigh Hunt claimed the plan as his own, perhaps to save appearances, and as soon as Byron decided to adopt it, he was prepared to announce it in *The Examiner*.[79] But such an announcement did not appear. By the time that word of the new scheme could have reached London and John Hunt's answer could have come to Pisa, the first number of *The Liberal* had appeared. Objections from John Hunt were to be expected, and in all probability they materialized. By October 10, Byron was "perfectly willing that the magazine should be proceeded with," for he believed that John had "done so much as to render the Examiner plan

---

[73] Hobhouse's diary, September 5, 1822 (*Recollections*, III, 2). This rather long entry reported events occurring well after September 5.

[74] Hunt, *Lord Byron*, p. 48.   [75] *Ibid.*, p. 57.   [76] *Ibid.*, p. 48.

[77] Hobhouse's diary, September 5, 1822 (*Recollections*, III, 2).

[78] Hazlitt, "On Jealousy and Spleen of Party," *Works*, XII, 379. Hazlitt believed that Hobhouse's reasons for the suggestion were simply that "the 'Liberal' scheme, he was afraid, might succeed: the newspaper one, he knew, could not."

[79] Leigh Hunt to Elizabeth Kent, September 26, 1822 (Stout, "Studies Toward a Biography of Leigh Hunt," pp. 171-72). In a letter to John Hunt dated March 17, 1823, Byron claimed the suggestion as his own (*L. & J.*, VI, 172).

impossible."[80] The direct effects of Hobhouse's visit were annulled, but the confusion that it had caused undoubtedly injured the editorial partnership behind *The Liberal*.

Through the summer months, it had become apparent that the Counts Gamba were not to be allowed by the authorities to return to Ravenna or Pisa and were becoming progressively less welcome at Lucca. Byron had finally decided that he and the Gambas should locate at Genoa.[81] Mary Shelley made arrangements at Albaro near Genoa for houses. For Byron, she rented the Casa Saluzzo at £24 yearly; and despite the recent strain between Leigh Hunt and herself,[82] she took the Casa Negroto, at £20 yearly, for herself, her son Percy Florence, and the Hunts.[83] In late September and early October, the Pisan group made their way to Genoa—Byron and Teresa Guiccioli in a pilot boat, Trelawny in another, and the Hunts in a felucca.[84] There were points on the way which became painful reminders to the Hunts of the hopes with which they had made the journey from Genoa to Pisa eleven weeks before. After they had left the Palazzo Lanfranchi, they stayed briefly at the inn at Leghorn, which they had visited once before.[85] At Lerici the parties met, and Trelawny took Hunt to the Villa Magni, where Shelley had lived. They "paced over its empty rooms and neglected garden. The sea fawned upon the

---

[80] Leigh Hunt to John Hunt, October 10, 1822 (Brewer, *Library*, I, 119). In a letter to Douglas Kinnaird, December 23, 1822, Byron reported, "I even proposed to them to give up the notion of the journal. L[eigh] H[unt] agreed, but J[ohn] H[unt] *would* publish it" (*Corr.*, II, 240).

[81] Origo, p. 323. Luigi Torelli recorded the decision in his diary: "Milord has at length decided on going to Genoa. Some say he is already tired of his favourite Guiccioli, others that he is bent on going to Athens, and purchasing adoration from the Greeks" (Ross, p. 763).

[82] The strain was caused by disagreement over possession of Shelley's heart, which Trelawny had snatched from the funeral pyre; and by the fact that Hunt believed that Mary had not made Shelley happy during his last years (Mary Shelley, *Letters*, I, 209-10; *Gisborne and Williams*, pp. 88-89).

[83] Hunt, *Autobiography*, p. 349.   [84] Hunt, *Lord Byron*, pp. 58-61.

[85] Marianne Hunt's diary for September 18, 1822 (*Bulletin and Review of the Keats-Shelley Memorial Association*, II [1910], 71).

shore, as though it could do no harm."[86] And at Genoa, Leigh Hunt was reminded of the difference between their present feelings and those with which they first beheld the city.[87]

Byron claimed that the new routine at Albaro offered very infrequent contact,[88] but Hunt found that their association, "though less than before, was considerable." Despite the deterioration of their relationship, they maintained at least the appearance of "good terms."[89] Byron was most pleasant, Hunt later recalled, "when he had got a little wine in his head" and was "the proper natural Byron as he ought to have been." In the morning, however, "the happy moment had gone, and nothing remained but to despair and joke."[90] Shortly after the arrival at Genoa, on October 9, Byron was writing to John Murray in a way that would leave little doubt as to the nature of the situation:

> I am afraid the Journal *is* a *bad* business, and won't do; but in it I am sacrificing *myself* for others—*I* can have no advantage in it. I believe the *brothers H.* to be honest men; I am sure they are poor ones. They have not a rap: they pressed me to engage in this work, and in an evil hour I consented: still I shall not repent, if I can do them the least service. I have done all I can for Leigh Hunt since he came here; but it is almost useless: his wife is ill, his six children not very tractable, and in the affairs of this world he himself is a child. The death of Shelley left them totally aground; and I could not see them in such a state without using the common feelings of humanity, and what means were in my power, to set them afloat again.[91]

Obviously the letter was somewhat inaccurate. Worse perhaps,

---

[86] Hunt, *Autobiography*, p. 347.   [87] *Ibid.*, p. 349.

[88] Byron to Murray, December 9, 1822 (*L. & J.*, VI, 148). Benjamin Robert Haydon reported that Lady Blessington had told him, as evidence of Byron's insincerity, that "when she asked him [Byron] about the Hunts, he always affected never to have seen them above once or twice a week, 'a notorious story, Mr. Haydon' " (*Table Talk* [2 vols.; London, 1876], II, 382).

[89] Hunt, *Lord Byron*, p. 64.   [90] Hunt, *Autobiography*, p. 353.

[91] Byron, *L. & J.*, VI, 122-25.

it was indiscreet, for in the back parlor of Murray's publishing house it was to become an instrument used against Leigh Hunt and *The Liberal*.

§ *iii*

Leigh Hunt's letter to John advising him of the death of Shelley became the basis for the obituary in *The Examiner*.[92] Here the circumstances of the accident were recorded, with the remark that Shelley "had been to Pisa to do a kind action, and he was returning to his country abode at Lerici to do another."[93] This was the first public notice in England of Shelley's death, and it formed the basis for many of those which followed.[94] Comparatively few of these mentioned the proposed periodical. Richard Carlile's *Republican* of August 16 simply copied the obituary from *The Examiner*.[95] Other comment was either neutral or unfavorable. In September, *The Gentleman's Magazine* simply noted "that Mr. Shelley had gone to Pisa to establish a periodical work, with the assistance of Lord Byron and Mr. Leigh Hunt."[96] The remarks in *John Bull*,[97] though more general, were less objective:

---

[92] John Gisborne to Thomas Jefferson Hogg, August 12, 1822 (*Gisborne and Williams*, p. 87).

[93] *The Examiner*, No. 758 (August 4, 1822), p. 489.

[94] For illustration and discussion of the obituaries of Shelley, see White, *The Unextinguished Hearth*, pp. 321-38; and George L. Marsh, "The Early Reviews of Shelley," *Modern Philology*, XXVII (1929), 73-95.

[95] *The Republican*, VI (1822), 380. This weekly newspaper was published from 1819 to 1826 by Richard Carlile. He began the work and published twelve of its fourteen volumes in Dorchester Gaol, where he was confined from 1819 to 1825.

[96] *The Gentleman's Magazine*, XCII, Part II (1822), 283. This monthly journal was begun by Edward Cave in 1731, with the intention of collecting and reprinting the best from the many half-sheets and other serials in London at the time. The work existed until 1868. Its sympathies were clearly with the Tories. From 1792 to 1826 John Nichols was editor.

[97] *John Bull*, a weekly newspaper, was established on December 17, 1820, by Theodore Hook and Daniel Terry, with the admitted purpose of aiding the King against Queen Caroline by any possible means. Terry soon dropped out, but Hook continued as editor. The work appeared until 1892.

Mr. Byshh Shelly [*sic*], the author of that abominable and blasphemous book called *Queen Mab*, was lately drowned in a storm somewhere in the Mediterranean. His object in visiting that part of the world, it was said, was to *write down* Christianity. The visitation is, therefore, striking; and the termination of his life (considering his creed) not more awful than surprising.[98]

On October 26, after the first number of *The Liberal* had appeared, *The Bard* carried a poem, supposedly in imitation of Byron, "Rejected Addresses by L. B.," in which a clever reference to the new magazine was probably at least intended:

> Poor Shelley, thou hast given them the slip;
> Thou scorn'd to rank among a race of minions;
> Curse on the wave that struck thy freighted ship!
> And left the mighty void of friendship in one's
> Breast; where shall we find another lip,
> To speak such learn'd and *liberal* opinions?[99]

Blackwood's, which might have been expected on this occasion to make further comments upon the Pisan group, actually carried no obituary of Shelley and remained silent for several months regarding the association of Byron and Hunt. This is a

---

[98] *John Bull*, No. 87 (August 11, 1822), 693. On August 12, Robert Stewart, Viscount Castlereagh, the Foreign Secretary, committed suicide. The following day the Coroner's Jury ruled that he had been "delirious and of insane mind" (*The Times*, No. 11,637 [August 14], 2-3). This provided material for the parody appearing in the obscure *British Luminary and Weekly Intelligencer* (No. 203 [August 18, 1822], p. 685) and reprinted in *The Republican* (VI [1822], 408):

> The Marquis of L——, the author of those detestable measures which gave up the South of Italy to the most coarse and leaden despotism in Europe— delivered up Genoa to a tyrant, in the face of a British pledge of honour— and who indemnified the employment of torture in Ireland to extort confession; lost his life on Monday last in a fit of insanity, just as he was about to proceed to the Continent with the object of doing his best for the extinction of dawning freedom in Spain and Greece. The visitation is therefore striking; and the termination of his life (considering *his* creed) not more awful than surprising.

[99] *The Bard*, October 26, 1822, p. 11 (quoted from Marsh, p. 89). Graham describes this periodical as "an inconsequential journal of verse put out for eight monthly numbers, by F. G. and G. Whiteson" (*English Literary Periodicals*, p. 368).

striking manifestation of a belief that probably prevailed among
the critics and members of the press, which *The Literary Chronicle*
made explicit in its obituary of Shelley:

> It has been stated, and we believe with truth, that Lord Byron,
> Mr. Shelley, and Leigh Hunt, were about establishing a periodical
> work at Pisa, destined of course for England, and which has been
> looked for with considerable anxiety. The league is now dissolved,
> and with it, we should think, all thought of the threatened journal.[100]

This was, of course, not the case, but several months were to
pass before some became aware of the fact.

§ *iv*

In the middle of the summer of 1822, Leigh Hunt as editor
of the proposed periodical faced several problems. One, of
course, concerned matters relating to the printing and physical
appearance of the new work. On January 27, Hunt suggested
to Byron, "The size of the publication could be as you pleased,
larger or smaller than an ordinary thick pamphlet, but printed
in good open type like a book."[101] It is not improbable that
Leigh made similar suggestions to John, but his reaction to the
first number of *The Liberal* after it had arrived at Genoa[102] and
John's report to Leigh in February, 1823,[103] indicate that the
decisions concerning numbers of copies, costs, and advertising
belonged primarily to John. In many instances, this fact could
be attributed to the distance between the editor and the publisher, but it is not unlikely also that it was an outgrowth of
former practices.

---

[100] "Biography," *The Literary Chronicle and Weekly Review* No. 169 (August 10,
1822), p. 504. This literary newspaper appeared from 1819 until 1828, when it
was incorporated with *The Athenæum*, founded January 2, 1828.

[101] The Berg Collection of the New York Public Library.

[102] Payson G. Gates, "A Leigh Hunt-Byron Letter," *Keats-Shelley Journal*, II
(1953), 13—hereafter referred to as Gates, "Letter."

[103] Unpublished letter from John Hunt to Leigh Hunt, February 25, 1823
(British Museum MS. ADD. 38108, f. 258).

From the beginning, the question of a title for the new work was somewhat troublesome. Shortly after Leigh Hunt's arrival, the name *Hesperides*, which Byron had suggested, was adopted. "You may announce the title at once," Hunt wrote Elizabeth Kent on July 8, "for I think it certain."[104] However, more than six weeks later, Byron told Medwin, "The name is not yet decided upon,—half-a-dozen have been rejected."[105] Indecision continued for some time. By September 29, when *The Examiner* carried an announcement that the new work was in the press,[106] John Hunt was apparently not aware of the final decision for a title. Presumably news reached him during the following week, for on October 6 *The Examiner* carried an advertisement which mentioned the title as well as a special announcement that a title had been chosen, " 'The Liberal,'—a title which conveys in the most comprehensive manner the *spirit* in which the work is written, and falls in happily with the general progress of opinion (we do not mean in a political so much as in a general sense) throughout Europe."[107] The choice was Byron's.[108] Through subsequent advertisement in *The Examiner* and elsewhere, it soon became quite familiar in literary places.[109]

---

[104] Hunt, *Corr.*, I, 189.

[105] Medwin, *Conversations*, p. 404. This occurred after Medwin's return to Pisa, August 18, 1822.

[106] *The Examiner*, No. 766 (September 29, 1822), p. 615.

[107] *Ibid.*, No. 767 (October 6, 1822), p. 633.

[108] Hunt, *Lord Byron*, p. 47. Edmund Blunden has suggested that the title was derived from that of a Brussels journal (*Shelley* [New York, 1947], pp. 351-52). *Le Libéral*, supposedly a daily, was published with this title from November 16, 1816, to March 31, 1817, and with the title *Le Vrai Libéral* until July 21, 1821. The owner, Lecomte de Pestre, was prosecuted and sent to prison in 1821 "pour articles de nature à troubler la tranquilité de l'état" (André Warzée, *Essai historique et critique sur les Journaux belges: Journaux politiques* [Bruxelles, 1845], p. 74).

[109] William Thackeray attributed the "wide currency" of the word *liberal* and *liberalism*, both in England and on the Continent, to Byron and Hunt's choice of a title for their periodical ("Liberalism," *Cornhill Magazine*, V [1862], 70-71). See the entries for the word *liberal* in the *New English Dictionary*. It is evident that the critics who were to attack the use of the word for the title were thinking for the most part of the older meanings, those related to class and education rather than to politics.

The most important problem which Leigh Hunt faced was, of course, the accumulation of materials. He was optimistic. "Our first number will shortly appear," he wrote in late July.[110] Byron, however, was more realistic. "Leigh Hunt is sweating articles for his new Journal," he wrote Moore a month later.[111] Leigh Hunt expected to use the various works contributed by Byron, of course, but even on this score there was some difficulty. Byron decided to withdraw from publication his "Letter to the Editor of 'My Grandmother's Review,' " and Leigh Hunt explained to John that "it is of old date,"[112] but before his letter could reach London, the piece had appeared in the first number of *The Liberal*. John Hunt probably applied to Murray for "The Vision of Judgment" almost immediately after receiving word from either Leigh or Byron. In August, it was known that John Hunt was to publish the work.[113] One difficulty existed regarding the form of publication, for Byron's early vagueness gave way, first to a definite desire that the poem be published in the new journal, then to vacillation between this idea and the wish for publication of "The Vision of Judgment" as a distinct work.[114] A far more serious difficulty, of which Byron and the Hunts were not to be aware for some time, was created when John Hunt applied to Murray for "The Vision of Judgment," for Murray gave him neither the Preface

---

[110] Hunt to Horace Smith, July 25, 1822 (Thomas J. Wise, *A Shelley Library* [London, 1924], p. 107).

[111] Byron to Moore, August 27, 1822 (*L. & J.*, VI, 109).

[112] Leigh Hunt to John Hunt, October 10, 1822 (Brewer, *Library*, I, 119).

[113] In August, *Blackwood's* (XII [1822], 236) announced: "Mr John Hunt will shortly publish 'The Vision of Judgment,' by Quevedo Redivivus, suggested by the composition of Mr Southey, so entitled. We understand this production is from the pen of Lord Byron." It is worth mentioning that this announcement was copied in October by the American miscellany, *Atheneum; or, Spirit of the English Magazine* (XII [1822], 48). This appears to have been the first of the very few American comments in any way referring to *The Liberal*.

[114] As Leigh Hunt forwarded Byron's various instructions to John, the situation became thoroughly confusing. "I do not recollect whether I wrote to you two or three letters," Leigh wrote John on August 14, "or upon which of them you are acting" (Byron, *L. & J.*, VI, 124 n.).

to the poem nor the corrected proof, as Byron had specified. "Have you got the *Preface* to the Vision?" Leigh asked John in October. "He says the poem ought not to appear without it."[115] But his warning reached London after some of the first reviewers of *The Liberal* had already charged down upon Byron's poem.

Aside from these two pieces, the only work by Byron to appear in the first number of *The Liberal* was his "Epigrams on Lord Castlereagh," one quatrain and two couplets in which he rejoiced at the suicide of the Foreign Secretary.[116] They were written after August 27,[117] the result of an "impulse of the moment," intended for publication in *The Examiner*.[118] On September 18, Byron sent the quatrain to Douglas Kinnaird, who gave it to John Hunt according to Byron's instructions.[119] Presumably, the two couplets were sent to London at approximately the same time, and John decided shortly before publication of *The Liberal* to use the "Epigrams" in the magazine rather than the newspaper.

Shelley's translation of the Walpurgisnacht scene from Goethe's *Faust* apparently came into Leigh Hunt's hands some time after Shelley's death. Shelley had once translated passages from *Faust* merely for practice,[120] but when he returned to the

---

[115] Leigh Hunt to John Hunt, October 10, 1822 (Brewer, *Library*, I, 119).

[116] Hunt, *Lord Byron*, p. 53. Charles W. Dilke ("The Liberal," *Notes and Queries*, Ser. 8, IV [1893], 10) reprinted the remarks made by Charles Armitage Brown—who was in Italy while Hunt was editing *The Liberal*—on the Contents page of his own copy of *The Liberal*. Although Brown's list of authors cannot be taken as final proof of authorship, it adds to the accumulation of evidence.

[117] In a letter to Thomas Moore dated August 27, 1822, Byron clearly revealed that he was not aware that Castlereagh's death was suicide (*L. & J.*, VI, 109). Byron described Castlereagh to Thomas Medwin as "the only public character whom I thoroughly detest, and against whom I will never cease to level the shafts of my political hate" (*Conversations*, p. 352). On January 2, 1820, he had sent a mock epitaph of Castlereagh to Moore, who particularly hated Castlereagh (*L. & J.*, IV, 394).

[118] Hunt, *Lord Byron*, p. 53.

[119] Byron to Kinnaird, September 18, 1822 (*Corr.*, II, 231).

[120] Curtis C. D. Vail, "Shelley's Translation from Goethe's Faust," *Symposium*, III (1949), 187-213.

work in March, 1822,[121] it was with the intention that this, like a translation of "several scenes" from Calderon's *Magico Prodigioso*, might serve "as the basis of a paper for our journal."[122] It is possible that he also planned to contribute his translation of Plato's *Symposium*,[123] which he had finished in 1818.[124] Of these, however, only Goethe's "May-day Night" was to appear in *The Liberal*.[125]

Leigh Hunt had reason to expect a contribution from Edward Trelawny, possibly for the first number. "I should like much to put the last poor tribute from an unliterary and sincere friend—to Shelley—in your journal," Trelawny wrote to Byron. The piece would be personal, "a recorded witness to his virtues and worth in private life from one unconnected with him in literary writing or opinions."[126] Trelawny was

---

[121] George Bancroft, the American, who was visiting Pisa at this time, noted that "Shelley is translating Faust: Shelley of whom you may have heard many foolish stories, of his being a man of no principles, an atheist & all that: but he is not" ("Letters and Diaries of George Bancroft," ed. M. A. DeWolfe Howe, *Scribner's Magazine*, XXXVIII [1905], 505).

[122] Shelley to John Gisborne, April 10, 1822 (*Works*, X, 371). Shelley here complained "how weak! how incompetent to represent Faust" was an English translation of certain scenes which he had at hand. "I have only attempted the scenes omitted in this translation," he wrote. Vail (p. 192) identified the translation referred to here as "Retach's series of outlines illustrating 'Faust,' which was published in London in 1820 by Boosey and Sons together with an 'Analysis of the Tragedy' (author unknown)."

[123] The translation had been mislaid, and Shelley searched for it for a year. On July 4, 1822, he wrote to Mary, "I have found the translation of the 'Symposium' " (*Works*, X, 413). William Michael Rossetti (*Shelley* [London, 1886], p. 123) made the suggestion that at this time Shelley was looking for the work particularly "for insertion in the *Liberal*."

[124] Shelley to Thomas Love Peacock, August 16, 1818 (*Works*, IX, 320).

[125] *The Liberal*, I, 121-37. The authorship of this work can offer no problem, for the translation was attributed to Shelley in an advance review of *The Liberal* appearing in *The Examiner* (No. 768 [October 13, 1822], p. 652) and in the introduction to the work itself in *The Liberal*. Leigh Hunt attributed the piece to Shelley (*Lord Byron*, pp. 221-27; "Lord Byron—Mr. Moore—and Mr. Leigh Hunt," *The Tatler*, No. 114 [January 14, 1831], p. 454), as did Dilke (p. 10). Mary Shelley reprinted "May-day Night" in *Posthumous Poems of Percy Bysshe Shelley* (London, 1824), pp. 399-415.

[126] Trelawny to Byron, September 2, 1822 (Rosalie Glynn Grylls, *Trelawny* [London, 1950], p. 95).

eventually to develop this idea as the theme of his *Recollections of the Last Days of Shelley and Byron*, published in 1858, but for the moment he had an account of Shelley's death, presumably written earlier,[127] rather than a personal tribute, which he sent to Leigh Hunt. However, when the essay, "Loss of the Don Juan," had not appeared in two numbers, Trelawny showed impatience. "Is that narrative of the wreck published in the 'Liberal'?" he asked Mary in April. "I have been applied to for it from a very good work, and they pledge to instantly insert it."[128] But the unpublished article remained with one of the Hunts and was to be used in much altered form in 1828 in Leigh Hunt's *Lord Byron and Some of His Contemporaries*.[129]

The remaining materials for the first number of *The Liberal* were by Leigh Hunt,[130] the result of what Byron called his "sweating."[131] They were in some instances superior but more often mediocre in quality. In time, Leigh Hunt came to recognize this, excusing it on the basis of "ill health, and the

---

[127] In August (ca. 27), Mary Shelley wrote to Maria Gisborne concerning the cremation of Shelley, "I will say nothing of the ceremony since Trelawny has written an account of it to be printed in the forthcoming journal" (Mary Shelley, *Letters*, I, 187). This was one of ten or more such accounts. See Leslie A. Marchand, "Trelawny on the Death of Shelley," *Keats-Shelley Memorial Bulletin*, IV (1952), 9-34.

[128] Trelawny to Mary, April 2, 1823 (*S. & M.*, III, 931).

[129] Hunt, *Lord Byron*, pp. 195-200. Trelawny's article (British Museum MS ADD. 39168) was published by H. J. Massingham (*The Friend of Shelley* [New York, 1930], pp. 172-81) without distinction between Trelawny's original and Leigh Hunt's emendations (Marchand, "Trelawny on the Death of Shelley," p. 111). The failure to publish the article in some number of *The Liberal* can hardly be attributed to delay. Objections might have come from Byron or—if it reached London in the year of *The Liberal*—from John Hunt, on the grounds perhaps that its appeal would be too limited; or, as has recently been suggested, from Mary, in fear that a publication concerning Shelley might antagonize Shelley's father, from whom she hoped to receive some support for her son (Leslie A. Marchand, "Notes," in *Byron: A Biography* [3 vols.; New York, 1957], III, 113).

[130] Hunt to Elizabeth Kent, November 7, 1822 (Stout, "Studies Toward a Biography of Leigh Hunt," p. 175). This attribution does not appear in the letter as it is published in Hunt's *Correspondence* (I, 198-200). See also Hunt to Vincent Novello, September 9, 1822 (Clarke, *Recollections of Writers*, p. 218).

[131] Byron to Moore, August 27, 1822 (*L. & J.*, VI, 109). In this same letter, Byron irritated sore wounds by remarking that both Hunt and he thought "it somewhat shabby in *you* not to contribute."

calamitous death of his friend, and the new, unlooked-for, and most unpleasant circumstances under which he found himself situated with Lord Byron."[132] Of the eight pieces by Leigh Hunt which were to appear in the first number of *The Liberal*, all but one represented literary types in which Hunt might be expected to work. The exception was a short story, "The Florentine Lovers,"[133] an account of two lovers caught between their warring families based upon an episode in Marco Lastri's *L'Osservatore Fiorentino*.[134] It is possible that Hunt turned to this book, and even wrote the story, at the suggestion of Mary Shelley, who had read Lastri's book in April, 1821.[135] In some respects, the narrative is successful, but Hunt did serious harm by interrupting its progress on three different occasions.[136]

Of the other seven pieces which Leigh Hunt was to contribute to the first number of *The Liberal*,[137] only two were clearly original works—the Preface to the new periodical, which Hunt wrote to satisfy an obvious need and which has but slight literary merit,[138] and "Letters from Abroad, No. 1.—A Description of Pisa."[139] The latter appears to have been the indirect

---

[132] *The Tatler*, No. 114 (Jan. 14, 1831), p. 454. Cf. Hunt, *Autobiography*, p. 350.

[133] *The Liberal*, I, 51-80. Charles Armitage Brown listed Leigh Hunt as the author of this tale (Dilke, p. 10). Hunt himself admitted authorship by including it in a collection of his work, *The Seer; or, Commonplaces Refreshed* (2 parts in 1 vol.; London, 1840-41), Part II, pp. 49-59.

[134] Marco Lastri, "S. Maria Sopr'Arno, E Due Celebri Amanti, Ippolito E Dianora," *L'Osservatore Fiorentino sugli edifizi della sua patria, per servire alla storia della medesima* (3rd ed.; 8 vols.; Florence, 1821), VIII, 27-33.

[135] From April 10 through 14, Mary recorded reading *L'Osservatore Fiorentino*, finishing it on the last day mentioned (*Mary Shelley's Journal*, pp. 151-52).

[136] First Hunt turned aside briefly to remark, "How delicious it is to repeat these beautiful Italian names, when they are not merely names" (*The Liberal*, I, 53). The second interruption is a dialogue between the "Author" and the "Reader" on the subject of lovers (*Ibid.*, I, 66-68). Finally, the narrator breaks off for half a page to defend his own frequent use of the word "and" (*Ibid.*, I, 70).

[137] Charles Brown attributed all seven to Hunt (Dilke, p. 10).

[138] *The Liberal*, I [v]-xii. Internal evidence supports Hunt's authorship of the Preface—the style, familiarity with the intentions of the three chief contributors, the type of literary references, and the unrestrained praise of Shelley.

[139] *The Liberal*, I, 97-120. This was partly reprinted by Hunt in the chapter entitled "Lord Byron in Italy—Shelley—Pisa," *Autobiography*, pp. 333-47.

result of Hunt's earlier proposal to Byron that the periodical could open "with your account of a land journey to Italy, which I might follow in the next number with that of a sea-one."[140] Hunt's descriptions of his voyage found in his later autobiographical works[141] were obviously based upon a journal, from which he admittedly took the account of his arrival at Genoa that forms a major part of the second of his "Letters from Abroad."[142] Byron seems to have ignored Hunt's suggestion, which is hardly surprising, so that Hunt came to depend totally upon himself for travels and geographic descriptions. Otherwise, he composed, from his literary background, "Rhyme and Reason, being a new Proposal respecting Poetry in Ordinary"[143] and "A German Apologue."[144] Finally, three of Leigh Hunt's contributions were translations—"Ariosto's Episode of Cloridan, Medoro, and Angelica" from *Orlando Furioso*,[145] "The Country Maiden from Politian,"[146] and an "Epigram of Alfieri."[147]

---

[140] Unpublished letter from Hunt to Byron, January 27, 1822 (the Berg Collection).

[141] Hunt, *Lord Byron*, pp. 433-91; *Autobiography*, pp. 289-313.

[142] *The Liberal*, I, 269-88.

[143] *Ibid.*, I, 81-89. Hunt listed "Rhyme and Reason" among that small group of his works in *The Liberal* which "I would save, if I could, from oblivion" (*Lord Byron*, p. 62). He reprinted it in *The Seer* (Part II, pp. 59-61).

[144] *The Liberal*, I, 91-95. Barnette Miller (*Leigh Hunt's Relations with Byron, Shelley and Keats* [New York, 1910], p. 112) asserted, without giving a source, that "A German Apologue" was by Shelley; she was possibly influenced by the fact that Shelley made the translation of *Faust*, and, according to the Preface (*The Liberal*, I, vii), was to have been concerned with German literature.

[145] *The Liberal*, I, 139-59. The source was *Orlando Furioso*, XVIII, clxiv, I–XIX, xxxvii, 4. Hunt reprinted the translation in part in *Stories from the Italian Poets* (London, 1846) and in full in *Stories in Verse* (London, 1855) as "Medoro and Cloridano." In *The Poetical Works of Leigh Hunt* (London, 1857; ed. Thornton Hunt, London, 1860), it appeared as two pieces, "Friends and Foes" and "Angelica and Medoro." See *The Poetical Works of Leigh Hunt*, ed. Milford, pp. 448, 731-32.

[146] *The Liberal*, I, 161-63. The source was the thirty-third of the "Canzoni a Ballo e Canzonette di Messer Angelo Poliziano," *Opere Volgari di Messer Angelo Ambrogini Poliziano* (Florence, 1885), p. 218.

[147] *The Liberal*, I, 163-64. This is the twenty-seventh of the "Epigrammi" entitled "Paragone d'armonia fra tre lingue moderne," *Le Opere di Vittorio Alfieri* (12 vols.; Padua, 1809-10), XII, 45.

§ v

Since all the writing in the first number was the work of the original partners, it was unnecessary to pay contributors. Costs, therefore, arose exclusively from the printing and distribution of the journal. Aside from commissions or discounts given those who sold the work, these amounted to £400. Seven thousand copies were printed, for which paper cost £205, the actual printing £98, and stitching £35. The remainder, £62, was spent for advertising.[148]

The Examiner, of course, handled some of the advertising. On September 29, it carried an announcement:

The long-expected Periodical Work from Pisa is in the press, and will shortly appear. The *Vision of Judgment*, a satire upon the Laureate, which contains also a true and fearless character of a grossly adulated Monarch, forms a prominent portion of the First Number; besides which, there are miscellaneous Essays of various kinds, descriptive and speculative, among them an account of the beautiful city whence the work emanates, and the interesting recollections with which it is associated.[149]

The following week, a list of the contents of the first number of *The Liberal* appeared.[150] Aside from these, there was a notice which is now preserved on a newspaper clipping in the British Museum:

The long-promised periodical work from Pisa is nearly ready for publication. Lord Byron's chief (but not his only) share in it, is the *Vision of Judgment*, which is a *quiz* upon the laureate's extraordinary poem under that title, though some other characters, of rather more importance than Mr. S., are also very freely handled

---

[148] Unpublished letter from John Hunt to Leigh Hunt, February 25, 1823 (British Museum MS. ADD. 38108, f. 258).

[149] *The Examiner*, No. 766 (September 29, 1822), p. 615. It has not been possible to learn what charges *The Examiner* made to *The Liberal* for carrying advertising, but there were charges, since John was the publisher rather than a partner, and he considered Leigh to be no longer an owner of *The Examiner*.

[150] *The Examiner*, No. 767 (October 6, 1822), p. 640.

in it. In particular a deceased royal personage, regarding whom every species of *Cant* has been exhausted by almost every party, is treated not much better, which will be a bone for the loyal and pious critics to pick.[151]

Although this certainly did not appear in *The Examiner*, the similarity to the announcement in that newspaper of September 29 is obvious. Since the title for the new periodical was not given, it seems probable that this appeared before *The Examiner*'s announcement of the title on October 6. On October 9, Byron wrote Murray, "That damned advertisement of Mr. J. Hunt is out of the limits: I did not lend my name to be hawked about in this way."[152] He was clearly not referring to *The Examiner*'s announcement of September 29, in which his name was not used.[153] On the following day, October 10, Leigh wrote John that Byron had received a letter "from Murray inclosing the advertisement you sent round to the booksellers" and believed "it would have been as well had you omitted the direct mention of the names in advertising a periodical work, in which others too will write."[154] It is possible that this, a publisher's circular—on which John Hunt might well have advertised other publications, so that it would resemble a newspaper— was the notice given above. Had it been printed and come to the attention of John Murray at the time of the announcement in *The Examiner*, September 29, it might have reached Byron by October 9; but there is no reason to believe that the circular did not precede the newspaper announcement by several days, allowing sufficient time for the mails to carry it to Byron.

---

[151] Byron, *L. & J.*, VI, 125 n. Prothero described this as "found in a volume of *Byroniana* in the British Museum, consisting of newspaper cuttings. No clue is given to the paper in which it appeared." The British Museum has no further information concerning this holding.

[152] Byron, *L. & J.*, VI, 125-26.

[153] Prothero, however, believed that Bryon's comment probably referred to *The Examiner's* announcement of September 29 (*Ibid.*, VI, 125).

[154] Brewer, *Library*, I, 119.

In addition, John Hunt published in the "Literary Notices" of *The Examiner* of October 13 an extremely long account of the forthcoming number of *The Liberal*.[155] This was not to be "anticipative criticism," but "mere notice," of which the purpose was "to supply a few brief allusions to the contents of this long-expected first number, and to illustrate our observations by passages from its most characteristic articles." All of the articles were praised of course, but the Preface to *The Liberal* and "The Vision of Judgment" were extensively quoted. Byron's poem, it appeared, might require preliminary defense. "We cannot for a moment pretend not to foresee the horror which this Vision will excite in pious personages, among whom the original Vision excited no horror at all." The course was simply to attack Southey's "Vision of Judgment," Byron's model, in which the hypocrisy of cant and flattery "shuts out the perception of the thing called *blasphemy* altogether." If Southey had the right "to penetrate into the 'heaven of heavens,' in order to 'presume' a judgment upon human character, the same liberty is open to other people; and the fact of differing on the judgment delivered, makes no sort of distinction in the indecorum, if such it be."

The dependence of *The Liberal* upon the resources of John Hunt and the advertising facilities of *The Examiner* was clearly extensive. Any disproportion which might be attributed to such dependence arose in part at least from the fact that the number of publications which were willing to carry advertisements of *The Liberal* was apparently quite limited. Of the newspapers, *The Morning Chronicle*, the liberal Whig work, carried more notices of the new periodical[156] than did the moderate Tory *Times*[157]

---

[155] *The Examiner*, No. 768 (October 13, 1822), pp. 648-52.

[156] *The Morning Chronicle*, October 7, 9, 11, 14, 15, 17, 19, 23, 26, 29; November 1, 4, 6, 11, 15, 20. This newspaper was founded in 1769 by William Woodfall. In 1817, John Black, a champion of reform, became editor.

[157] *The Times*, October 16, 17, 21. In 1817, Thomas Barnes, a friend of Leigh Hunt since boyhood, became editor of *The Times*.

or *The Morning Herald*.[158] Among the periodicals, it is more surprising that the October *Blackwood's* carried a notice[159] than that advertisements appeared in *The Monthly Repository* of the same month[160] and in *The Monthly Magazine* of November.[161]

John Hunt published the first number of *The Liberal* on October 15, 1822.[162] It was bound in a dull, red-brown paper cover, on the front of which, enclosed in an ornamental rectangular frame, appears the title: "THE / LIBERAL. / VERSE AND PROSE FROM THE / SOUTH. / TO BE CONTINUED OCCASIONALLY. / N⁰ 1. / LONDON, 1822: / PRINTED BY AND FOR JOHN HUNT, / 22, OLD BOND STREET. / PRICE FIVE SHILLINGS." The title page follows, showing some variations from the cover.[163] The

---

[158] *The Morning Herald*, October 31, 1822. It has not been possible to see a complete file of this newspaper; the available file begins with this number, so that it is likely that other advertisements of *The Liberal* appeared during the latter half of October. *The Morning Herald* was founded in 1780 by the Reverend William Bate. It first supported the Prince of Wales in his opposition to the King, but as the Prince became more conservative, the newspaper moved to a position which was nominally Tory.

[159] "Monthly List of New Publications," *Blackwood's*, XII (1822), 506.

[160] "New Publications," *The Monthly Repository of Theology and General Literature*, XVII (1822), 635. This was founded in 1806 as an organ of the Unitarians. In 1836, Leigh Hunt and Richard Hengist Horne were to become editors for the last year of publication.

[161] "List of New Publications in October," *The Monthly Magazine, and British Register*, LIV (1822), 360. This journal, established in 1796 by Richard Phillips, became a strong supporter of liberal writers.

[162] The first number of *The Liberal* had been advertised for October 14 in *The Morning Chronicle* of October 7. Maria Gisborne might have referred to this notice when she wrote to Mary Shelley on October 8, "Mr. Gisborne tells me that the 'Liberal' is advertised for publication on Monday next" (*Gisborne and Williams*, p. 93). On Friday, October 11, *The Morning Chronicle* announced *The Liberal* for "Tuesday next [October 15]," on October 14 for "Tomorrow," and on October 15 the advertisement opened simply, "The New Periodical Work from the South." *The Times'* notice of October 17 opened, "On Tuesday last."

[163] "THE / LIBERAL. / VERSE AND PROSE FROM THE / SOUTH. / VOLUME THE FIRST. / LONDON, 1822: / PRINTED BY AND FOR JOHN HUNT, / 22, OLD BOND STREET." The first four lines, which do show verbal agreement with those on the cover, were not, however, set from the same type.

verso is blank. The Contents follows,[164] with two Errata listed
at the bottom of the page.[165] The verso is blank, followed by
8 pages of the Preface ([v]-xii), 162 pages of the text ([3]-164),
and 18 pages of advertisements.[166]

§ *vi*

In the Preface, Leigh Hunt primarily attempted to meet the
charges which had been made in anticipation of *The Liberal*
and to state what the intentions of the writers were to be. The
critics had predicted that they were "to cut up religion, morals,
and everything that is legitimate." If these things were benevo-
lent and just, Hunt argued, "then we should do our best to
leave religion and morals as we found them." But since they
were actually filled with ambiguity and hypocrisy, as "nine-
tenths of all the intelligent men in the world" were aware, "then

---

[164] In the Contents, the Preface is listed for page 5 although it actually opens
on an unnumbered page [v]. "The Vision of Judgment" is listed for page 15
while in fact it begins on the unnumbered [3]. Otherwise the list is accurate:
"A Letter to the Editor of 'My Grandmother's Review,' " p. 41; "The Florentine
Lovers," p. 51; "Rhyme and Reason, being a new Proposal respecting Poetry
in Ordinary," p. 81; "A German Apologue," p. 91; "Letters from Abroad, No. I.
—A Description of Pisa," p. 97; "May-day Night; a Poetical Translation from
Goethe's Faust," p. 121; "Ariosto's Episode of Cloridan, Medoro, and Angelica,"
p. 139; "The Country Maiden," p. 161; "Epigram of Alfieri," p. 163; "Epigrams
on Lord Castlereagh," p. 164.

[165] The first of the Errata was for "The Florentine Lovers," the second for
"Letters from Abroad":

Page 62, lines 29 and 30—and page 68, line 15, for "*Signora* Veronica,"
read "*Gossip* Veronica."

Page 109, line 10, for "about the size of Stratford Place," read "about *half*
the size."

[166] These eighteen lines of advertisements appear to have been an insert, which
was included in the binding of the separate numbers but not in the binding of
Numbers 1 and 2 as Volume I, for Number 1 ends with the full Signature L
(16 pages), and Number 2 begins with Signature M. The advertisements include
the "Publication List" of Sherwood, Neely, and Jones (pp. 1-8); a notice by
Simpkin and Marshall for the fourth edition of Barry O'Meara's *Napoleon in Exile*
(pp. 1-4); a list of "Elegant and Popular Works Published by Thomas Tegg"
(pp. 1-2); and an announcement by R. and S. Prowett of the sale of "a valuable
Collection of Books, in English and Foreign Literature" (pp. 1-4).

indeed we are willing to accept the title of enemies to religion, morals, and legitimacy." Furthermore, their writing would be political, "inasmuch as all writing now-a-days must involve something to that effect." But it would not be restricted and would include "liberalities in the shape of Poetry, Essays, Tales, Translations, and other amenities, of which kings themselves may read and profit." The term *liberal* is, therefore, "to be taken in its largest acceptation, old as well as new," and the writers to be considered as "advocates of every species of liberal knowledge." But "by a natural consequence in these times," such men must "go the full length in matters of opinion with large bodies of men who are called Liberals."

It is not surprising that Leigh Hunt should introduce the name of Lord Castlereagh at this point, with "his famous Six Acts . . . his treatment of Bonaparte, his patronage of such infamous journals as the *Beacon*,[167] his fondness for imprisoning, and for what his weak obstinacy calls his other strong measures." Though Castlereagh has died, these measures have survived and must be considered in response to the call for liberality toward the memory of Castlereagh. Furthermore, the supporters of Castlereagh have offered no example. "The other day, when one of the noblest of human beings, Percy Shelley . . . was lost on the coast of Italy, the *Courier* said, that 'Mr. Percy Shelley, *a writer of infidel poetry*, was drowned.' Where was the liberality of this canting insinuation?"[168] Now, Hunt pointed out, the

---

[167] *The Beacon*, Nos. 1-38 (January 6—September 22, 1821). This weekly journal, published at Edinburgh, represented an extreme point of view. "It appears as the Champion of our Civil Rights," the editor claimed for the paper in the Prospectus circulated prior to publication, "and of the Government under which we enjoy them. It claims the honourable distinction of maintaining the cause of Social Order, with the zeal which has hitherto belonged entirely to its enemies."

[168] Hunt referred to *The Courier* (No. 9,616 [August 5, 1822], p. 3): "Shelley, the writer of some infidel poetry, for the republication of which a man of the name of Clarke, either has been, or is about to be, prosecuted, is dead." *The Courier* was started in 1792 by John Parry, who sold it in 1799. Peter Street, one of the owners, made the daily one of the strongest supporters of the Government

death of Castlereagh had altered the situation: "could we not turn such a death against the enemies of Mr. Shelley, if we could condescend to affect a moment's agreement with their hypocrisy?" This, however, was not the intention, which, it would seem from the concluding paragraph, was far more noble:

Wherever, in short, we see the mind of man exhibiting powers of its own, and at the same time helping to carry on the best interests of human nature,—however it may overdo the matter on this side or on that, or otherwise partake of the common frailty through which it passes,—there we recognize the demi-gods of liberal worship;—there we bow down, and own our lords and masters;—there we hope for the final passing away of all obscene worships, however formalized,—of all the monstrous sacrifices of the many to the few, however "legitimatized" and besotted.

Hunt was clearly attempting to reconcile a political conception of liberalism with one that embraced intellectual freedom, but it seems that in his own mind his ardor for the former occasionally interfered with his full acceptance of the latter. The result was somewhat confusing and would do little to broaden or intensify sympathy for *The Liberal*. Yet, despite the excitement with which the magazine had been anticipated and the occasionally threatening suggestions which Hunt made in the Preface, only two works, "The Vision of Judgment" and the "Epigrams on Lord Castlereagh," carried direct political significance.

Although the Preface to "The Vision of Judgment" was not printed with the poem at this time, there was some indication that Robert Southey, rather than George III, was the primary object of Byron's satire—in the phrase following the title, "Suggested by the Composition so entitled by the Author of

---

among London newspapers. In 1822, it was acquired by William Mudford and continued as a Tory paper until it was purchased by Whig interests in 1830. It ceased to exist in 1842.

'Wat Tyler,' " and in the epigraph, which was addressed to Southey with reference to his own poem, "A Daniel come to judgment! yea, a Daniel! / I thank thee, Jew, for teaching me that word" (*The Merchant of Venice*, IV, i, 342). Byron was attacking not the form of government by which George had ruled but that group, represented in this instance by Southey, which had carried on the process of government during much of George's reign. With reference to the political writings of Quevedo y Villegas,[169] Byron assumed the name "Quevedo Redivivus." The "Epigrams on Lord Castlereagh," which Leigh Hunt had clearly not expected to find in *The Liberal*, shared only political sentiment with "The Vision of Judgment," but even this was crudely presented:

> Oh, Castlereagh! thou art a patriot now;
> Cato died for his country, so did'st thou;
> He perish'd rather than see Rome enslav'd,
> Thou cut'st thy throat, that Britain may be sav'd.
>
> .   .   .   .   .   .
>
> So Castlereagh has cut his throat!—The worst
> Of this is,—that his own was not the first.
>
> .   .   .   .   .   .
>
> So *He* has cut his throat at last!—He! Who?
> The man who cut his country's long ago.

It is possible that in Hunt's "The Florentine Lovers" the ultimate triumph of Dianora d'Amerigo de' Bardi and Ippolito Buondelmonte de' Buondelmonti against the prejudices of their warring families should be given political interpretation, but otherwise, the writings in the first number of *The Liberal* are non-political.

Byron's "Letter to the Editor of 'My Grandmother's Review' " was quite dated by 1822 and probably suffered by inclusion in *The Liberal* without explanatory notes. A prose

---

[169] Francisco Gomez de Quevedo y Villegas (1580-1645).

satire, the "Letter" was part of a literary quarrel which Byron
had begun in the First Canto of *Don Juan*:

> For fear some prudish readers should grow skittish,
> I've bribed my Grandmother's Review—the British.

> I sent it in a letter to the Editor,
>   Who thanked me duly by return of post—
> I'm for a handsome article his creditor;
>   Yet, if my gentle Muse he please to roast,
> And break a promise after having made it her,
>   Denying the receipt of what it cost,
> And smear his page with gall instead of honey,
> All I can say is—that he had the money.[170]

Although Byron did not doubt that his remarks would create
an unfavorable reaction on the part of *The British Review*, he
never suspected that William Roberts, the editor of the
journal,[171] would take his accusation literally.[172] Yet *The
British Review* of August, 1819, carried William Roberts' defense
against the charge, which was primarily a denial that Byron
could have been the author of *Don Juan*, rather than a refutation
of the charge that the author of the poem bribed *The British
Review*. "No peer of the British realm can surely be capable of
so calumnious a falsehood," Roberts observed. It implicated

---

[170] *Don Juan*, I, ccix-ccx (*Poetry*, VI, 76).

[171] William Roberts (1767-1849), a member of the Bar, who held Tory and
Evangelical principles, helped found *The British Review and London Critical Journal* in
1811. Dissatisfaction with both *The Edinburgh Review* and *The Quarterly Review*
was partly responsible, for the new periodical, though largely concerned with
criticism, was to express the "opinions of that part of the public, who view religion
as a vital principle" (Arthur Roberts, *The Life, Letters, and Opinions of William
Roberts* [London, 1850], pp. 37-38).

[172] "To be sure I took in the British Roberts finely," Byron wrote Murray on
October 8, 1820. "He fell precisely into the glaring trap laid for him: it is incon-
ceivable how he could be so absurd as to think us serious with him" (*L. & J.*,
V, 92). There is no suggestion in the biography of William Roberts that he or
his son Arthur ever became aware of Byron's facetiousness. Arthur complained
that Byron did not "do what he both could and should have done, by confessing
and apologising for the wrong" (Roberts, p. 50).

the accuser himself. Byron would not have done this; nor would he have shown such little "discernment" as to make an accusation like this against "a Review which has so long maintained, in the cause of public and private virtue, its consistency and purity, independence of all party and of all power." Besides, added Roberts, "If Lord Byron had sent us money, and we had been so entirely devoid of honesty, feeling, and decency, as to have accepted it, his Lordship would have had sense enough to see, that to publish the fact would have been at once to release us from the iniquitous contract."[173]

Almost immediately after Byron saw the review he wrote his "Letter to the Editor of 'My Grandmother's Review.'" It opens, "My Dear Roberts," and is signed by "Wortley Clutterbuck," who describes himself as "a believer in the Church of England . . . and an occasional reader, and great admirer of, though not a subscriber to, your Review, which is rather expensive." In any event, the purpose of his letter, Clutterbuck continues, is to commend Roberts for mentioning publicly the false accusation. Charges such as this must be refuted, for the sake of the reviews and thereby for the sake of the editors themselves. But there are aspects of this charge which Roberts overlooked, Clutterbuck believes, such as the phrase "my grandmother's review." Perhaps the author of *Don Juan* meant that Roberts was his grandmother, but he should not have made such an assertion, for it is unfair "to judge of sex from writings, particularly from those of the British Review," in which certain of the best articles "attributed to a veteran female" were actually by Roberts himself. If the author of *Don Juan* were in earnest, therefore, not making "a mere figurative allusion to your supposed intellectual age and sex, my dear friend, it follows, whether you be she or no, that there is such an elderly lady still extant." The poem cannot be by Byron, Clutterbuck

---

[173] "Don Juan," *The British Review*, XIV (1819), 266-68.

concludes, for Byron has no grandmother. The question of Byron's innocence would seem settled; on the other matter, that of the bribe, Clutterbuck has an afterthought:

I don't mean to insinuate, God forbid! but if, by any accident, there should have been such a correspondence between you and the unknown author, whoever he may be, send him back his money: I dare say he will be very glad to have it again: it can't be much, considering the value of the article and the circulation of the journal; and you are too modest to rate your praise beyond its real worth.

Hunt's "Rhyme and Reason" is a proposal that the English imitate the Italian *rimatori* in their use of one-word lines of verse, as a means of saving words, space, paper, and print, and of avoiding the risk of prosecution without sacrificing meaning.[174] For the conventional title "On Time" Hunt offered an example, "Child / Beguil'd / Boy / Joy / Man / Span / Sire / Expire. / So / Go." "A German Apologue" is Hunt's account of Mercury's quest for three women—"undeniably beautiful, unexceptionably orthodox, and irreversibly chaste"—who might take the place of the three Graces; Mercury hears of three such women but learns that the previous day Pluto took them away to become the three Furies. The first of the "Letters from Abroad" is a rambling essay, as personal as many of Leigh Hunt's writings for *The Examiner*, in which he was con-

---

[174] Despite Hunt's protests, Byron insisted that Hunt wrote "Rhyme and Reason" as a satire upon the love poetry of Thomas Moore, which Byron called "Looks and Tones" ("Lord Byron—Mr. Moore—and Mr. Leigh Hunt," *The Tatler*, No. 114 [January 14, 1831], p. 455).

[175] In a footnote (*The Liberal*, I, 111), Hunt recommended *A Comment on the Divine Comedy of Dante Alighieri* by John Taaffe (1787-1862), one of the Pisan group. Though printed in Italy, this book was published anonymously by John Murray. On December 5, 1822, Hunt wrote to Taaffe regarding the footnote, "It should have been longer, had I possessed longer time or better health. Sincerer it cannot be. But there will be a long one by and by, with an extract or two" (Brewer, *Library*, II, 145). There is no evidence that Leigh Hunt carried out this intention.

cerned with many of the points of historical and literary significance at Pisa.[175]

The remaining "liberalities" were the three translations in
verse and Hunt's imitation of the Alfieri Epigram. Shelley's
"May-day Night" from *Faust*, which Leigh Hunt described in
a brief introduction to the work as "the very highest triumph
both of poetry and translation," is strikingly simple and effective, certainly the finest poetic achievement of the translations
in *The Liberal*. Hunt's "Ariosto's Episode of Cloridan, Medoro,
and Angelica" is quite even, with but slight forcing of rhymes
and wrenching of vocabulary, such as some of his translation
displays. But his treatment of Politian's "La Pastorella" gives
an impression of triviality and perhaps sentimentality.[176]

Despite the fact that only three contributed to this first
number of *The Liberal*, there was variety. However, the quality
was uneven, and, so far as the critics were concerned, the mass of
material which was not objectionable achieved very little effect,
but in quality and in kind "The Vision of Judgment" at least
seemed to justify the spirit with which they had anticipated
The Liberal. The reaction to the first number of the periodical
was doubtless more extensive than Byron or the Hunts had
expected, and certainly it was more violent than the actual
nature of *The Liberal* justified.

---

[176] See Appendix I, n. 3.

IV

Reaction and Review

§ i

SHORTLY AFTER LEIGH HUNT LEARNED THAT JOHN HUNT HAD
not received from John Murray the Preface to "The Vision of
Judgment," he sent word to Byron, with the hope that "the
realizations on the 7,000 [copies] will compensate for all defects."[1]
Leigh could be optimistic because he had not seen the poem,
but Byron knew what legal dangers were involved in publishing
the work without the Preface. He wrote at once to John Murray,
angrily accusing him of carelessness or indifference, but then
suggesting malicious premeditation. "If you have (as seems
apparently to be the case) purposely kept back the preface to
the *Vision*, I can only say that I know no words strong enough
to express my sense of such conduct."[2] He enclosed this in a
letter to John Hunt, from whose hands Murray was to receive
it unsealed.[3] At the same time, Byron appears to have requested

---

[1] Mary Shelley to Byron, probably October 21, 1822 (Mary Shelley, *Letters*,
I, 198).

[2] Byron to Murray, October 22, 1822 (*L. & J.*, VI, 127).

[3] "Lord Byron and Mr. Murray," *The Examiner*, No. 876 (November 14, 1824),
p. 723. In this account of his dealings with Murray, John Hunt recalled that
Byron's letter had come "from Italy, without seal or wafer," with instructions
that he "take a copy and forward it open." Out of courtesy, however, John Hunt
sealed the letter and sent it to Murray, who returned it unopened. Hunt then took
the letter himself, open as Byron had intended, and gave it to Murray, who
was extremely embarrassed. "It was impossible to pity him," John Hunt recalled,
"the retribution was so entirely the fruit of arrogance and ill-manners." R. E.
Prothero (*L. & J.*, VI, 126) has printed a letter from Douglas Kinnaird to John
Murray dated December 18, 1822, in which Kinnaird apparently enclosed a letter

that John publish in *The Examiner* an announcement concerning the missing Preface.[4] John complied on November 3, explaining that there was a Preface, which demonstrated "more completely how Mr. Southey has subjected himself and his cause to this sort of attack," but "for some reasons best known to himself, Mr. Murray, the bookseller, who was to have been the original publisher of the Vision, contrived to evade sending the preface to the present publisher."[5]

John Murray had been causing other difficulties. After the arrival of Byron's letter of October 9, with its condescending comments upon the Hunts, Murray lost no time in circulating the letter among the group who frequented the back parlor of his publishing house. John and Henry Hunt heard rumours concerning the letter, which Henry attempted to answer in *The Examiner* by charging that the letter was a "forgery," which he dared Murray to publish.[6] Theodore Hook would appear to have anticipated the challenge in *John Bull* on the same day, October 27, with a garbled account of the contents of Byron's letter: " 'Hunt is a bore, he is,' says his Lordship, 'a proser; Mrs. Hunt is no great things; and their six children perfectly intractable.' "[7] Henry Hunt enclosed this and probably some further description of the supposed contents of the rumored letter, together with a copy of his own remarks in *The Examiner*,

---

from Bryon. However, as George Dumas Stout ("Studies Toward a Biography of Leigh Hunt," p. 184) has pointed out, it is impossible that Kinnaird could enclose a letter written four days after December 18. He obviously referred to an earlier letter from Bryon.

[4] On October 26, Leigh Hunt wrote to John, "Lord Byron had nothing further to say to you on Murray's business. I thought he might alter his mind a little perhaps in a day or two, but he did not, and wishes the paragraph still to appear, leaving it nevertheless as before to your own judgment" (Brewer, *Library*, II, 154).

[5] "The Liberal," *The Examiner*, No. 771 (November 3, 1822), p. 697.

[6] *Ibid.*, No. 770 (October 27, 1822), p. 679. Henry's authorship is not certain, but Leigh's letter of November 14, in which he thanked Henry "for the zeal with which you thought it necessary to take notice of the gossip you speak of" (Brewer, *Library*, II, 157) strongly suggests that Henry wrote the comment in *The Examiner*.

[7] *John Bull*, No. 98 (October 27, 1822), p. 781.

and sent them to Leigh. But Leigh was inclined at the moment to dismiss the matter as lightly as possible, blaming it primarily upon John Murray's pettiness. There were, of course, certain painful aspects of the situation, Leigh Hunt told Byron. "My 'wife and six small' come rather hard upon me in the business,— but a little reflection takes the heat out of my cheeks: and as to your 'proser,' God knows I should never think it worth a savager answer than to lay hold of one of my puns, and say you're a 'worser.' " The actual danger lay not in a break between them, he reminded Byron, but in the ammunition furnished their enemies by what *appeared* to be a break between them. However, the matter should be closed, and "nothing more need be said on the subject, if it can possibly be helped, or unless you yourself shall think fit to say anything." Leigh would reply to Henry's letter and show Byron "as usual what I write."[8]

Leigh Hunt wrote two letters to his nephew. One was to be used in *The Examiner* if Murray had not published the letter from Byron. "We give importance to nonsense of this kind by attending to it," he said. The other was to appear in the event that Murray had publicly demonstrated the existence of Byron's letter, and it did as much as possible to dismiss the entire situation: "If one person, violating the confidence of a splenetic moment of Lord Byron's, endeavours to turn one or two ill-phrases of his to our injury (the epithets his Lordship makes use of), persons of respectability could give an account, if they pleased, of twenty speeches from the same quarter to very different purposes."[9] Leigh allowed Byron to see these letters, but then he delayed sending them to Henry. He conceived the

---

[8] Hunt to Bryon, November 11, 1822 (Brewer, *Library*, II, 122).

[9] *Ibid.*, II, 157. The tone of the second letter suggests that Hunt possibly took his cue in part from Byron himself, who replied to Hunt's early remonstrances with the simple explanation that he "libelled his friends all round" ("Lord Byron and Leigh Hunt," *The Examiner*, No. 1,043 [January 27, 1828], p. 52).

idea that Byron might write a kind of retraction which could appear in *The Examiner*, and Mary Shelley wrote to Byron to propose this. The situation as it now stood, she remarked, could easily injure *The Liberal*, which was, after all, Hunt's means of subsistence. It now appeared to be merely "a work of charity— a kind of subscription for Hunt's family."[10] Byron replied, denying that he had any "intention to insult Hunt's poverty," for which he actually honored him. "I engaged in the Journal from good-will towards him, added to respect for his character, literary and personal; and no less for his political courage, as well as regret for his present circumstances," Byron continued. "I did this in the hope that he might, with the same aid from literary friends of literary contributions . . . render himself independent." On the suggested retraction, Byron appears to have made no comment.[11] Hunt was dissatisfied and believed that "something better might have been done," Mary reported.[12] Hunt knew that Byron was sorry, "but he ought to have cut the matter short by saying as much now in public," for which, Hunt believed, Byron lacked the courage.[13]

Byron did write to John Murray, whose actions he considered "indiscreet," in order to terminate their publishing connection entirely.[14] He was now to turn to John Hunt, for whom on occasion he expressed high respect,[15] but in his apparent deter-

---

[10] Mary Shelley to Byron, probably November 9, 1822 (Mary Shelley, *Letters*, I, 200-2).

[11] Byron to Mrs. [Shelley], undated (*L. & J.*, VI, 174). Moore, who first published this letter (*Byron*, II, 398), omitted part, so that it is impossible to be certain that Byron said nothing regarding Mary's suggestion.

[12] Mary to Byron, undated (Mary Shelley, *Letters*, I, 202).

[13] Hunt to Elizabeth Kent, November 22, 1822 (*Corr.*, I, 200).

[14] Byron to Murray, November 18, 1822 (*L. & J.*, VI, 138). Byron had been on the point of leaving Murray and turning entirely to John Hunt on October 31, when he wrote to Hunt that he had "received a letter from the Honble Douglas Kinnaird, enclosing a note from Mr. M" (*Ibid.*, VI, 134). This probably referred to the Preface of "The Vision of Judgment."

[15] Edward Trelawny wrote Mary Shelley from Cephalonia on September 6, 1823, that Byron was "delighted with Hunt as a publisher" (*S. & M.*, III, 975). Surgeon Major-General Henry Skey Muir wrote in his diary for October 1,

mination of the moment to stand beside Leigh Hunt, Byron
was clearly moved by a sense of obligation rather than desire.
If the periodical scheme were to fail, he would be responsible
to an even greater degree for Hunt and his family. The efforts
of Murray and Byron's other London friends to injure *The
Liberal* were extremely foolish, he argued. "Now, do you see
what you and your friends do by your injudicious rudeness?"
he asked Murray at Christmas. "Actually cement a sort of
connection which you strove to prevent."[16] Yet Byron continued to reveal his uneasiness in the association with "these
Sunday paper patriots,"[17] so that, as *The Literary Museum*
remarked in December, "Many contradictory reports relative
to Lord Byron's connexion with the Liberal are in circulation."[18]

§ *ii*

The first number of *The Liberal* arrived in Genoa in early
November, "accompanied both with hopes and fears."[19] Byron
and Leigh Hunt "were very much pleased" with the work,
which was "nicely printed & got up" and looked "both neat
& rich." They believed that it might have been thicker and less
"spun out." In spite of all else, Byron was for the moment
interested in the periodical and made suggestions for the next
number.[20] But the "fears" which Hunt was to recall were to be
"too speedily realized."[21] In all likelihood, it could not have

---

1823, that Byron "said of Leigh Hunt, that he was a poor helpless creature, but
that his brother was really a clever fellow" (H. Skey Muir, Jr., "Byroniana,"
Notes and Queries, Ser. 6, IX [1884], 81).

[16] Byron, *L. & J.*, VI, 156.

[17] Byron to Hobhouse, December 14, 1822 (*Corr.*, II, 238).

[18] "Lord Byron and the Liberal," *The Literary Museum, or Records of Literature,
Fine Arts, Science*, No. 34 (December 14, 1822), p. 543. This rather obscure weekly
review existed from 1822 to 1824, first as *The Museum* but then as *The Literary
Museum*. It was Tory in its political sympathies, but apparently not extremely so.

[19] Hunt, *Autobiography*, p. 350.

[20] Byron and Leigh Hunt to Henry Hunt, undated (Gates, "Letter," pp. 13-15).

[21] Hunt, *Autobiography*, p. 350.

been otherwise, since the general tone of the reaction to this first number was belligerent.

Private opinions, of which there are not many recorded instances, offered exceptions, but then the reactions of individuals did not constitute the financial and legal threat to *The Liberal* that the antagonism of the majority of the press created. Charles Lamb, a friend both of Southey and of Leigh Hunt, but certainly no admirer of Byron, was at one time to consider "The Vision of Judgment" as the "one good-natured thing" that Byron ever wrote.[22] A pair as diverse as William Hazlitt[23] and Henry Crabb Robinson[24] were later to record their admiration for Shelley's "May-day Night." But, according to P. P. Howe, in 1822 Robinson expressed his contempt for *The Liberal* as a whole: "This worthless work will scarcely reach a second, certainly not a third number."[25] The tone was more nearly characteristic. "Ld. Byron seems to be a fool for working in the Liberal," Lord Blessington remarked. "It might do for Bysshe Shelley."[26] To the Reverend H. H. Milman, it was simply that Byron was doing "everything which people who hate, fear, and envy him, would have especially wished him to do."[27] Even Southey appeared to be generally contemptuous of the work although he was not altogether indifferent. "I have only seen some newspaper extracts from this journal, among them the description of myself," he told his brother. "He may go on

---

[22] E. V. Lucas, *Life of Charles Lamb* (2 vols.; London, 1905), II, 380.

[23] William Hazlitt, "The Posthumous Poems of Percy Bysshe Shelley," *The Edinburgh Review*, XL (1824), 494-514.

[24] Henry Crabb Robinson to Johann Wolfgang von Goethe, January 31, 1829 (*The Diary, Reminiscences, and Correspondences of Henry Crabb Robinson*, ed. Thomas Sadler [2 vols.; Boston, 1869], II, 81).

[25] P. P. Howe, *The Life of William Hazlitt* (London, 1949), p. 352. This does not appear in the published *Diary* of Robinson and could not have been written, except by mistake, for October 2, 1822, the date to which Howe assigned it.

[26] Lord Blessington to John Galt, December 5, 1822 (courtesy of Mr. Ralph Brown of B. F. Stevens and Brown, Ltd., London).

[27] H. H. Milman to John Murray, December 27, 1822 (Smiles, *A Publisher and His Friends*, I, 107).

with such satire till his heart aches, before he can excite in me
one uncomfortable emotion." He felt an advantage over Byron
and "no necessity for striking a blow at one who has so completely condemned himself. I wish the Liberals joy of their
journal."[28] A few days after this, he had read *The Liberal* and
pronounced it "quite what it ought to be." It would last no
more than two numbers, and even in this event, prosecution
was likely, and a quarrel between Byron and Hunt was nearly
certain.[29] There was, however, some active condemnation,
made without any attempt to display indifference. Edward
Irving, in London as minister at Hatton Garden Chapel, was
to condemn both Southey's and Byron's poems: "with the one,
blasphemy is virtue when it makes for loyalty; with the other,
blasphemy is the food and spice of jest-making. Barren souls!"[30]
But the most scathing, and at the same time perhaps the most
contemptuous, of the private comments was that made by
Thomas Carlyle in late October or early November:

Byron's Magazine, or rather Hunt's, "The Liberal" is arrived in
Town; but they will not sell it—it is so full of Atheism and Radical-
ism and other noxious *isms*. I had a glance of it one evening; I read
it through and found two papers apparently by Byron, and full of
talent as well as mischief. Hunt is the only serious man in it, since
Shelley died: he has a wish to preach about politics and bishops and
pleasure and paintings and nature, honest man; Byron wants only to
write squibs against Southey and the like. The work will hardly do.[31]

---

[28] Robert Southey to Dr. Henry Southey, October 30, 1822 (*The Life and
Correspondence of the Late Robert Southey*, ed. Charles Cuthbert Southey [6 vols.;
London, 1850], V, 126).

[29] Southey to John Rickman, November 3, 1822 (*Selections from the Letters of
Robert Southey*, ed. John Wood Warter [4 vols.; London, 1856], III, 344). On
November 16, he made substantially the same statements to Neville White (*Life
and Correspondence*, V, 126 n).

[30] "The Rev. Edward Irving, A. M." *The Examiner*, No. 807 (July 13, 1823),
p. 53. See Irving, *For the Oracles of God, Four Orations for Judgment to Come* (Philadelphia, 1824), p. 248.

[31] Thomas Carlyle to Jane Welsh, undated (*The Love Letters of Thomas Carlyle
and Jane Welsh*, ed. Alexander Carlyle [2 vols.; London, 1908], I, 95-96).

The more significant reaction to *The Liberal* appeared in the newspapers and periodicals, of course, but it is worth noting that the range of comment and in some instances the specific and recurring comments in the press correspond generally with what has been found in the limited number of recorded private reactions.

§ *iii*

The newspapers had an obvious advantage over the magazines, particularly since *The Liberal* was published in the middle of the month, so that with but slight exception none of the monthly journals brought forth their comments upon *The Liberal* until the newspapers had given theirs and had really said very much of what was to be said at all about the new periodical. In most instances the attack was primarily directed toward "The Vision of Judgment," which was considered evil, occasionally dangerous, but more frequently a failure. The question of the appropriateness of a reviewer's reprinting passages from the poem remained in dispute. Leigh Hunt was most frequently considered contemptible, occasionally as honest though stupid. The critics treated Shelley with hesitation, differing widely as to the merits of "May-day Night." And they ranged, in their handling of Byron, from something akin to respect for his rank and genius to an outright assertion that he was deteriorating in ability as only the depraved could. The alliance between Byron and Hunt was, according to the remarks of most of the critics, futile, and *The Liberal* itself was destined for rapid failure.

St. James's Chronicle, a thrice-weekly, carried in its issue for October 12-15 the first Tory review of *The Liberal*.[32] Although the author had at least "been able to look through" Byron's

---

[32] "The Liberal," *St. James's Chronicle*, No. 10,131 (October 12-15, 1822), p. 2. This newspaper was begun in 1761 as an independent Whig journal, but it became in time an organ for the Church and State group. It existed until 1866.

"The Vision of Judgment," his review was based largely on the
preliminary notice in *The Examiner* of October 13, and it was
copied almost at once by *The Gentleman's Magazine* for its
October issue.[33] Although literary circles had expected "blasphemy and impurity of every kind to a certain extent" in this
work of "translated cockneys," the reviewer remarked, they
could not "anticipate all the atrocity of 'the Liberal,' " which,
however, has been matched by "a stupidity greater than the
best men could have hoped." Byron himself was "becoming
so dull," illustrating "the words of the Prophet, which, no
doubt, apply to intellectual excellence as well as temporal
prosperity, 'Pride bringeth to destruction, and lewdness to
decay.' " He had attempted a parody of Southey's poem but
failed, for his "Vision of Judgment" simply "does not wear the
same clothes," and is filled with "the most shocking profaneness" and unjustified attack on "that sainted monarch." The
single passage "free from positive blasphemy" was that concerning Southey, which the reviewer quoted with an apology.
Actually, Byron rather than Southey was a changeling, as
Southey had often been called, for only of Byron could it be
charged,

that he abandoned the Christian Religion for the religion of Childe

---

[33] "The *Liberal*. The New Periodical Work from Italy," *The Gentleman's Magazine*,
XCII, Part II (1822), 348-51. The editor acknowledged the source of the review,
"our old literary favourite, the 'St. James's Chronicle.' " In the suggestion of
the striking failure of Byron's genius in *The Liberal*, *St. James's* was first in the
field, possibly giving the suggestion to others. In a review of *The Liberal* reprinted
"*From the Guardian*" in *The Windsor and Eton Express and General Advertiser* (October
26, 1822, p. 3), the writer remarked that Byron's "systematic determination to
mislead the intellect, to corrupt the feelings, and to violate all the decencies of
society" had replaced his "original genius." There was satisfaction in perceiving
"that the hardening of the heart carries with it the debasement of the understanding; and that the deeper this unhappy man plunges into the filth of blasphemy
and lasciviousness, the more does he lose the brilliance of his original genius,
and sink the ardent poet into the drivelling scoffer" (W. G. Bebbington, "The
Most Remarkable Man of His Age: Byron in *The Windsor and Eton Express and
General Advertiser*," *Keats-Shelley Memorial Bulletin*, VII [1956], 28-29).

Harold; that he changed his disgust, at Mr. Moore's too warm painting, for a taste indicated by the incestuous ravings of Manfred; that he resigned his respect for the free government of Britain, for a love of democracy which he has inculcated in theory, and a preference for Turkish or Austrian despotism, which he has manifested in practice; that, once the admirer of Milton, Dryden, Pope, he has become the associate of the Cockney Bluestockings, and the panegyrist of Lady Morgan; or to give one which comprehends all other degrees of metamorphosis and degradation, he has sunk from the station of an English nobleman, and the highest place in English literature, to be the colleague of Mr. Leigh Hunt, the author of Don Juan, and a contributor to the Liberal.

On Saturday, October 19, four days after the publication of *The Liberal*, four weekly newspapers carried notices, in each case simply the first of two or three installments of a review. The most restrained of these appeared in *The Literary Museum*. At first, the reviewer, "prevented by the courtesy of the craft from noticing it in any other way," gave an extract from Leigh Hunt's "Rhyme and Reason," which he attributed to Byron during the recent period of Popean influence.[34] Later, this attack was more direct. It was aimed first at the choice of title. "We do not think it *liberal* to deny that other parties may contain as good and generous people as that to which we belong," remarked the reviewer. "And we think that the man who could write those brutal Epigrams on Lord Castlereagh . . . is the last man who should dare to call himself *liberal*." He turned then to certain other pieces in the periodical. "The Vision of Judgment" was "very profane, and in sufficiently bad taste" but no worse than Southey's poem; the "Letter to the Editor of 'My Grandmother's Review' " merely demonstrated Byron's base conduct; and "The Florentine Lovers" was "a pretty enough tale, spoiled by the egotism of the Narrator."

---

[34] *The Literary Museum*, No. 26 (October 19, 1822), p. 405.

8

On the positive side, there was the first of Leigh Hunt's "Letters from Abroad," which was well written and contained "much interesting information," the reviewer believed, while Shelley's "May-day Night" was "the first article in point of merit" in *The Liberal*, "executed so as to make us regret that we have not the whole drama translated by him."[35]

"My dear Byron, See what you have brought yourself into by liking Leigh Hunt's verses," *The Literary Register* began, in parody of Hunt's dedication of *Rimini*. The remarks were far more angry than those of *The Literary Museum*, and far less literary, for they were concerned primarily with the personalities from which came the pieces in the first number of *The Liberal*. Hunt, though accredited with the "Epigrams on Lord Castlereagh," was for the time dismissed as an unnecessary adjunct in the literary association, who "scents food for the nobler animal." But Byron himself deserved only contempt. His principal contribution to *The Liberal*, "the most profligate and outrageous insult that was ever yet offered to the serious opinions of the majority of mankind," consisted exclusively of "profaneness and obscenity: profaneness like that which a mighty, though fallen, intelligence would pour out at a hell-debauch . . . obscenity floundering in its own mire." The work therefore could not be quoted. "There is not a line in 'The Vision of Judgment' which we could read for a wife, a child, or a mother, and we shall not print a line of it for our readers," continued the writer, urging that everyone ignore the work. "If this contagion must exist among us, let it exist unspoken of, if possible unnamed; like some talisman of fiendish construction and pestilential tendency, whose influence must remain suspended in our silence, only to break and become capable of harm from our communion with it." There were to be other developments of the theme of the supposed Byronic depravity,

---

[35] *Ibid.*, No. 27 (October 26, 1822), pp. 422-23.

but none perhaps so forceful as this. The remainder of the review itself showed signs of anticlimax in its brief comments upon the various articles in *The Liberal* and, on the following Saturday, in its ridicule of Hunt's translation from Ariosto and Politian, "too matchless and monstrous a compound of nonsense and—nonsense and nonsense!"[36]

Although *The Literary Chronicle and Weekly Review* took time to comment on the inappropriateness of the title of *The Liberal* —"without a spark of liberality, generosity, or even good nature in it"—the primary purpose was to make specific reference to articles rather than general comments upon the work itself. The reviewer condemned the Preface as demonstrating Leigh Hunt's "mawkishness," the "Epigrams on Lord Castlereagh" as "stupid and brutal," and the first of the "Letters from Abroad" as uninspiring, "a description of Pisa, every line of which Mr. Leigh Hunt could have written as well at Hampstead as in Italy." Although Hunt's translation of Ariosto was "rather spirited," his version of Politian exemplified "the true cockney style." And Shelley's work, though totally unobjectionable, was "destitute of every other merit." "The Vision of Judgment" was, of course, regarded with horror—"a blasphemous parody of a profane piece of absurdity of the same name"—with the suggestion that certain passages in the poem were "more deserving of the notice of the Attorney General than the critic." Surprisingly, Byron's "Letter to the Editor of 'My Grand-mother's Review' " was considered "a very playful piece of satire, and, perhaps, the best article in the work." And besides this, there was "The Florentine Lovers," "a pretty tale" which, "if not possessing the most merit, is, at least, one of the least objectionable papers in 'The Liberal,' which, we suspect, as a

---

[36] "The Liberal: Verses [*sic*] and Prose from the South," *The Literary Register of the Fine Arts, Sciences, and Belles Lettres*, No. 16 (October 19, 1822), pp. 241-43; No. 17 (October 26, 1822), pp. 260-62. This periodical was published from July 6, 1822, to July 26, 1823.

whole, must have greatly disappointed the expectations of the public."[37]

In noticing *The Liberal* for three consecutive weeks, William Jerdan, editor of *The London Literary Gazette*, tended to refute his own claim that the new periodical was "only as impotent as disgusting, as foolish as egotistical, and as despicable as indecent." He proclaimed the fall of Byron, even in his futile attempt to exploit the possibilities offered by Southey's "senseless production." Jerdan quoted extensively from "The Vision of Judgment" on the grounds that "no harm can be done" and probably some good, for "we think it must disgust every one and sicken the most inveterate admirers of Lord Byron's muse and principles." For the same reason, he copied the "Epigrams on Lord Castlereagh." "Their decency, their playful humour, their superlative wit, their pure feeling, and above all, their unequalled point, render them altogether worthy of finishing this exhibition of unsophisticated liberality and philosophical perfection," Jerdan remarked in closing the first installment. The following week he rejoiced, "The Liberal is almost dead already." Nevertheless, there would be some effort to save it, and Byron would bring Hazlitt to Pisa "to throw a little spirit into future Numbers, and prevent their being so inhumanly disgraced by Lordly spleen and sycophantic, even if congenial, prostitution." He turned to many of the individual items in the journal, but he could add little, and in the third week he concluded his review with satisfaction:

We have now very fully exhibited and discussed this publication; and we find, on casting up the account, that Lord Bryon has

---

[37] "The Liberal. Verse and Prose from the South. Volume the First," *The Literary Chronicle and Weekly Review*, No. 179 (October 19, 1822), pp. 655-58; No. 180 (October 26, 1822), pp. 675-77. This Saturday paper was begun in 1819 and existed until 1828. According to Walter Graham (*English Literary Periodicals*, p. 317), it was characterized by "somewhat wrongheaded, perhaps, but vigorous and arresting criticism." It is worth noting that *The Literary Chronicle* was advertised in the back pages of the first number of *The Liberal*.

contributed impiety, vulgarity, inhumanity, and heartlessness; Mr. Shelley, a burlesque upon Göthe; and Mr. Leigh Hunt, conceit, trumpery, ignorance, and wretched verses. The union of wickedness, folly, and imbecility, is perfect; and, as they congratulate the Devil, so do we congratulate the Authors of the Liberal.[38]

On Saturday, October 26, *The Courier* turned to the "*scoundrel-like* publication." Its "cursory examination" of the contents of *The Liberal* inspired comments only on the Preface, "The Vision of Judgment," and the "Epigrams on Lord Castlereagh," and these contributed little to the rapidly accumulating criticism of these works. The chief claim of *The Courier*'s review to special notice is a kind of virulent eloquence which its reviewer achieved in reference to Byron. Leigh Hunt was a Sporus-like character, "a manufacturer of lack-a-daisical prose—and namby pamby poetics," while Shelley was "the infidel Shelley, of whom we should speak in no compromising terms, were he still capable of future mischief." Byron, however, was far more dangerous than either of these had been, for it was his "master-hand" which guided *The Liberal*:

With a brain from heaven and a heart from hell—with a pen that can write as angels speak, and yet that riots in thoughts which fiends might envy—with the power to charm, instruct, and elevate— but with the ruling passion to provoke our loathing and deserve our scorn—this compound of rottenness and beauty—this unsexed Circe, who gems the poisoned cup he offers us, and exhorts our admiration of its rare and curious workmanship, while the Soul sickens at the draught within—seems to have lived only that the world might learn from his example, how worthless and how

---

[38] "The Liberal," *The London Literary Gazette, and Journal of Belles Lettres, Arts, Sciences*, No. 300 (October 19, 1822), pp. 655-58; No. 301 (October 26, 1822), pp. 678-79; No. 302 (November 2, 1822), pp. 693-95. This important critical journal was founded in 1817 by William Jerdan and edited by him until 1850. In 1862, it was merged with the *Parthenon*. The theme of these reviews with regard to Byron seems to follow the pattern that has been traced by Robert W. Duncan ("Byron and the London *Literary Gazette*," *Boston University Studies in English*, II [1956], 240-50).

pernicious a thing is genius, when divorced from religion, from morals, and from humanity.[39]

In *John Bull* the following day, Theodore Hook remarked that it was an "unpleasant task, for the sake of public justice, to quote into our paper some of the nonsensical blasphemy which has appeared, during the week, in a Magazine called the Liberal." He pointed to the "bad grammar and Cockney English" in "The Vision of Judgment" and accused Byron of having done the translation from Politian. More important, Hook made a suggestion with reference to the younger Hunts which was soon to be developed further, "We should think the [Hunt] children must have done the greatest part of the first number of *The Liberal*."[40]

It is somewhat surprising that there was no comment from such consistently conservative papers as *The Morning Post*[41] and *The New Times*,[42] which were possibly of that school that sincerely believed that total neglect of *The Liberal* would bring about its rapid downfall. It is less surprising that there was only slight support for *The Liberal* among the Whig and Radical papers. Journals like Richard Carlile's *Republican* and William Cobbett's *Political Register*[43] were concerned with political rather than literary comment. The more moderate Whig newspapers were hesitant to make favorable literary comment

---

[39] "The Liberal," *The Courier*, No. 9,677 (October 26, 1822), pp. 2-3.

[40] *John Bull*, No. 98 (October 27, 1822), pp. 780-81.

[41] In 1772, this newspaper was founded as *The Morning Post and Daily Advertiser*. In 1796, it was acquired by Daniel Stuart at a time when circulation had fallen. In seven years, however, he brought the paper to second place among the morning dailies.

[42] *The New Times*, unlike the moderately conservative *Post*, took an extreme Tory-constitutionalist position. It was founded in 1817 by Dr. John Stoddart after his release from *The Times* because of his extremely anti-French writings, which had persisted after Waterloo.

[43] William Cobbett founded *The Political Register* on January 1, 1802. He was at first a supporter of the Tories, but he weakened in this support and finally came to oppose them. He was fined in 1804 in connection with his writings in his newspaper, and fined and imprisoned in 1809.

in the face of the seemingly extreme political and religious point of view of *The Liberal*.

Except for the remarks in *The Examiner*, the only favorable review of the first number of *The Liberal* was that which appeared on October 20 in *The British Luminary and Weekly Intelligencer*. "At length this long expected publication from Italy has appeared, and, generally speaking," began the reviewer, "we apprehend it will not disappoint the anticipation formed of it." He concerned himself largely with "The Vision of Judgment," which he compared to Southey's poem, in itself a work "not more reverential and decent because less witty." Byron's "Letter to the Editor of 'My Grandmother's Review' " seemed to this reviewer "an inconceivably keen piece of satire." He praised Hunt's "The Florentine Lovers" and "Letters from Abroad," but he merely mentioned Shelley's translation, at least setting it apart in this way from "the remaining pieces . . . of minor pretension." Although at times the reviewer was hardly enthusiastic about much of the first *Liberal*, he was confident that the writers would carry forth their intentions. "This number will produce skirmishing," he remarked in conclusion, "but the conductors seemed prepared for war, and their ability to maintain it, the present specimens, we opine, will prove with tolerable significance."[44]

The Morning Chronicle did not review the first number of *The Liberal*, but it made reference to the new periodical as a point of departure for an attack upon the Constitutional Association.[45] "We should not wonder if a certain Association

---

[44] "The Liberal," *The British Luminary and Weekly Intelligencer*, No. 212 (October 20, 1822), p. 754.

[45] At the time of its inception, the Constitutional Association printed and circulated its definition of the Law of Libel, part of which is very much to the point in connection with the history of *The Liberal*:

The law of libel is founded upon a single, plain, and familiar principle—a principle sanctioned alike by morality and religion, "That no individual shall injure the reputation of another." Men in a state of society have a right to be protected in their property, their persons, and their character. . . . In

were at this moment pondering in solemn conclave over the article entitled *Rhyme and Reason* (in *The Liberal*)," it suggested on October 25,[46] and the following day it presented a series of rhymes occurring in "Rhyme and Reason," for which it supplied lines:

What	Tools	Backs	Seat
Use	Host	Throne	Sell
Rot	Fools	Tax	Complete
Abuse.	Most.	Alone.	Hell.

The Bridge-street Gang's I know not *what*,
　　Nor what its social *use*,
Unless it be to favour *rot*,
　　And patronise *abuse*.
For this, indeed, they're worthy *tools*,
　　In this great cause a *host;*
And very good at finding *fools*,
　　For such are plunder'd *most*.
M-rr-y and S-w-ll at their *backs*,
　　They cant of Church and *throne;*
Poor starving rogues with libel *tax*,
　　And leave the rich *alone*.
Snug in their profitable *seat*,
　　No one must pamphlets *sell*

---

like manner, but with a far stronger claim, the interests of the community at large, or in other words, the state, in which all the interests of all are combined, demand protection. Whatever, therefore, has a tendency to ridicule the doctrines and institutions of religion—to relax the obligations of morality—to violate public decency—to vilify the person and dignity of the Sovereign—to defame the constituted authorities of the empire, and the reputation of public men, or to disturb the quiet and repose in private life, in whatever manner expressed, is libellous and ought to be suppressed ("The Law of Libel," *The Beacon*, No. 12 [March 24, 1821], p. 95).

For three or four months, the Constitutional Association was quite successful in its work of suppression, but then the Grand Jury found a true bill against its members for oppression and extortion. They were acquitted, but the trial served to arouse the public to the dangers of such an association.

[46] "Libel," *The Morning Chronicle*, October 25, 1822, p. 3.

To prove the Hypocrites *complete*
Are sure to go to *hell*.[47]

In defense against the critics of *The Liberal*, two items
appeared in *The Examiner*. One was supposedly a letter to the
editor, written with reference to the comments which had
appeared in *The London Literary Gazette*:

Depend upon it, Sir, that an Editor who gives *three or four* columns
of extract from the most *piquant* passage of the *Vision of Judgment*,
is no enemy to the sale of the *Liberal*, though he may find it necessary to save appearances with the proprietors of the puffing machine,
by seeming to condemn it. And then the style of the abuse—how
could you mistake any thing so wilfully and extravagantly over-
done?[48]

The other effort of *The Examiner* on behalf of *The Liberal*
at this time was an article, "Odious Cant—George the Third
and Lord Castlereagh," which appeared on November 3 and
10.[49] Despite the title, the case of Castlereagh was considered
in the first installment of this article, possibly because John
Hunt feared legal reprisals for publishing the "Epigrams"
rather than "The Vision of Judgment."[50] "The feeling which
antimates the Epigrams is unquestionably one of satisfaction
and triumph," but this merely reflected the reaction of millions
of Castlereagh's victims to the news of his death. It was necessary,

---

[47] "Rhyme and Reason," *Ibid.*, October 26, 1822, p. 3. The series of rhymes
occurred in *The Liberal*, I, 88. Three days later, October 29, 1822, this paper
carried sixteen rhyming words from the same source, for which it again supplied
lines as a means of attacking the Constitutional Association.

[48] "The Secret of Over-Acted Zeal," *The Examiner*, No. 771 (November 3,
1822), p. 693.

[49] "Odious Cant—George the Third and Lord Castlereagh," *Ibid.*, No. 771
(November 3, 1822), pp. 689-91; No. 772 (November 10, 1822), pp. 705-7.

[50] "We . . . shall only for the present express our surprise, that when the Gang
[the Constitutional Association] determined to take advantage of the cant about
the character of the dead, they did not indict the Epigrams on Castlereagh
instead of the account of George the Third" (*Ibid.*, No. 777 [December 15, 1822]
pp. 789-90).

in reading these lines, to make a distinction between "the man we think of only with pity" and "the minister we remember with loathing." Though the man died, the works of the minister survived. "The *Courier* talks of *scoundrel-like*. It would have its readers believe, that because a man expresses an honest indignation against a detested statesman, that therefore he is incapable of relenting towards a departed private enemy." The case of Byron's opinion of George the Third was even less difficult than this, for he attributed merely weakness, rather than malice, to the late King. "Can any thing be more obvious, than the strong and even careful distinction made by the Poet between the active wickedness of the courtiers, and the passive though most disastrous weakness of the sovereign?" Byron had strongly defended George's personal character, but he could hardly overlook the late monarch's madness, caused by "pure fatuity and lack of brains." The description, therefore, was a fair one, so that the only remaining question, with which the article closed, was that of the poet's rights: "Why cannot his [George's] eulogists bear that others should fairly express *their* opinions, and endeavour to shew the mischief that may be done by a weak monarch in the hands of unprincipled corruptionists?"

§ *iv*

As the newspapers ceased to comment, the monthly journals were beginning to appear, bringing forth remarks on *The Liberal* which were not very unlike those which had already been published in the daily and weekly press.

The only periodical other than *The Gentleman's Magazine* to carry a review of *The Liberal* in its number for October was *The New European Magazine*. Despite the resolution to review "*only* those works which were likely to *interest*, *edify*, or *amuse*," the reviewer felt compelled to notice "this newly arrived Manifesto of the Pisan Conspirators" because of "the very

supremacy of weakness and wickedness in which those Pro-
fessors of the '*Satanic School*' have indulged in its compilation."
The "evil intention is indeed evident," he continued, but the
work itself was without talent, surpassed even "by the forgotten
vanities and impertinencies of the *Examiner* Newspaper, in
those halcyon days when it was the organ of Cockney taste."
All the articles were condemned. The Preface was like Leigh
Hunt's former "hebdomadal lucubrations," and Shelley's
translation from *Faust* made "that which was before dim, most
profoundly obscure." But "The Vision of Judgment" offered
the outstanding example of the combination of weakness and
wickedness, for it was a work "so vulgar, and so dull, that the
contempt it will draw upon it's [*sic*] author will long outlive
the memory of the deed; and its baseness will be remembered
while not a line of it will be quoted." And Byron himself has
deteriorated, by "natural profligacy" rather than by "villainous
company," so that "for the first time" the reviewer found reason
to "pity the degraded Leigh Hunt in being his associate and
toad-eater."[51]

In November, three periodicals—*The Literary Speculum, The
Council of Ten,* and *The Edinburgh Magazine*—noticed *The
Liberal.* The first of these belittled the Byron-Hunt partnership
and thoroughly condemned the new magazine, but was largely
concerned with individual pieces in the work. But here, the
only contribution was a comment upon the "Epigrams on Lord
Castlereagh," which the reviewer assigned to Leigh Hunt:

We dare say, if Mr. Leigh Hunt should take it into his head some day
to blow out the portion of brains with which nature has furnished
him, it would be no very pleasing reflection for Mrs. Leigh Hunt,
to read her husband's life, character, and behaviour, sketched and
commented on by the pen of malignity, and the peculiar circum-

---

[51] "The Liberal," *The New European Magazine*, I (1822), 354-63. This work
existed for two years, from 1822 to 1824, dedicated to the cause of "Bible, Crown,
and Constitution."

stances of his death thrust upon her attention on every occasion with unfeeling brutality.

For the journal in its entirety, the writer made the suggestion which, surprisingly, had not appeared before, that the work was simply not worth the five shillings asked for it, for it "scarcely contains more than half the quantity of any two shilling magazine of the day." Possibly, the writer suggested, quality compensates for deficient quantity, "and so it would prove, were it as apparent to the reader as it doubtless is to the writers." But it clearly was not apparent, and this fact foretold early failure of the magazine.[52]

The reviewer in *The Council of Ten* chose to develop two propositions which were now quite familiar. The first of these was the misuse of the term *liberal*, of which he considered the Preface an illustration. On the basis of "the rapid, rambling, and *tranchant* style," he assigned the Preface to Byron, whose other works, the "Vision" and the "Epigrams," clearly offered further support for his argument. This brought the reviewer to his second assertion, that "the genius even of Lord Byron is clogged and depressed by this conjunction with Mr. Hunt." He made the suggestion that Byron pay Hunt £1000 to break off the association, and, in a letter addressed to Byron with which this writer for *The Council of Ten* closed his review, he offered the alternatives: "When you step out of your proper sphere, be assured, that you are only a common man; and 'The Liberal' *at best* will be no better than an ordinary magazine. On the other hand, my Lord, what a wide field of fame and utility is open to you. What glorious prizes are still within your reach."[53]

---

[52] "The Liberal," *The Literary Speculum*, II (1822), 422-32. This journal was begun in 1821 as a monthly, but toward the end of its career in 1822 it became irregular.

[53] "On Liberality. 'The Liberal; Verse and Prose from the South.' Postscript to Lord Byron," *The Council of Ten*, II (1822), 149-78. This was a monthly periodical with obvious Tory sympathies. It flourished in 1822 and 1823, rather pompously setting itself up to comment upon matters, both political and literary,

The writer of one of the letters signed "Jonathan Oldmixon" appearing in *The Edinburgh Magazine,* like the reviewer in *The New European Magazine,* saw *The Liberal* as the result of evil combining with impotence. As might be expected, he suggested that this indicated that Byron had "taken leave of his genius." Worse, "he himself seems to be conscious of the state of helpless impotence, and immature imbecility into which he has at length fallen." His apparent mirth, therefore, arose merely from desperation and "resembles what we may conceive of the damned, attempting to drown, for a moment, the dreadful consciousness of their misery, in a wild fit of desperate and delirious laughter." Blasphemy and desecration of the dead would be expected, but although these expressed his fury, they revealed none of "the sublime and terrible energy of despair." Despite his totally evil intentions, Byron produced only "the most commonplace drivelling and impotency; and when he thinks he is distilling the most pungent and deadly venom, it turns out to be only the deglutition of a little rabid slaver, calculated rather to defile than injure."

The unique contribution of *The Edinburgh Magazine* had nothing to do with criticism of the first number of *The Liberal,* but was a suggestion relating to the ownership of the new periodical. "We can perfectly conceive, that the *real* proprietor of a work, and the *ostensible* publisher whose name figures in the imprint, may be two persons as different in their identity as Mr. John Murray, Albemarle Street, and the present Editor and Proprietor of the Examiner." The reasons for the suspicion —"we do not say, whatever we may *conjecture*"—were Murray's previous willingness to publish the early cantos of *Don Juan* and the fact "that Mr. John Murray's Edinburgh Agents,

which seemed to require or deserve comment. Its editors chose as an epigraph the following lines from Byron's *The Two Foscari* (II, i, 196):

Loredano : We have decided.
Doge :   We?
Loredano :   The Ten in Council.

Messrs Oliver & Boyd, were the persons who subscribed 'The Liberal' to the trade in this city."[54] The accusation gained little or no support, because of the improbability of the charge as well as the likelihood that Bradfute, rather than Oliver and Boyd, was the agent for *The Liberal* in Edinburgh.[55] "A Scotch magazine insinuates, in no very indirect terms, that Mr. M. is covertly concerned in the publication of the Liberal," reported *The Literary Museum* in December, pointing to the "squinty syllogism. . . . He who is the concealed publisher of one work may be the concealed publisher of another." This, however, was hardly acceptable, and the writer could not "be induced to believe that Mr. M. has any participation in the property of the Liberal."[56] Apparently no other publication considered the charge worth noticing.

In December, *La Belle Assemblée*, a fashion magazine, observed that Byron had "descend[ed] from his impregnable fortress of poetry" by participating in *The Liberal*. "Having long in his enchanting poetry instilled erroneous opinions in those who listened to him," he was now vulnerable, and the critic of *La Belle Assemblée* was "happy in having an opportunity of combating the *Liberals of the South*, in plain language." He promised that in the following number he would "give a specimen, with some remarks, that may not be lost on the public."[57] But none appeared.

---

[54] "Oldmixon's Account of 'The Liberal,' " *The Edinburgh Magazine, and Literary Miscellany*, N.S. XI (1822), 561-73. This periodical was begun in January, 1785. It merged with *Scots Magazine* in 1802 and retained the title of both periodicals until July, 1817, when it adopted the name given above. It ceased publication in June, 1826.

[55] On January 12, 1823, Thomas Carlyle told Jane Welsh, "Mr. Bradfute I think is the publisher here" (*The Love Letters*, I, 148). It is probably significant that when *The Literary Examiner* began to appear in the summer of 1823, Bell and Bradfute were listed as the Edinburgh agents for the work (*The Examiner*, No. 809 [July 27, 1823], p. 495).

[56] "Lord Byron and The Liberal," *The Literary Museum*, No. 34 (December 14, 1822), p. 544.

[57] "Lord Byron," *La Belle Assemblée, Being Bell's Court and Fashionable Magazine*, N.S. XXVI (1822), 526-27. The magazine, founded in 1806, was concerned

At the same time, *The Imperial Magazine* proposed that *The Liberal* had been "sent into the world as a mental barometer, or an instrument of experiment, to measure, by the extent of its circulation, the quantity of vice with which the community is saturated." Even adverse critical comment would call attention to *The Liberal* and stimulate its circulation; nevertheless, *The Imperial* rather systematically reviewed the contents of the magazine. There were "several articles, which, if not worthy of strong recommendation, are at least amusing." However, "irreligion, and a contempt of what has been revered as sacred or venerable among the virtuous and loyal, constitute the more prominent articles of the cargo which the *Liberal* has imported from a foreign shore." The circulation had probably been disappointing for the writers, "less extensive than some others, which, though similar in their tendency, are less gross in their attack upon the virtuous feelings of mankind." The public was apparently proving that it was not saturated with vice, and the reviewer could hope that although the cargo in *The Liberal* had "indeed escaped the dangers of the sea," it might yet "be wrecked on the coast of oblivion."[58]

The British Review for December carried its brief notice of the first number of *The Liberal* appended to a review of the *Poems* of Bernard Barton.[59] In the course of 1822, William Roberts had stepped down as editor of the *Review*,[60] but certain

---

primarily with fashions and the social arts. It was generally conservative, as might be expected, but it was only incidentally concerned with politics and religion. It ceased to appear in 1832.

[58] "The Liberal," *The Imperial Magazine*, IV (1822), 1139-42.

[59] "Poems by Bernard Barton," *The British Review*, XX (1822), 405-22. Bernard Barton, the "Quaker Poet," lived from 1784 to 1849. He was the author of "Stanzas Addressed to Percy Bysshe Shelley" (1820) and *Verses on the Death of Percy Bysshe Shelley* (1822), in both of which he pointed to Shelley's ability and errors.

[60] Although *The British Review* existed until 1825, Arthur Roberts reported that it "was finally discontinued in the year 1822" (p. 63) and that it continued under his father's "sole management until it was finally abandoned" (p. 38); it is possible that the difficulty between the two dates, 1822 and 1825, can be resolved by Arthur Roberts' own qualification in his recollection that "an attempt indeed

phrases in the remarks on *The Liberal* suggest that these were his. From the start the reviewer was hesitant, suspicious that his words "may not be quite in place." Yet he insisted "upon the surest grounds of knowledge, that not a word of the letter written by the noble lord . . . to the editor of this journal has ever been read by him; so little has been his curiosity concerning it, and so ineffectual the vengeance intended to be executed upon him."[61] In reality, the reviewer could hardly consider Byron's use of the *Review* as an "indication of his holding its criticisms in contempt," for he had in front of him at the time a letter written by Byron in gratitude for remarks which had appeared in *The British Review* concerning the first two cantos of *Childe Harold*,[62] and he was "pretty confident that the series of criticisms upon his Lordship's productions which have succeeded that article, down to the last on 'Don Juan,' have not sunk us in his real respect." However, if the attack which Byron made upon *The British Review* did arise from hostility, then its only significance, concluded the reviewer, was "the proof it has afforded to the public of the power of the 'British Review' to provoke and to deserve vengeance."

Blackwood's kept its silence until December. At first, in the sixth of the "Noctes Ambrosianæ," *The Liberal* was most generally discussed. "The Vision of Judgment" was considered "vastly inferior to Beppo, to say nothing of the exquisite Don Juan," and Shelley's translation seemed to be "an admirable *morceau*," but Leigh Hunt's Ariosto was "Cockneyfied," and

was made, soon after, to revive it in a smaller form and under another editor; but the attempt was utterly abortive" (p. 63).

[61] Arthur Roberts reported that his father "never troubled himself to read" Byron's "Letter to the Editor of 'My Grandmother's Review' " (p. 51).

[62] The review had appeared in June, 1812 ("Childe Harold's Pilgrimage; a Romaunt," *The British Review*, III [1812], 275-302). The letter referred to was probably that which Arthur Roberts published as written by Byron on June 30, 1812: "Lord Byron presents his compliments to Mr. Longman, and requests that he will do Lord Byron the favour to transmit his best thanks to the conductor of the 'British Review' for the present of that work, and for the very gratifying critique contained in the last number" (Roberts, pp. 44-45).

"The Florentine Lovers" was "an abortion." Byron was chided, but Hunt was regarded with contempt and dislike. If they were to knock away Byron's "handcuffs, (I mean the Cockneys)," Christopher North remarked, they would "see Byron is a sweet fellow yet."[63] The pattern which *Blackwood's* was to follow, generally if not completely, was becoming apparent. At this time there was nothing of the suggestion, already quite familiar, that Byron was losing popularity. In fact, in the article immediately following this, "Odoherty on Werner," William Maginn commented on this type of argument:

> There are a set of blockheads, such as "the Council of Ten," (who, by the way, are the gravest asses going), who pretend to think that the sale of Byron's works has been knocked down merely by the public indignation against the immoralities of his Don Juan, and the baseness and blasphemy of his Pisan production, "The Liberal." But this is mere humbug. The public curiosity is always stimulated by an astonishing degree of clever blackguardism; and a book of real wickedness and real talent, although it may not always be exhibited in the Boudoir, is pretty sure to find its way into every house that has any pretensions to be "*comme il faut.*"[64]

In the seventh of the series "On the Cockney School of Poetry," which appeared in this same issue under the title "Hunt's Art of Love," the writer, presumably John Wilson, commented on the faults apparent in "The Florentine Lovers," but then directed his remarks to the total absurdity of Hunt's position itself. What could Byron mean by it? he asked. "A Bear at College was all very well;—but, my lord, think on it,—a Cockney at Pisa! Fie, my lord." It was natural to see Hunt in his proper situation, as menial to a lord, but it was nevertheless ironic to observe "the man who, for years, kept abusing nobility; and now sneaks fawningly, with hat in hand, to 'my dear Byron,' and is quite happy to do any little dirty job

---

[63] "Noctes Ambrosianæ, No. VI," *Blackwood's*, XII (1822), 695-709.
[64] "Odoherty on Werner," *Ibid.*, XII (1822), 710.

9

imposed on him by the aristocratical pride of the domineering peer." From the relationship, the fact "that Satan should stoop to associate with an incubus," can demonstrate only "that there is degeneracy in hell."[65]

These were comments primarily concerned with personal rather than literary matters. In the issue of January, 1823, *Blackwood's* offered something approaching a conventional review of *The Liberal*. Entitled "The Candid. No. 1," it came forth in the guise of an article recently left on the doorstep of "Maga," which Christopher North decided to publish, first as a means of disposal, then because *The Liberal* was not "merely that grinning idiot which it appears to be . . . but it is also knavish." However, the author of this review, like some of the others, confined his remarks almost exclusively to "The Vision of Judgment," which he considered a failure, "a jest that does not excite a smile, drawled out through nine-and-thirty pages." Byron, who had been falling off gradually in the quality of his productions, suddenly declined sharply. The company which he kept was largely responsible for this, but it had at least one other effect, the reviewer concluded, for it was likely "that the composers of The Liberal have attempted to hoax their readers by imitating and burlesquing the style and manner of each other."[66]

Despite politics, *The Quarterly Review* carried nothing directly relating to *The Liberal*, possibly at the request of John Murray.[67] In January, 1823, *The New Monthly Magazine* merely mentioned

[65] "Hunt's Art of Love," *Ibid.*, XII (1822), 775-81.

[66] "The Candid, No. I," *Ibid.*, XIII (1823), 108-24.

[67] Robert Southey's article in January ("The Progress of Infidelity," *The Quarterly Review*, XXVIII [1823], 494-546) possibly carried indirect references. The word *liberals* was used as synonymous with *infidels*. Here, he made the reference to "dear little T[hornton] H[unt]," who had received no religious training. The following October, Charles Lamb replied to this remark ("Letter of Elia to Robert Southey, Esquire," *The London Magazine*, VIII [1823], 400-407), and at one point remarked about Southey's depicting of Satan in his "Vision." "A noble Lord, your brother Visionary," Lamb wrote, "has scarcely taken greater liberties with the material keys, and merely Catholic notions of St. Peter."

"the appearance of 'The Liberal' from the South: so called by the god-father of the Serpentine River, who gave it that name because it was neither serpentine nor a river."[68] Here was perhaps more gentle treatment than the Hunts had expected. On the other hand, *The Monthly Magazine*, from which some support might have been anticipated, gave admittedly delayed notice in December to "a meteoric production called *the Liberal.*" Although Southey certainly deserved the treatment he received, the reviewer here regretted "that good education, superior talents, and gentlemanly character, should be so abused as they are by all the parties in these personal controversies."[69] Among the monthly journals there was only one which offered any suggestion of support for *The Liberal*, and this, Galignani's *Paris Monthly Review* for January, 1823, was at best indirect. The support came in the guise of a letter from a reader who had written a verse on Southey's poetic development, "a sort of epitaph," appropriate because it was improbable "that the Laureat [*sic*] will ever recover from . . . The Liberal."[70]

What appears to have been the unique American notice of the first number of *The Liberal* was published in *The Albion* on December 21, 1822. It was admittedly based upon the review in *The London Literary Gazette* of October 19 rather than upon an examination of *The Liberal* itself. "The book we believe has not yet reached the United States," the reviewer reported, "and God forbid it ever should; it is enough that one nation is cursed with its impiety and blasphemy." He was, therefore,

---

[68] "Annus Mirabilis! or, A Parthian Glance at 1822," *The New Monthly Magazine*, VII ([*Original Papers*] 1823), 24. This reference was copied, as part of the entire article, in the third volume of *The Weekly Entertainer and West of England Miscellany*, No. 4 (January 27, 1823), p. 50.

[69] "Literary and Critical Proemium," *The Monthly Magazine*, LIV (1822), 452.

[70] *Paris Monthly Review of British and Continental Literature*, No. 12 (January 1823), p. 578. This was published for fifteen numbers between January, 1822, and April, 1823. Of these, the first twelve, through January, 1823, appeared with the title given above. The remaining numbers were published as *Galignani's Magazine and Paris Monthly Review*.

limited in his discussion to the three pieces on which the
Gazette had commented—the Preface, "The Vision of Judgment," and the "Epigrams on Lord Castlereagh." He barely
mentioned the first, and, as might be expected, he found that
the "Vision" was more wicked than any of Byron's earlier
works. The "sentiments" of the "Epigrams" seemed to be
"anything but human, and the lines anything but poetry."
The review, at best a very mechanical piece of criticism—"what
we considered a solemn duty we owed to our readers"—closed
with the hope "that the blasphemous pages of the '*Liberal*' will
never be reprinted on this side the Atlantic," and with the
promise that "the reviler of our holy religion shall always be
held up to public scorn, however elevated his rank or brilliant
his talents."[71]

§ *v*

If the number of reviews indicates the extent of the disturb-
ance which *The Liberal* caused, the existence of individual works
inspired by the new periodical simply emphasizes the fact.
In January, *The Edinburgh Magazine* announced,

A poem will make its appearance in a few days, entitled Falearo,
or the Neapolitan Liberal. The work is written in cantos, in the
stanza of "Don Juan," and containing satirical, humourous, and
quizzical remarks, on the principal personages and institutions of
Great Britain. The author announces himself as a member of "the
Satanic School."[72]

Since this is the only evidence to come forth, the reality of the
poem is questionable. This was not the case, however, with
three other works—*A Critique on "The Liberal," The Illiberal,*

---

[71] "The Liberal—Lord Byron," *The Albion, or British, Colonial, and Foreign
Weekly Gazette*, No. 27 (December 21, 1822), pp. 214-15. Dr. John S. Bartlett
founded this paper in New York in 1822 and then served as its editor for approximately twenty-five years. The paper existed until 1875.

[72] "Works Preparing for Publication," *The Edinburgh Magazine*, N.S. XII (1823),
106.

and *The London Liberal*—which were produced between the publication of the first and second numbers of *The Liberal*.

A Critique on "The Liberal" was simply a review of the first number of the magazine, not unlike those which appeared in the press except that it was an anonymous pamphlet of sixteen pages.[73] It was written by those who claimed to be "no established reviewers," but men who felt themselves "called upon by . . . public duty to give . . . opinions" because of *The Liberal*'s attack on "religion and morality." They insisted that their criticism, unlike that of some reviewers who were motivated only by a zealous faith, would be reasonable. Nevertheless, the results are similar. While they admitted the talents of the writers of *The Liberal*, they pointed out that in this instance "from some singular cause, all their usual ability seems to have forsaken them." They objected to the title of the new work. They directed the major force of their attack, "an accusation of blasphemy," at "The Vision of Judgment," but they were careful to note that even in this Byron had failed. The one exception to this final assertion, a point in which the writers of *A Critique on "The Liberal"* made a contribution, was the suggestion that only the description of Satan's approach to the scene of judgment "bears the signature of Byron; it is a departing gleam of Childe Harold, such as he was once, before the fogs of scepticism and Liberalism obscured the bright star of his genius." Despite its weaknesses, "The Vision of Judgment" would have its effect. Besides the pain that it would give to "our present august majesty and his family," there was the danger of any kind of public ridicule, even that which was unaccompanied by talents. "What the people hear made a laughing stock and butt, they will learn to despise," so that it is desirable that "the eyes of the Public . . . be opened to their danger." This has been the mission of the *Critique*, to point out

---

[73] *A Critique on "The Liberal"* (London: Printed for the Author by William Day, 1822).

that the efforts of the writers of *The Liberal* are "more calculated to lead us to pity and pray for them, than to repose our faith upon the strength of their judgment; and we hope that they will so change that they will make their talents useful, to themselves and to society."

The Illiberal: Verse and Prose from [the North was a personal and literary satire, printed in late 1822 as a pamphlet of twenty pages by G. Morgan, 25 Fleet Street. The identity of the author has not been established despite the firm but undocumented assertion of Thomas J. Wise that *The Illiberal* "was written by William Gifford."[74] Although the title page lists T. Holt, 1 Catherine Street, as the publisher, and both C. Chapple of Pall-Mall and Chappel of the Royal Exchange as vendors of the work, it is probable, as Wise suggested, that the pamphlet was never published.[75] There is no evidence that the work was a later forgery, and the suggestion that a spurious title page was used by the real printer, in order to avoid a possible libel action, can at least be qualified by the fact that those listed as printer, publisher, and vendors of the work were not imaginary.[76]

---

[74] Thomas J. Wise, *The Ashley Catalogue* (11 vols.; London: Private circulation, 1922-36), I, 167. Materials in the British Museum relating to the Ashley Library offer no suggestion concerning Wise's reason for attributing the satire to Gifford.

[75] Wise (*Ibid.*, I, 168) assumed, again without indicating his reasons, that *The Illiberal* "was suppressed before publication and was never issued, and the present copy is the only known survivor." It was, he continued, "found lurking in a quantity of waste which came from the warehouse of Messrs. Richard Bentley & Son, and was secured by Mr. W. B. Tegetmeir, who held it to be one of the most curious and attractive of his books. I purchased it from Mr. Tegetmeir in 1892."

[76] The names of G. Morgan and T. Holt occur with great irregularity in the files of *Kent's London Directory* and the *Post Office London Directory* for the early 1820's. Obviously, a negative generalization based upon the absence of a name from the directories is unsafe, for the lists were far from complete. Chapple and Chappel[!] appear more regularly here, and can be located elsewhere. Chapple was listed as printer and/or publisher of at least seven works in *The London Catalogue of Books Published in Great Britain, 1816-1851*, and, in the back pages of the first number of *The Liberal*, he was listed as a vendor of *The Literary Chronicle*. "Chappell and Son, Royal Exchange" were the publishers of *The Bard*, Part I, according to a notice in *The Morning Chronicle*, October 31, 1822.

The main body of the work is a dramatic episode, divided into two acts, the first of which includes two scenes; the second, three.[77] The action centers upon the preparation of materials for a second number of *The Liberal* by "Lord B——N . . . . . *The Magnus Apollo*" and "Mr. H——T . . . . *Versifier*," with the aid of "The Little Aitches, *Imported from the Land of Cockneys, as Assistant Scribblers to the Liberal.*" Lord B——N is a caricature of the supposed Byron of *Childe Harold* as much as a representation of the wicked author of *Don Juan*. Mr. H——T is the essence of cockneyism, both in person and in literary production. The climax of the episode comes, after Lord B——N has reported a dream about Shelley in hell, with the appearance of a letter from the "Ghost of Percy B. Shelly" [*sic*] and somewhat later of the Ghost itself; Lord B——N, aware of the full significance of the apparition, repents. Both the Ghost and the conclusion of the episode are conventional devices in such satire, and they were used by the writer just as would be expected in a work that is as obvious as it is mediocre.

In December, 1822, *Blackwood's* carried the announcement, "In the press, The Antidote, Verse and Prose, from the North. To be continued occasionally."[78] This was probably the first advance notice of *The London Liberal; An Antidote to "Verse and Prose from the South*," which was intended as an instrument for the refutation of many of the statements expected in *The Liberal*. The identity of the sponsors or editors or of the writers of various articles remains unknown. The publishers were W. Simpkin and R. Marshall of Stationers'-Hall Court, Ludgate Street, and William Sams, 1 St. James's Street; and the printer was William Clowes, Northumberland-Court.[79]

---

[77] See Appendix I.

[78] "Works Preparing for the Press," *Blackwood's*, XII (1822), 791. This was copied by *The Paris Monthly Review* (No. 12 [January 1823], p. 619).

[79] Neither the British Museum nor the Bodleian Library, in which a copy of *The London Liberal* is to be found, has any information concerning sponsorship,

Although the advertisements for *The London Liberal* found in *John Bull*,[80] *The Examiner*,[81] and *The Times*[82] indicate that the magazine appeared during the first week of January, 1823, the exact date of publication is uncertain.

Of the twenty-three articles in *The London Liberal*,[83] six, covering a total of sixty-six of the magazine's one hundred and forty-four pages, were concerned directly with *The Liberal*—the Introduction, "The Stars of Pisa," "The Vision of Parnassus. By Andrew Mucklegrin," "The Liberal 'Amenities' from the South," "Invitation from a Late Bard to a Cockney Poet," and "Letters from Abroad. Letter I.—Ostend." Three articles, covering fourteen pages, contained attacks upon Hunt, Shelley, and Byron, without reference to *The Liberal*—respectively, "Dinner by the Amateurs of Vegetable Diet,"[84] "De-

editorial direction, or authorship. The records of the firm Simpkin Marshall, Ltd. were destroyed by enemy action in 1940.

[80] *John Bull*, No. 108 (January 5, 1823), p. 1.

[81] *The Examiner*, No. 780 (January 5, 1823), p. 15. It is not surprising that *The London Liberal* was advertised in *The Examiner*, for any attention which *The Liberal* received, even from a hostile quarter, might increase its sales. This would be particularly true of a work which based its title on that of *The Liberal*. It is of further interest to call attention again to the fact that in the back pages of the first number of *The Liberal*, Simpkin and Marshall advertised the fourth edition of O'Meara's *Napoleon in Exile*.

[82] *The Times*, No. 11,761 (January 6, 1823), p. 4. This advertisement was identical with that in *The Examiner* on the previous day. It opened, "This day is published, price 3s. 6d." The full title, contents, and the name of the publisher followed.

[83] The articles are as follows: Introduction, p. 1; "The Stars of Pisa," p. 9; "The Vision of Parnassus. By Andrew Mucklegrin," p. 24; "The Liberal 'Amenities' from the South," p. 43; "Invitation from a Bard to a Cockney Poet," p. 61; "The Wife of Giartho, An Andalusian Story," p. 62; "Imitation of the Opening of Ovid," p. 92; "Memory and Music," p. 93; "A Letter," p. 94; "Hours Gone By," p. 100; "To Myself," p. 100; "Imitation from Horace," p. 101; "On Vulgarity," p. 103; "Style. A Prating Fragment," p. 120; "Dinner by the Amateurs of Vegetable Diet. Extracted from an old Paper," p. 121; "Allemar and Ellen; a Tale, (For Recitation)," p. 129; "Sue," p. 131; "Twin Sisters," p. 131; "The Muleteer," p. 132; "Detached Thoughts on Atheism. By a modern Spartan," p. 133; "Byronian," p. 138; "To Mr. Malthus," p. 139; "Letters from Abroad. Letter I.—Ostend," pp. 140-44.

[84] "Dinner by the Amateurs of Vegetable Diet" was reprinted by A. H. Koszul, *La Jeunesse de Shelley* (Paris, 1910), pp. 420-27.

tached Thoughts on Atheism," and "Byronian." The remaining materials included discussions of current affairs, literary criticism, narratives, and short poems of various kinds. Some of these articles were controversial, but none made significant reference to either *The Liberal* or its founders.

The Introduction to *The London Liberal* was a prolix statement of the writers' purposes, which were not to be restricted by the direction that *The Liberal* followed. "We shall certainly always keep a sharp look out a-head for the *Corsair* of Pisa, the most formidable, perhaps, of those rovers that infest the literary ocean," remarked the writer. "But we shall also attempt to assist our brethren of 'the regular service,' in clearing the seas of pirates of every magnitude and weight of metal." With respect to *The Liberal*, the intention was to oppose the opinions of its writers but to recognize private virtues and to refrain from personal attacks. "If . . . zeal should sometimes outrun discretion, and make us lose sight, for a moment, of courtesy," the writer added, "we can only plead in excuse the sacredness of the cause we espouse."

The writers were extremely zealous. In "The Stars of Pisa," the article which immediately followed the Introduction, the device used was a letter to the editor, which went "a little farther," the editor remarked, "than we ourselves would willingly have done." In the opening paragraph, the writer described "a conjunction . . . some time ago in the literary horizon between three planets of very unequal magnitudes." One was "an orb of surpassing brightness, but its beams are better calculated to dazzle than to enlighten," another "*was* a fiery comet," while "the last, and assuredly the least, is a subordinate satellite, whose feeble light occasionally twinkling through the mists of affectation, may amuse us by its coruscations, but has neither steadiness to guide, nor strength to illumine, nor fire to animate." The writer soon dropped the metaphor and commented upon his own disappointment in

The Liberal. "What," he asked, "is there, or was there, in the character of its authors to justify such hopes or fears?" Byron was nothing as soon as he had moved from "his own circle . . . depicting the workings of selfish pride and rancorous animosity." Shelley had merely exerted "a vague, blind, Polyphemus-kind of force," and "his intellectual appetite was essentially depraved." Hunt had reached the age at which his "cerebellum, which by courtesy of England may be called brain, has been for some time in a course of ossification."

The work of each of the three members of the earlier Pisan alliance was parodied—Byron's in "The Vision of Parnassus," Shelley's in "Invitation from a Late Bard to a Cockney Poet," and Hunt's in "Letters from Abroad. Letter I.—Ostend."[85] The first of these, a narrative in the first person running through sixty-eight stanzas, was clearly based upon "The Vision of Judgment." The narrator and his host John, who are strikingly like Hunt and Byron as the critics and public imagined them in Italy, sit drinking after dinner when the host hands a book to his guest and asks him to read. It is *The Liberal,* which the guest reads until first his host, then he himself, fall asleep. In a dream, the guest is taken to Parnassus, where Byron's works are brought to trial before a jury of "nine muses and three graces." The prosecution reads from *Don Juan, Cain,* and *The Liberal*—which "set the jury, judge, and all a dozing"—and calls John Murray as a witness. Byron's works are convicted as objectionable, and are banished. The "Invitation from a Late Bard to a Cockney Poet" is perhaps an imitation of Shelleian form, though the subject makes it ridiculous rather than humorous. Far more successful is "Letters from Abroad. Letter I.—Ostend," in which Ethelinda Wiggin writes to Miss Mortimer, in the fashion that the critics might have supposed that one of Leigh Hunt's washerwomen would have written to

---

[85] See Appendix II.

another. The essential absurdity, of course, lies in the fact that Ethelinda writes from her point of debarkation, "O my dear friend, only think of MY BEING ABROAD." Her description is marked by provincialism and a preoccupation with the mundane.

The only direct review, "The Liberal 'Amenities' from the South," made little or no contribution to the already existing criticism of *The Liberal* or to the rather deficient quality of *The London Liberal*. It attacked *The Liberal* because its principles were "inimical to good taste and sound morals." It found the Preface trivial. It considered that "The Vision of Judgment" abounded "in a light and contemptible ribaldry on sacred subjects, which we shall not dignify with the title of blasphemy." Hunt's works, though "tolerably free from his characteristic affectations," showed "little merit." Only Shelley's translation from *Faust* had value, "a gem of the first water, among a collection of valueless, though some of them brilliant, pebbles." Despite the difficulty and complexity of Goethe's poem, Shelley proved in working with it that, though his "taste and reason" were perverted, "he was a man of the very highest order of poetical imagination." The review closes with the suggestion that, though the reviewer considers *The Liberal* harmless, "a higher tribunal, and one more competent to pronounce upon the case," should examine the work.

The fact that a second number of *The London Liberal* never appeared can be attributed to the quality of the work. Aside from this, the purpose, indicated by the title and the prefatory remarks, was restricted: as *The Liberal* ceased to appear as a threat, the *Antidote* would hardly seem necessary. Furthermore, *The London Liberal* seems to have received very little encouragement from the press, which might have been expected to be generally sympathetic. *The New Times*[86] and *The Morning*

---

[86] "Lord Byron," *The New Times*, January 4, 1823, p. 4.

Post[87] reprinted the passage on Byron from "The Stars of Pisa," but *The Imperial Magazine* for February dismissed *The London Liberal*: "its pretensions are not of a character deserving particular notice."[88] This same month, *The Gentleman's Magazine* pointed out that in the case of *The London Liberal* the writers failed because their ignorance of life robbed their essays of all interest. "What is the use of telling the publick [*sic*], that Lord Byron's principles are very reprehensible, that an adder is venomous?" the critic asked with reference to their purpose. Then, in conclusion, he turned to the method: "Nor is it a subject, like folly, for facetious modes of treatment."[89] Apparently, many of the Tories silently agreed with him.

§ *vi*

By early November, there were plans for a second edition of the first number of *The Liberal*, which would include the Preface to "The Vision of Judgment" and the corrections that appeared in the proof. Leigh Hunt had come to recognize that legal difficulties might arise from the first publication of the poem, but he was inclined to believe that "they will most likely not meddle with it."[90] Nevertheless, during the December Sessions the Grand Jury in Middlesex indicted John Hunt after a charge had been brought by the Constitutional Association. The indictment first charged generally:

John Hunt, late of the parish of St. George, Hanover-square, in the county of Middlesex, bookseller, being a person of wicked and malicious disposition, and wickedly and maliciously contriving and intending to injure, defame, disgrace, and vilify, the memory, reputation, and character of his late Majesty King George the

---

[87] "Lord Byron," *The Morning Post*, January 9, 1823, p. 4.
[88] "Literary, Scientific, and Religious Gleanings," *The Imperial Magazine*, V (1823), 195.
[89] "The London Liberal," *The Gentleman's Magazine*, XCIII, Part I (1823), 159.
[90] Byron and Leigh Hunt to Henry Hunt, undated (Gates, "Letter," pp. 14-15).

Third, the Father of our Sovereign Lord the now King, and of divers others the descendants of his said late Majesty, members of the Royal Family of this realm; and also contriving and intending to cause it to be believed that his said late Majesty was a bad King, guilty of misrule, and a protector of tyrants, and that his death was unlamented and unregretted even by those who attended his burial, and thereby to disturb and disquiet the minds and destroy the comfort and happiness of our said Lord the now King and other the said descendants, and to bring them into public scandal, infamy, disgrace, and contempt, with and amongst all the subjects of this realm, on the second day of December, in the year of our Lord one thousand eight hundred and twenty-two, at the parish aforesaid, in the county aforesaid, with force and arms, falsely, wickedly, maliciously, unlawfully, did print and publish, and cause to be printed and published, in a certain printed book, to wit, in a certain printed book called *"The Liberal,"* a certain false, scandalous, malicious, and defamatory libel, of and concerning his said late Majesty, and also of and concerning his reign, death, and burial.

The indictment charged more specifically that the work in *The Liberal* had suggested that George the Third was "a person of mean and avaricious disposition," "an enemy to the liberties of his people and of other nations," and "a person of bad and vicious character." The charges were fully documented with phrases and lines from "The Vision of Judgment," which were much to the point and in themselves would seem to substantiate the charges.[91]

The Examiner did not comment until December 15, when it came forth to insist on the absurdity of the situation. "The Mock-Constitutional Association have indicted the *Liberal* for a pretended libel in the *Vision of Judgment*" with the hope of

---

[91] *The Examiner*, No. 780 (January 5, 1823), pp. 5-6. As the indictment was printed here, only passages containing reiterative legal language were omitted. An identical selection appeared in *The Times* (No. 12,085 [January 16, 1824], p. 2).

winning public notice, if not public favor, for the Association
had fallen into difficulties and needed to do something "to
raise them out of the mire." The difficulty with their present
course of action, *The Examiner* continued, lay in the possibility
that in order for them to prosecute Byron's poem, they might
have to drag Southey's "unfortunate hexameters out of their
obscurity." This would prove "an awkward hitch," since
Southey "had intruded himself and his bad passions into the
very presence of Deity," while Byron in his "Vision" "has
carefully confined his 'supernatural scenery' to the outside of
Heaven's gate, and has meddled with no higher personages
than the Archangel and the Arch-Fiend." The blasphemy of
Southey's poem could not be ignored despite its gravity, but
Byron's was merely "satirical and ludicrous." There was only
one escape for the Constitutional Association, *The Examiner*
proposed—simply for Southey "to consent to an indictment of
his Vision, let judgment go by default, and come into court
contrite," so that there would be a precedent for the conviction
of *The Liberal*.[92]

By December 23, news of the indictment reached Genoa.
Byron wrote to Douglas Kinnaird, requesting that James
Scarlett, the noted attorney,[93] "or other able counsel," be
retained for John Hunt. Byron offered to come to England
himself "if *that* will remove the prosecution from *his* shoulders."[94]
Although Leigh Hunt admitted that Scarlett had "weight of a
certain kind with the Jury," he feared such a choice for counsel,
"knowing how such men as Scarlett are apt to trim toward
'ears polite.'" However, he left the final choice to John,
cautioning him against any attempt to serve as his own counsel.
In any event, he observed, the prosecution could not obtain

[92] *The Examiner*, No. 777 (December 15, 1822), pp. 789-90.
[93] James Scarlett, later the First Baron Abinger (1769-1844). He was to become
attorney general under Canning and then Wellington.
[94] Byron to Kinnaird, December 23, 1822 (*Corr.*, II, 239-40).

a verdict.[95] Scarlett was chosen, perhaps at the insistence of Byron. "I am willing to retain counsel (at my expense), and the best going, for Mr. J. Hunt," Byron emphasized to Kinnaird. He reiterated his pledge "to be *both ostensible* and *responsible* for the poem; and to come home, and face the consequences as the *author*."[96]

Leigh Hunt doubted the usefulness of such a step as Byron's return to England, for he believed that the Constitutional Association would move to prevent any practical results from it,[97] and John himself "frequently objected, declaring that they would not prosecute the author, but the publisher."[98] There is no reason to doubt that Byron was sincere, at least with regard to the *idea* of going home,[99] but he received very little support.[100] He soon dropped the scheme entirely, though he occasionally gave advice for the defense of John Hunt. The indictment clearly complicated the situation and probably made Byron more uncomfortable in his association with the Hunts, but it also forced him closer to them, for the moment at least, in a kind of mutual defense.

After the printing of the indictment in January, *The Examiner* made no further comment until May 11, 1823, when it published the *reductio ad absurdum*, "More Indictments," a parody of the indictment of John Hunt, in which the Earl of Walde-

---

[95] Unpublished letter from Leigh Hunt to John Hunt, December 26, 1822 (courtesy of the Pierpont Morgan Library).

[96] Byron to Kinnaird, December 30, 1822 (*Corr.*, II, 245).

[97] Byron to John Hunt, January 8, 1823 (*L. & J.*, VI, 159).

[98] Byron to Kinnaird, March 13, 1824 (*Corr.*, II, 290).

[99] The idea was not new with Byron. On October 4, 1821, when he first sent "The Vision of Judgment" to Murray, Byron suggested that if Murray were to find another publisher for the work he should assure him that "if he gets into a scrape, I will give up *my name* or person" (*L. & J.*, V, 386-87). He made the same offer to Murray in the event that *Cain* were prosecuted (Medwin, *Conversations*, pp. 258-59).

[100] Edward Trelawny at least favored the idea, for on January 11, 1823, he wrote to Mary Shelley, "I shall be anxious to hear what is going on in England regarding the 'Liberal,' seeing that it is prosecuted. What course will Lord Byron take? Go to England, I hope" (*S. & M.*, III, 910).

grave as the author of his *Memoirs* and Walter Savage Landor
as the author of *Gebir* were charged with libel of George the
Third; and Horace Walpole as author of *Memoirs of the Last
Ten Years of George the Second* was indicted for unfavorable
reports about Frederick, Prince of Wales, "the *Grandfather* of
our Sovereign Lord the now King."[101] In May and June, after
a jury had been named for the case of John Hunt, *The Examiner*
carried a series of articles attacking the system of picking
Special Juries.[102] Through the remainder of 1823, *The Examiner*
gave only very brief reports of the legal activities in preparation
for the trial.

The extent of the commercial value which the indictment
held for *The Liberal* is uncertain. Byron believed that "the
prosecution will at least help his [John Hunt's] sale,"[103] and
The Monthly Magazine for January apparently agreed with him.
"Public opinion had decided and the publication in question
had become harmless by not being read," it observed, but now
"the expected tragi-comedy at Westminster, in creating great
public interest, will at least serve the purpose of a thousand
puffs and advertisements."[104] However, "great public interest"
did not become great public sale. On the other hand, it is
unlikely that in London the booksellers suppressed *The Liberal*
as Thomas Carlyle reported that they did in Edinburgh.[105]

Leigh Hunt specified that the Preface to "The Vision of
Judgment" should "be printed, both for the Liberal, & in the

---

[101] "More Indictments," *The Examiner*, No. 798 (May 11, 1823), pp. 305-7.

[102] "Special Juries," *Ibid.*, No. 799 (May 18, 1823), pp. 321-23; No. 801 (June 1,
1823), pp. 353-55; No. 803 ([Monday] June 16, 1823), pp. 385-86. This series
of articles was probably the substance of the pamphlet which John Hunt published
in November at a price of two shillings, *On the Law of Libel; with a Detailed Exposure
of the Special Jury Picking System*. It was of course advertised in *The Examiner* (No. 824
[November 16, 1823], p. 752).

[103] Byron to Kinnaird, December 23, 1822 (*Corr.*, II, 240).

[104] *The Monthly Magazine*, LIV (1823), 538.

[105] On January 12, 1823, Thomas Carlyle wrote to Jane Welsh, "The Vice-
society is prosecuting for Byron's articles [*sic*], and men are shy of selling them"
(*The Love Letters*, I, 148).

Examiner," and that the changes indicated in the corrected proof of the "Vision" could appear "as Errata or rather 'Right Readings withheld by Mr Murray.' "[106] At one point, John brought forth a second issue of the first edition, which carried two more Errata at the bottom of the Contents page,[107] but the nature of these indicates that this second issue had nothing to do with the corrected proof of "The Vision of Judgment" which John Murray had withheld.[108] On the whole, John Hunt tended to keep Leigh's suggestions in mind during the preparation of the second edition. He first advertised in *The Examiner* on December 22,[109] and one week later he printed excerpts from the Preface to the poem, with the remark, "Had not one Mr. Murray perpetrated the suppression, we exceedingly doubt whether the other Mr. Murray could have had the assurance (which is saying much) to have preferred the indictment."[110] This helped advertise the new edition, of course, and Leigh's other suggestion, that proof changes be published as "Errata," would clearly save the expense of resetting parts of Byron's poem, so that the plan was adopted.

On January 1, 1823, the second edition of the first number of *The Liberal* appeared, both in separate covers and bound with the second number, which was published the same day, as Volume One.[111] The general title page shows no variation

---

[106] Byron and Leigh Hunt to Henry Hunt, undated (Gates, "Letter," pp. 14-15).

[107] Stout ("Studies Toward a Biography of Leigh Hunt," p. 183) first pointed out that there was a first issue of the first edition, then a second issue of the first edition, before the second edition appeared.

[108] The Errata are as follows:

   Page 20, line 5, for "dwell," read "well."
   Page 109, line 10, for "about the size of Stratford Place," read "about *hal* [half] the size."

The first of these concerns a non-controversial line in "The Vision of Judgment," the second, a sentence in the first of the "Letters from Abroad."

[109] *The Examiner*, No. 778 (December 22, 1822), p. 816.

[110] *Ibid.*, No. 779 (December 29, 1822), pp. 825-26. Attorney Charles Murray of the Constitutional Association was "the other Mr. Murray."

[111] M. J. Ryan ("The Adventures of Lord Byron's Prefaces," *Bookman's Journal*, XVI [1928], 421) reported that the second edition of the first number of *The*

from that of the first edition; the verso is blank. The Contents reveals slight difference from the first edition in the listing of two titles;[112] at the bottom of the page, three Errata concerned with lines in "The Vision of Judgment" appear, bringing the total to seven.[113] On the verso is the "Advertisement to the Second Edition." Eight pages of the general Preface ([v]-xii) follow, in form identical with that of the first edition. The title and epigraph for "The Vision of Judgment" follow on an unnumbered page, as in the first edition, but instead of the text of the poem, there appears the Preface for five pages ([i]-v). The text of the poem then begins at the bottom of v, with the second stanza coming at the top of page 4, on which there is at least one minor variation from that of the first edition.[114] Signature B begins with page 5 and is the same as that used in the first edition.

In the "Advertisement to the Second Edition," John Hunt attempted "to explain the omission in the first edition of the Preface to the Vision of Judgment, as well as those mistakes, obviously too considerable for mere errors of the press, which are noticed as *errata*." He placed the blame directly upon John Murray, both for withholding the materials in the first place

Liberal appeared only as part of Volume One, bound up with the second number. However, the existence of separate copies of the second edition in their original covers, which I have had the opportunity to examine, clearly refutes this statement.

[112] For page 81, the listing occurred, "Rhyme and Reason, or a New Proposal to the Public respecting Poetry in Ordinary," rather than "Rhyme and Reason, being a new Proposal respecting Poetry in Ordinary." For page 97 appears "Letters from Abroad. Letter I.—Pisa," rather than "Letters from Abroad, No. I.—A Description of Pisa."

[113] The three additional Errata are as follows:

Page 6, line 6, instead of "a *worse* king never left a realm undone," read "a *weaker* king ne'er left a realm undone."

Page 7, line 16, instead of "a bad ugly woman," read "an unhandsome woman."

Page 23, line 6, instead of "amidst the *war*," read "amidst the *roar*."

The first two clearly soften the meaning, while the last makes meaning where none existed before.

[114] Stanza III, line 7 reads "stripp'd" in the first edition, "stripped" in the second.

and for delaying to turn them over after John Hunt had learned of the real situation, so that the second edition appeared much later than originally intended.

The other attempted explanation appearing in this edition was, of course, Byron's Preface to "The Vision of Judgment," which he had written more than a year before. But it now appeared too late. The indictment remained, as probably everyone except Leigh Hunt had expected, and the legal machinery continued to move toward the eventual trial of John Hunt. The second edition served little purpose at the time, except perhaps to increase slightly the number of sales of *The Liberal*.

After the indictment, John Hunt could not expect to be granted an injunction against piracy of "The Vision of Judgment" in Great Britain.[115] One pirated edition appeared in 1822, presumably in December, with the imprint of T. M. Rowe.[116] At least two editions contained Southey's "Vision" as well as Byron's, one *"Printed for W. Bumpus, Fleet Street"* and another of *"W. Dugdale, 23 Russell Court, Drury Lane."*[117] John Hunt, following the only course open to him, commented in *The Examiner*:

Some fraudulent persons, taking advantage of the interest respecting the Vision of Judgment, excited by its prosecution by the Bridge-street Gang, advertise a pirated Edition of that Poem, along with Mr. Southey's "Vision." That piracy does not contain this important Preface, nor the Author's Corrections for the Poem itself, which are only to be found in the Second Edition of the Liberal.[118]

The Liberal met difficulties other than the indictment. "The French Bourbons have shown a most complimentary fear of it,"

---

[115] There was, of course, no restriction upon American publication. At least one edition, containing both Southey's poem and Byron's, appeared at the time, *The Two Visions; or, Byron vs. Southey* (New York: Borradaile, 1823).

[116] *The Vision of Judgment. Suggested by the Composition so entitled by the Author of Wat Tyler,* By a Noble Author (London: Printed and published by T. M. Rowe, 1822).

[117] Wise, *A Byron Bibliography,* II, 39.

[118] *The Examiner,* No. 782 (January 19, 1823), p. 64.

The Examiner reported in late December. "The police have strict
orders to prevent its introduction; and such is the notion
entertained of the danger of any connection with it, as well as
of the justice of the said Bourbons, that the foreign booksellers
in London, who correspond with Paris, declined sending copies
in their parcels, lest the whole cargo should suffer for that one
article!"[119] Apparently the Austrians, or at least Austrian
authorities in Italy, followed the example, for in March, 1823,
Byron—whose mail had frequently attracted the curiosity of
the Austrians[120]—was suggesting to John Hunt, "It will be
useless to forward *The Liberal*, the insertion of which will only
prevent the arrival of any other books in the same parcel. That
work is strictly prohibited."[121]

---

[119] *Ibid.*, No. 778 (December 22, 1822), p. 812.

[120] Medwin (*Conversations*, p. 104) reported that Byron attributed his departure
from Venice, in part at least, to the Austrian interception of his books and papers.

[121] Byron to John Hunt, March 17, 1823 (*L. & J.*, VI, 174).

V

The Second Number

§ *i*

IN OCTOBER AND NOVEMBER, LEIGH HUNT WAS PREPARING
materials for the second number of *The Liberal*, which he hoped
could "appear in the height of the Christmas Season." The
situation was to become quite different from that which he had
experienced in the summer. *The Liberal* was to receive contributions from Mary Shelley and Charles Armitage Brown in Italy,
and from William Hazlitt and Thomas Jefferson Hogg in
England, as well as works of Byron, Shelley, and Hunt himself.
And Byron, for the moment at least, seemed interested, suggesting that *The Liberal* appear in "six numbers a year instead of
four" and "that the number of pages should always *exceed*
200."[1]

Leigh Hunt himself had various materials at hand. Probably
one of the first to be written was "Letters from Abroad.
Letter II,—Genoa," which was largely made up of entries in
the journal which Leigh Hunt had kept at the time of his arrival
in Italy.[2] He had three translations from Alfieri—Numbers 1
and 26 of the "Epigrammi"[3] and Number 167 of the "Sonetti"[4]
—which he entitled "Alfieri's Benediction," "An Ultra

---

[1] Byron and Leigh Hunt to Henry Hunt, undated (Gates, "Letter," pp. 12, 15).
[2] *The Liberal*, I, 269-88. Reproduced in part in the chapter entitled "Genoa,"
Autobiography, pp. 354-67.
[3] "Epigrammi," *Le Opere di Vittorio Alfieri* (12 vols.; Padua, 1809-10), XII, 35,
44-45.
[4] "Sonetti," *Ibid.*, XI, 271.

License," and "Portrait of Himself, by Alfieri."[5] By late
October he had finished two other works which he was sending
to John. He described "The Giuli Tre,"[6] a summary with some
translation of Giambatista Casti's "I Tre Giuli,"[7] as "a piece
of Italian pleasantry, consisting of 200 sonnets, all about a
dun's worrying a man for a sum of money amounting to about
eighteen pence."[8] The second of the two pieces, "Virgil's
Hostess,"[9] was a comment on Virgil's "Copa," to which
certain passages, in both the original and translation, were
added.[10] The purpose of the article was clearly to emphasize
the quality in unusual, little-known works such as this. Leigh
Hunt finished "The Dogs,"[11] which he dedicated "To the
Abusers of The Liberal," on November 9.[12] The poem,
consciously "in the Don Juan style,"[13] was based upon an
account of Wellington's half-starved soldiers having to feed
scarce and coveted biscuits to Wellington's hounds, which had
appeared in a work entitled *Journal of a Soldier of the 71st
Regiment during the War in Spain.* Despite the fact that the work
is perhaps only slightly better than mediocre, Leigh Hunt was

---

[5] *The Liberal*, I, 395-96, 399. Charles Armitage Brown attributed all of the
Alfieri translations to Leigh Hunt (Dilke, p. 10). "Portrait of Himself" was
reproduced in *The Poetical Works of Leigh Hunt* (London, 1857; ed. Thornton
Hunt, 1860).

[6] *The Liberal*, I, 207-25. Reprinted in *Poetical Works* (1857, 1860).

[7] *Opere di Giambatista Casti* (Brussels, 1838), pp. 203-39.

[8] Leigh Hunt to John Hunt, October 26, 1822 (Brewer, *Library*, II, 155).

[9] *The Liberal*, I, 377-84.

[10] The work in manuscript was first entitled "Virgil's Copa" (British Museum
MS. ADD. 38108, ff. 247-56).

[11] *The Liberal*, I, 245-67. This was originally entitled "The Pack of Hounds"
and was in sixty-seven, rather than the later fifty-one, stanzas (British Museum
MS ADD. 38108, ff. 204-46). It was first reprinted in the Milford edition of
Hunt's *Poetical Works*.

[12] Marianne Hunt recorded in her diary on November 9, 1822, "Mr. Trelawny
dines with Mary—brought Mr. H. a list of dogs [*sic*] names from the sporting
magazine for a poem he has finished to day on the Duke of Wellington's dogs at
Waterloo" (R. Brimley Johnson, *Shelley-Leigh Hunt: How Friendship Made History*
[2nd ed.; London, 1929], p. 337). It is interesting that Marianne confused
Waterloo with the Spanish peninsula.

[13] Byron and Leigh Hunt to Henry Hunt, undated (Gates, "Letter," p. 16).

sincerely proud of it. "If nothing else besides were put in but 'the Dogs,' " he told his nephew, Henry Hunt, in late November, "the Magazine would be well made up."[14] Of Leigh Hunt's works which were to go into the second number of *The Liberal*, the last that he composed was "The Suliotes,"[15] a translation of a manuscript in Italian by Captain Christo Perevò, in which were recorded the political and military history of the people of Suli from 1820 to 1822. In late October, Leigh wished "to get up an article upon the Greeks for our *Liberal*,"[16] and somewhat later, in early November, he had found "a merchant at Leghorn who has a Greek connexion," to whom he expected to apply.[17] It is more than possible that this was the "friend," mentioned in the introduction to the translation, from whom Hunt received the manuscript. Perhaps Byron made suggestions, for he was more familiar than Leigh Hunt with the subject matter,[18] but the style of the work is characteristic of Hunt.[19]

Byron's major contribution to the second number was the drama "Heaven and Earth."[20] The action was based upon the passage in *Genesis* (6: 1-2), "And it came to pass . . . that the sons of God saw the daughters of men that they *were* fair; and they took them wives of all which they chose." Byron interpreted "the sons of God" to mean angels, and "the daughters of men" were the descendants of Cain doomed in the Flood. The action closes with the rising of the waters about Japhet, the son of Noah, who waits in safety for the arrival of

---

[14] Unpublished letter from Leigh Hunt to Henry Hunt, undated; postmarked, "FPO/DE.9/1822" (courtesy of the Pierpont Morgan Library).

[15] *The Liberal*, I, 385-94.

[16] Leigh Hunt to John Hunt, October 26, 1822 (Brewer, *Library*, II, 156).

[17] Byron and Leigh Hunt to Henry Hunt, undated (Gates, "Letter," p. 16).

[18] Stout, "Studies Toward a Biography of Leigh Hunt," p. 460.

[19] There is at least the external evidence of the statement by Charles Armitage Brown that Leigh Hunt wrote "The Suliotes" (Dilke, p. 10). This was possibly the result of conjecture on Brown's part, for Leigh had written to Brown at Pisa in his quest for materials about the Greeks (Gates, "Letter," p. 16).

[20] *The Liberal*, I, 165-206.

the Ark. Byron began the play at Ravenna on October 9, 1821, and finished it in "about fourteen days."[21] On November 14, he sent the work to Murray, pointing out that this was possibly to be merely "*Part first,* as there is a suspension of the action, which may either close there without impropriety, or be continued in a way that I have in view."[22] Despite Byron's belief that his "new Mystery is less speculative than *Cain,* and very pious,"[23] Murray hesitated after having proofs printed.[24] William Gifford examined the work and made suggestions which Byron willingly accepted.[25] Yet "Heaven and Earth" remained unpublished though Byron complained of the situation and repeated his instructions for its publication.[26] On October 31, Byron, anticipating his break with Murray, wrote to John Hunt, turning over to him, among other pieces, "Heaven and Earth" and "Werner,"[27] "either or both of which would answer for *The Liberal.*"[28] Byron soon expressed his fears that "Werner" was too long for *The Liberal* although Leigh Hunt, who knew the drama only by description, disagreed

---

[21] Medwin, *Conversations,* p. 231. Mary Shelley recorded for December 14, "Shelley reads Lord Byron's 'Heaven and Earth' in the evening" (*Journal,* p. 163). Edward Williams made the same statement on that day, describing the work as one "which he [Byron] only finished the day before" (*Gisborne and Williams,* p. 117). The fact that Byron sent the poem to Murray on November 14, 1821, clearly refutes this of course. Williams remarked, "there are many pages in the manuscript without a single correction" (*Ibid.*), while the copy which Medwin saw, presumably the original or an early revision, "was so interlined as scarcely to be legible" (*The Life of Shelley,* p. 340).

[22] Byron, *L. & J.,* V, 473-75.

[23] Byron to Moore, March 4, 1822 (*Ibid.,* VI, 31).

[24] Byron to Murray, April 9, 1822 (*Ibid.,* VI, 47-48).

[25] Byron to Murray, July 6, 1822 (*Ibid.,* VI, 93).

[26] *Ibid.,* VI, 24, 30, 37, 40, 54, 60, 63, 120-21, 130; Byron, *Corr.,* II, 222, 225.

[27] Byron wrote the first act of "Werner" in 1815 and resumed work on the play in 1821. He sent the manuscript to Moore on January 29, 1822 (*L. & J.,* VI, 28), and on March 6 he ordered Moore to turn the work over to John Murray (*Ibid.,* VI, 34). Moore received "Werner" on February 12, 1822 (Russell, *Moore,* III, 326), but precisely what happened thereafter is uncertain because Murray apparently made no reply for some months to Byron's questions and comments concerning "Werner."

[28] Byron, *L. & J.,* VI, 134.

with him.[29] "Werner should start first by all means," Leigh wrote concerning the second number of *The Liberal*, but if it had not reached John's hands at this time, then obviously something else must open the number, "not Pulci because it is a translation." Only "Heaven and Earth" could be considered, but Leigh apparently doubted that Murray had sent this if he had withheld "Werner."[30] The situation was quickly resolved. John Murray, acting on the arrangements which he had previously maintained with Byron, had been preparing a separate publication of "Werner."[31] Somewhat later Leigh Hunt found consolation. "Since I have seen Werner," he wrote to John, "I much less regret that we did not have it."[32] John was preparing to open the second number of *The Liberal* with "Heaven and Earth," holding the translation from Pulci for the indefinite future.

Byron excluded from possible publication in *The Liberal* his reply to the criticism of the first and second cantos of *Don Juan*, which had appeared in *Blackwood's* (V [1819], 512-22), and his "Observations upon 'Observations,' " the second letter that he wrote in the controversy with William Lisle Bowles over the work of Alexander Pope.[33] Possibly he had not known or he

---

[29] Byron and Leigh Hunt to Henry Hunt, undated (Gates, "Letter," pp. 15-16). In a list of proposed contents of the second number of *The Liberal*, Leigh Hunt here put "Werner" first, followed by "The Dogs" in second place, "The Giuli Tre" in fourth, "Virgil's Hostess" in fifth, possibly the translation from Pulci in sixth, and "Minor Pieces" in seventh. Nothing had been decided for the third position.

[30] Unpublished letter from Leigh Hunt to Henry Hunt, undated; postmarked, "FPO/DE.9/1822" (the Pierpoint Morgan Library).

[31] "Werner" was published in January, 1823. On December 23, 1823, Byron wrote to Kinnaird, "I presume that some agreement has been concluded with Mr. Murray about *Werner*" (*L. & J.*, VI, 287).

[32] Unpublished letter from Leigh Hunt to John Hunt, December 26, 1822 (courtesy of the Pierpont Morgan Library).

[33] Gates, "Letter," p. 15. "Some Observations upon an Article in *Blackwood's Magazine*," written in March, 1820, remained unpublished until R. E. Prothero included it in *The Letters and Journals* (IV, 474-95). "Observations upon 'Observations.' A Second Letter to John Murray, Esq., on the Rev. W. L. Bowles's Strictures on the Life and Writings of Pope" was first published in *The Works of Lord Byron*, ed. Thomas Moore (17 vols.; London, 1835).

had forgotten that several rather trivial pieces had come into
John Murray's hands and, according to Byron's order, would
be surrendered to John Hunt. One was a translation, supposedly
of the First but actually of the Second Epigram, from Martial's
First Book.[34] Another was a couplet, entitled simply "From the
French," which Byron had originally sent to Thomas Moore
on August 2, 1821: "Ægle, beauty and poet, has two little
crimes; / She makes her own face, and does not make her
rhymes."[35] And finally, there was a parody of Air xxxviii,
"Good-morrow, gossip Joan," from *The Beggar's Opera* (II, xiii),
which Byron had sent in slightly varying forms both to Thomas
Moore[36] and to John Murray:[37]

> Why how now, saucy Tom,
>   If you thus must ramble,
> I will publish some
>   Remarks on Mister Campbell.

> Why how now, Parson Bowles,
>   Sure the priest is maudlin!
> (*To the Public*) How can you, d——n your souls!
>   Listen to his twaddling?

Byron did nothing to prevent the publication of these pieces,
so that they appeared among the Minor Pieces in the second
number of *The Liberal*.[38]

Expectations were high concerning the work of Shelley for
the second number of *The Liberal*, for they included his "Defence of Poetry," one of his most significant prose works. The
first of two parts of a proposed essay, this was written in early

---

[34] Identified as Byron's work (*Poetry*, VII, 303).

[35] Byron, *L. & J.*, V, 336. The text above is that of *The Liberal*, I, 396. In the
letter to Moore, the following differences appear: "Egle" rather than "Ægle";
"crimes," rather than "crimes;" and "*not*" rather than "not."

[36] Byron to Moore, February 22, 1821 (*L. & J.*, V, 252-53).

[37] Byron to Murray, May 8, 1821 (*Ibid.*, V, 276).

[38] *The Liberal*, I, 396-98.

1821 as an answer to Thomas Love Peacock's "Four Ages of Poetry," which had appeared in 1820 in the new *Literary Miscellany* of Charles and James Ollier. On March 20, 1821, Shelley submitted the article to Charles Ollier.[39] Since no more numbers of the Olliers' periodical appeared, Shelley did not write the proposed second part of the essay.[40] Somewhat later, when he decided to terminate his publishing connections with the Olliers, he requested John Gisborne, then in London, to retrieve his manuscripts, leaving the "Defence of Poetry" with the Olliers only if they intended to publish it.[41] Apparently, they succeeded in persuading Gisborne that they were "inclined to try another number" of the *Miscellany*, for he left the work with them.[42] Later, Charles Ollier allowed Peacock to borrow the manuscript until a time that he would wish to have it in hand again for publication, but Ollier never requested its return.[43] Mary Shelley then decided that the "Defence of Poetry" should go into *The Liberal*. She herself had a copy, probably an earlier draft. Since it was "somewhat perplexed, and difficult to write out" for transmission to London, she requested that John Hunt send to Peacock for the copy in his possession.[44] She herself asked Peacock, by way of Maria Gisborne, "to send it to Mr. John Hunt at the Examiner office."[45] Leigh Hunt sent further instructions regarding the preparation of the manuscript: "just alter the second line, or any other part that may be necessary, to hinder the look of its' [*sic*]

---

[39] Shelley, *Works*, X, 247.

[40] On September 25, 1821, Shelley wrote to Charles Ollier, "Pray give me notice against what time you want the second part of my 'Defence of Poetry' " (*Ibid.*, X, 328).

[41] Shelley to John Gisborne, January 26, 1822 (*Ibid.*, 353-54).

[42] Gisborne to Shelley, February 19, 1822 (*Gisborne and Williams*, p. 81).

[43] Peacock to Mary Shelley, September 2, 1822 (*The Works of Thomas Love Peacock*, ed. H. F. B. Brett-Smith and C. E. Jones [10 vols.; London, 1924-34], VIII, 231).

[44] Leigh Hunt to John Hunt, October 26, 1822 (Brewer, *Library*, II, 156).

[45] Mary Shelley to Maria Gisborne, November 6, 1822 (*Letters*, I, 199).

being an answer to an article in another work."[46] Apparently John acted as soon as he had received the first instructions, for by November 22 Mary received word that Peacock had given the manuscript to the Hunts.[47] At Albaro, it was fully expected as late as January that the second number of *The Liberal* would contain Shelley's "Defence of Poetry,"[48] but the article did not appear. What interfered is not known, but possibly confusion resulted from Mary's request that all of Shelley's works in Peacock's possession except the "Defence of Poetry" be sent to her for correction and approval.[49] John Hunt was again prepared to publish the article in the third number of *The Liberal*,[50] but somehow this plan also miscarried, and the "Defence of Poetry" did not appear until 1840,[51] when it was published from the manuscript which John Hunt had edited according to instructions.[52] Had the "Defence of Poetry" appeared in *The Liberal*, it would probably have done little to increase sales, but its omission was unfortunate, for the article would have heightened the general literary attainment of *The Liberal*.

"And by all means I wish *something* of Mr. Shelley's to appear *every time*," Leigh wrote to Henry Hunt. "I send a song for that purpose in case his admirable Essay on Poetry cannot appear."[53] He referred to "Song, Written for an Indian Air,"[54] which Shelley had composed on the opposite side of a transcrip-

---

[46] Byron and Leigh Hunt to Henry Hunt, undated (Gates, "Letter," p. 15). Peacock was to call Shelley's article in the form which John Hunt gave it, "a defence without an attack" (Shelley, *Works*, X, 248 n.).

[47] Mary Shelley to Maria Gisborne, November 22, 1822 (*Letters*, I, 206).

[48] Mary Shelley to Edward Trelawny, January 7 [1823] (*Ibid.*, I, 212).

[49] Mary Shelley to Maria Gisborne, November 22, 1822 (*Ibid.*, I, 206).

[50] Unpublished letter from John Hunt to Leigh Hunt, February 25, 1823 (British Museum MS. ADD. 38108, f. 257).

[51] *Essays, Letters from Abroad, Translations and Fragments of Percy Bysshe Shelley*, ed. Mrs. Shelley (2 vols.; London, 1840), I, 25-62.

[52] Shelley, *Works*, X, 248 n.

[53] Unpublished letter from Leigh Hunt to Henry Hunt, undated; postmarked, "FPO/DE.9/1822" (the Pierpont Morgan Library).

[54] *The Liberal*, I, 397. This was first reprinted as "Lines to an Indian Air," *Posthumous Poems of Percy Bysshe Shelley*, p. 63.

tion he had made of a song from Mozart's *La Clemenza di Tito*.[55]

Mary Shelley entered the circle of writers for *The Liberal* with "A Tale of the Passions,"[56] a story of the Guelph-Ghibelline conflict in the thirteenth century. She wrote this before the death of Shelley[57] but probably gave it to Leigh Hunt too late for insertion in the first number of *The Liberal*, for it was early November before he sent it to London "*an Italian story* of M[rs] Shelley's (a very good one)."

At the same time, Leigh submitted a "very respectable" article by Charles Armitage Brown,[58] "Les Charmettes and Rousseau."[59] Although this was nominally an account of Rousseau's six years at "Les Charmettes," the home of Mme. de Warens, it became actually a familiar, sympathetic discussion of Rousseau's actions and contributions. Before leaving England, Charles Brown had frequently written "musical critiques in the Examiner,"[60] and, apparently at Leigh Hunt's invitation, he had composed two articles for *The Liberal* by early November,[61] "Les Charmettes and Rousseau" and "Shakespear's Fools." Brown and Hunt decided that the first

---

[55] According to notes appended to the manuscript copy in the Pierpont Morgan Library.

[56] *The Liberal*, I, 289-325. Brown attributed the story to Mary (*Dilke*, p. 10). Mary herself wrote to Mrs. Thomas, a friend, "I send the second no. of the Liberal, you know my crime therein" (*Letters*, I, 214). "A Tale of the Passions" was first reprinted, in serial form without the name of the author or the source, in *The Weekly Entertainer, and West of England Miscellany*, VII (1823), 57-60, 65-68, 81-83, 137-40, 148-51. Many years later, it was again reprinted in *Tales and Stories by Mary Wollstonecraft Shelley*, ed. Richard Garnett (London, 1891), pp. 112-47.

[57] Elizabeth Nitchie (*Mary Shelley, Author of "Frankenstein"* [New Brunswick, New Jersey, 1953], p. 53) has noted that Shelley endorsed the manuscript.

[58] Byron and Leigh Hunt to Henry Hunt, undated (Gates, "Letter," p. 16).

[59] *The Liberal*, I, 327-45.

[60] Charles Brown, Jr., "Memoir" [of his father] (*The Keats Circle: Letters and Papers*, ed. Hyder E. Rollins [2 vols.; Cambridge, Massachusetts, 1948], I, lix).

[61] Brown wrote to Joseph Severn on November 7, 1822, "I hear they are much pleased with my article 'Les Charmettes and Rousseau'; and they have another which Hunt saw in Pisa, and said was very good indeed" (William Sharp, *The Life and Letters of Joseph Severn* [New York, 1892], p. 132).

would be signed "Carluccio,"[62] but for some reason "Les Charmettes" appeared above the name "Carlone" although in the third number of *The Liberal* "Shakespear's Fools" was to have the signature "Carluccio."[63]

Thomas Jefferson Hogg and William Hazlitt entered *The Liberal* by way of London. As early as January, Hogg had been ready to contribute. "I understand that you are going to commence a periodical work; of what nature is it to be?" he asked Shelley. "If my classic pen will be of any use, I shall be happy to contribute." He made but one request: "tell me what to write about, and I will write about it, excepting only politics, which I do not understand, and I have not time to learn."[64] Apparently, Shelley made no reply, and it seems that Leigh Hunt was not fully aware of Hogg's offer when he requested that John locate Hogg and tell him "that Lord B. as well as myself wishes he would write for us."[65] The result was Hogg's "Longus,"[66] an amusing appreciation, written with

---

[62] Brown to Thomas Richards, April 30, 1823 (*Some Letters and Miscellanea of Charles Brown*, p. 27).

[63] Brown's use of these signatures was to cause difficulties for later readers concerned with the problem of authorship. Leigh Hunt ("Lord Byron—Mr. Moore—and Mr. Leigh Hunt," *The Tatler*, No. 114 [January 14, 1831], p. 454) wrote, "One of the most genuine wits now living whose name we do not feel ourselves at liberty to mention without applying to him . . . was a writer in the *Liberal*." Many years later, S. R. Townshend Mayer (*Notes and Queries*, Ser. 5, VII [1877], 388) conjectured that "Les Charmettes and Rousseau" was by Charles Lamb and "Shakespear's Fools" by Charles Cowden Clarke. K. L. H. ("The 'Liberal' and Its Contributors," *Ibid.*, Ser. 7, IX [1890], 467) asserted that Brown was the author of both, which Charles Dilke confirmed three years later by his publication of the list that Charles Brown had made on the Contents page of his own copy of *The Liberal*. Somewhat in anticlimax, Hazlitt's grandson, W. Carew Hazlitt (*Lamb and Hazlitt* [New York, 1899], xxxvi), denied "that either of the essays, signed respectively *Carlone* and *Carluccio*, were written by Lamb."

[64] Hogg to Shelley, January 29, 1822 (*S. & M.*, II, 736-37).

[65] Leigh Hunt to John Hunt, October 26, 1822 (Brewer, *Library*, II, 156).

[66] *The Liberal*, I, 347-66. Charles Armitage Brown, who probably did not know Hogg, attributed "Longus" to "W. Hogg" (Dilke, p. 10). Winifred Scott (*Jefferson Hogg* [London, 1951], p. 177) identified Hogg as the author of "Longus" on the basis of the Hogg papers which she had examined. Other available correspondence, to be used elsewhere here, substantiates this.

an awareness of the ironic, of the Greek writer of the early Christian era.

William Hazlitt might have discussed the possibility of writing for the proposed journal when he visited John Hunt in Coldbath-fields Prison before John's release in May, 1822.[67] If this were so, he was possibly delayed by his concern with his divorce, which was being prepared at this time; or he might have hesitated because of his apparent dislike for Shelley[68] and his general disrespect for Byron.[69] Hazlitt was a friend of Leigh Hunt, and, according to Peter George Patmore, John Hunt was the only man "towards whom Hazlitt seemed to cherish a feeling of unmingled personal affection and regard."[70] Though this was likely an exaggeration, Hazlitt was probably well disposed to accept John Hunt's invitation to contribute to *The Liberal*, which, by Hazlitt's own account, followed the death of Shelley.[71] In late October, Leigh Hunt asked, "Is Hazlitt preparing anything yet?"[72] But by this time, he had been to Winterslow for the purpose of writing,[73] and he very soon gave John Hunt two articles, "On the Spirit of Monarchy" and "On the Scotch Character," for the second number of

---

[67] Catherine M. Maclean, *Born Under Saturn* (New York, 1944), p. 455. Peter George Patmore (*My Friends and Acquaintances* [3 vols.; London, 1854], III, 98) gave an account of Hazlitt's visits to John Hunt in prison.

[68] Hazlitt described Shelley as one with "a fire in his eye, a fever in his blood, a maggot in his brain, a hectic flutter in his speech, which marks out the philosophic fanatic" ("On Paradoxes and Common-place," *Works*, VIII, 148). Hunt came to Shelley's defense against such charges. See W. Carew Hazlitt, *Hazlitt Memoirs, Four Generations of a Literary Family* (2 vols.; London, 1897), I, 133-35.

[69] Patmore, III, 129.

[70] *Ibid.*, III, 98.

[71] "The cabal, the bustle, the significant hints, the confidential rumours were at the height when, after Mr. Shelley's death, I was invited to take part in this obnoxious publication (obnoxious alike to friend and foe)" (Hazlitt, "Of Jealousy and Spleen of Party," *Works*, XII, 379).

[72] Leigh Hunt to John Hunt, October 26, 1822 (Brewer, *Library*, II, 155).

[73] Mrs. Hazlitt wrote in her diary for July 6, 1822, that she had just met Hazlitt, who "said he meant to go to Winterslow, and try if he could write, for he had been so distracted the last five months he could do nothing" (*Liber Amoris*, ed. Richard Le Gallienne [London, 1893], lxii).

The Liberal.[74] In the first of these, Hazlitt proposed that the institution of monarchy arose from "the craving in the human mind after the Sensible and the One" and men's projection of their own hopes in the being of the monarch; pointing to the resulting abuses, he urged the restriction rather than the abolition of monarchy, for then the monarch would represent the people's will as much as the fulfilment of their emotional needs. "On the Scotch Character" is a somewhat more humorous article, possibly because the subject was of more restricted significance, but Hazlitt was as highly critical of the traits of the Scotch as of the institution of monarchy. Neither of these essays would be expected to attract to *The Liberal* a greater number of supporters than it antagonized. Leigh Hunt, who probably had no notion of the contents of the articles, was simply happy that Hazlitt had contributed them. "Remember me to Mr. Hazlitt," he told Henry Hunt, "and say how glad I am to hear of his joining with his artillery."[75]

Leigh Hunt also hoped to have Charles Lamb contribute to *The Liberal*,[76] but in this he was to be disappointed, possibly because of Lamb's dislike for Byron and his probable lack of sympathy with the aims of *The Liberal*. In addition, there was the unfulfilled expectation of an "article on Dancing" that

---

[74] *The Liberal*, I, 227-44, 366-76. Brown attributed both essays to Hazlitt (Dilke, p. 10). "On the Spirit of Monarchy" appeared in a pirated edition as a pamphlet (Falmouth: T. Philp, 1823 [?]); it is likely that the printer was not aware of the identity of the author (Geoffrey Keynes, *Bibliography of William Hazlitt* [New York, 1931], p. 61). Later it was printed with Godwin's "The Moral Effects of Autocracy" (London: Wakelin, 1835 [?]). Hazlitt's son William republished "On the Spirit of Monarchy" in *The Literary Remains of the Late William Hazlitt* (2 vols.; London, 1836), II, 441-68. W. Carew Hazlitt, the writer's grandson, positively identified the works of which Hazlitt was author: "The 'Liberal' lived into the fourth number, and Mr. Hazlitt contributed to it five papers: 'My First Acquaintance with Poets,' 'Arguing in a Circle,' 'On the Scotch Character,' 'Pulpit Oratory,' and 'On the Spirit of Monarchy'" (*Memoirs of William Hazlitt*, II, 73).

[75] Unpublished letter from Leigh Hunt to Henry Hunt, undated; postmarked, "FPO/DE.9/1822" (the Pierpont Morgan Library).

[76] Leigh Hunt to John Hunt, October 26, 1822 (Brewer, *Library*, II, 155).

Leigh Hunt sent to John for *The Liberal* in October,[77] which John was still to be considering in February, 1823, at that time as a possibility for the third number.[78] However, Leigh seems to have been confident in late November, when he wrote Henry that he had sufficient copy for the second number of *The Liberal*. He dispatched this by December 5.[79]

Payment had not been necessary for the materials used in the first number, since all of them were the work of the original collaborators. However, the situation changed with the coming of the second number. "We must pay, of course, in every instance, according to the best pay going," Leigh wrote John, adding somewhat confidently, "perhaps a little more would not be amiss."[80] John, rather than Leigh, decided upon the rate, but it appears that he heeded Leigh's suggestion. Although John possibly made specific arrangements with Hogg and Hazlitt at the time that he accepted their materials, the situation in Italy was extremely indefinite. Charles Brown, who mentioned to Joseph Severn that he was honored "to write in such good company," made the important point, "What I shall be paid I know not."[81] Leigh Hunt was probably no better informed when, in late December, he requested from John "accounts as frequent as well as particular as possible, of the sale of the Liberal, if it is only to avoid the wonder that

---

[77] Leigh Hunt to John Hunt, October 10, 1822 (*Ibid.*, I, 119).

[78] In an unpublished letter dated February 25, 1823, John Hunt mentioned to Leigh that he had "Lucian on Dancing" (British Museum MS. ADD. 38108, f. 257). This could have been either a translation or an article in which Lucian was mentioned. No indication of authorship appeared. Horace Smith wrote one familiar essay entitled "On Dancing" (*Gaieties and Gravities*; *A Series of Essays, Comic Tales, and Fugitive Vagaries* [2 vols., Philadelphia, 1825], I, 47-55); and in his *Festivals, Games, and Amusements, Ancient and Modern* (New York, 1831), two chapters (XVI-XVII) are entitled simply "Dancing." Either the essay or the chapters could have been the piece mentioned, but the first would more nearly seem to fit the aims and needs of *The Liberal*.

[79] Leigh Hunt to John Taaffe, December 5 (Brewer, *Library*, II, 145).

[80] Leigh Hunt to John Hunt, October 26, 1822 (*Ibid.*, II, 155).

[81] Charles Brown to Joseph Severn (Sharp, *Severn*, p. 132).

11

Lord B. often expresses at my not having more."[82] John replied on February 25, 1823, with an extremely informative financial statement. Mary Shelley was paid £36, he said, and Hazlitt £28, while Brown and Hogg received £18.18.0 each.[83] On the basis of the number of pages in the contribution of each of these writers, the rate would seem to be slightly more or less than £1 for each page,[84] substantially more than "twelve guineas per sheet," the minimum that Charles Brown had expected.[85] In addition, "The Suliote" was listed for a payment of £6.6.0, possibly the result of an arrangement for the use of the Perevò article that Hunt translated.

There were other increased expenses with the second number of *The Liberal*. Although 6,000 copies were printed this time, rather than 7,000 as in the case of the first number, there were well over 200 pages in the second number, so that it is not surprising that the cost of paper moved from £205 to £237. However, the printing, which John now turned over to C. H. Reynell of Broad Street, jumped disproportionately from £98 to £153. The stitching, which had taken £35 for the first number, dropped surprisingly to £22 for the second. And in the one expenditure in which choice could be freely exercised, advertising, John made reductions from £62 to £40. The total cost of the second number of *The Liberal*, nevertheless, remained

---

[82] Unpublished letter from Leigh Hunt to John Hunt, December 26, 1822 (the Pierpont Morgan Library).

[83] Unpublished letter from John Hunt to Leigh Hunt, February 25, 1823 (British Museum MS. ADD. 38108, f. 258). On January 31, 1823, Mary Shelley wrote Trelawny that she had "received £33 from the Liberal" (*Letters*, I, 214). It is possible that she was paid the difference of £3 during the first weeks of February, but mistakes or accidents could account for a continuing discrepancy.

[84] Mary's story covered thirty-seven pages, Hazlitt's two essays totalled exactly twenty-eight pages, Brown's article was slightly more than eighteen pages, and Hogg's slightly more than nineteen.

[85] Brown to Severn, November 7, 1822 (Sharp, *Severn*, p. 132). This, Brown reported, was the rate by which *The New Monthly Magazine* had paid him. If the "sheet" was octavo and the number of pages involved sixteen, then the rate would be 15/9 per page, which would suggest that the rate paid by John Hunt was more than ample.

high, £560.2.0, when compared with £400 spent in preparation of the first number.[86]

The Examiner carried the major part of the advertising of this number of *The Liberal*, beginning on December 1 with the announcement, "The Liberal, No. II will appear on the 1st of January 1823."[87] From December 22 through January 20, this was expanded to a list of the contents. From January 26 through February 9, 1823, the advertisements were reduced to mere mention of the second number of *The Liberal*, and from February 16 through March 23, the notices were directed only toward the sale of the first volume, which included, of course, the first two numbers.

Other than these rather conventional notices, *The Examiner* carried, in its issue of December 29, 1822, "a brief enumeration of the principal articles, with a few winged words upon their leading features." The chief purpose of this article, as of that preceding the appearance of the first number of *The Liberal*, was of course to increase the sale of the work; nevertheless, the writer, moved either by the desire to appear just or by sincere critical conviction, occasionally qualified his general praise. He argued that in "A Tale of the Passions," for example, "the catastrophe might have been managed more felicitously," and he remarked that "the critic of Longus has contrived to be at once both scholastic and lively, which is not very frequently the case, and we are sorry for it." It seems likely, particularly in view of the prosecution of "The Vision of Judgment," that a further purpose lay behind this article, to prepare the public for what at first might seem the improprieties of "Heaven and Earth." "Unless 'Paradise Lost' itself is to be attacked, even the unutterably contemptible and hypocritical vermin who are prosecuting the 'Vision of Judgment,' must be satisfied with the

---

[86] Unpublished letter from John Hunt to Leigh Hunt, February 25, 1823 (British Museum MS. ADD. 38108, f. 258).

[87] *The Examiner*, No. 775 (December 1, 1822), p. 768.

genuine scriptural tone preserved in the development of the
grand incident of this dramatic Mystery," the writer remarked.
"Demons and the wicked descendants of Cain alone speak and
argue as in character they are bound to do."[88]

Otherwise, *The Examiner* quoted in part "Longus" and
"Letters from Abroad,"[89] and in its entirety Shelley's "Song,
Written for an Indian Air,"[90] as a further means of bringing the
new number of *The Liberal* to the attention of the public. *The
Morning Chronicle*,[91] *The Times*,[92] and *The Morning Herald*[93] carried
notices of *The Liberal*, which was otherwise dependent upon
the gratuitous comments of other journals for further publicity.

The second number of *The Liberal* appeared as promised on
Wednesday, January 1, 1823,[94] with seventy-three more pages
of text than the first number,[95] and slight differences on the

---

[88] "The Liberal, No. 11," *Ibid.*, No. 779 (December 29, 1822), pp. 818-22.

[89] *Ibid.*, No. 780 (January 5, 1823), p. 13.

[90] *Ibid.*, No. 781 ([Monday] January 13, 1823), p. 28.

[91] *The Morning Chronicle*, December 26, 31, 1822; January 1, 9, 11, 14, 16, 21,
24, 27, and February 3, 1823.

[92] *The Times*, January 2, 3, 4, and 8, 1823.

[93] *The Morning Herald*, January 11, 1823.

[94] *The Examiner*, No. 779 (December 29, 1822), p. 831. *The Morning Chronicle*,
January 2, 1823, p. 3.

[95] The first issue of Number I, excluding the Preface, ran from [3] to p. 164;
Number II ran from p. 165 through p. 399. The contents of the second number
were "Heaven and Earth, A Mystery," p. 165; "The Giuli Tre," p. 207; "On the
Spirit of Monarchy," p. 227; "The Dogs," p. 245; "Letters from Abroad, Letter
II.—Genoa," p. 269; "A Tale of the Passions," p. 289; "Les Charmettes and
Rousseau," p. 327; "Longus," p. 347; "On the Scotch Character," p. 367;
"Virgil's Hostess," p. 377; "The Suliotes," p. 385; Minor Pieces: "Alfieri's
Benediction," p. 395; "An Ultra License. From Alfieri," p. 396; "From the
French," p. 396; "Song, Written for an Indian Air," p. 397; "Martial.—Lib. I.
Epig. 1.," p. 398; "New Duet," p. 398; "Portrait of Himself, By Alfieri," p. 399.
Regarding the contents of the second number of *The Liberal*, *The Gentleman's
Magazine* (XCIII, Part I [1823], 158) reported that "by a mistake of the printer,
we are referred to explanatory notes [to 'The Dogs'] which do not appear." I have
not seen such a copy as is described here, but it would seem that, since the last
stanza of this poem appears on page 263 and the notes to the poem on pages
264-67, the last stanza was also missing in the copy described. This would not
have disturbed the writer in *The Gentleman's Magazine*, however, for he found the
poem "unintelligible" in any event.

red-brown paper cover.[96] The most significant difference, perhaps, was external to the work itself, for the sense of disappointment that many of the reviewers had expressed with respect to the first number, despite their charges of blasphemous intention, had now spread, and there was far less interest, clearly none of the fear and uncertainty which had marked the anticipation of the first number. At most, the recollection of charges which had been made against "Cain"[97] caused curiosity about the forthcoming "Heaven and Earth."[98] But until December, 1822, this was entirely unrelated to the anticipation of the second number of *The Liberal*.[99]

§ *ii*

The nature of the reaction that followed publication could have been predicted. Comments were neither so numerous nor so extensive as those following the first number, and the anger of the commentators showed marked decrease. Many like Henry Crabb Robinson believed that a large portion of this number was "bad enough,"[100] but few considered it dangerous. *The Morning Chronicle*, which carried the only laudatory review,

---

[96] "No. II" and "1823" supplanted "No. I" and "1822," and "Printed for John Hunt" replaced "Printed by and for John Hunt."

[97] The charges against "Cain" were blasphemy. John Murray published the work in December, 1821, and was at one point temporarily refused an injunction against William Benbow's piracy and threatened by the Constitutional Association.

[98] In December, "Timothy Tickler" asked why "Heaven and Earth" had not appeared: "Is it for fear of that barbarous commonlaw, which prevents publishers of blasphemous books from pocketing their proceeds? If it comes out, and be such as I suspect, I hope honest Mr. Benbow will be at work without delay. Buccaneer *versus* Blasphemer is a pleasant civil war" ("Tickler on Werner," *Blackwood's*, XII [1822], 784).

[99] In December, *The Paris Monthly Review* announced that "Heaven and Earth" would appear in *The Liberal* (No. II [December 1822], p. 462). Somewhat in anticlimax, this was copied in *The London Magazine* in January (VII [1823], 117), with the addition of the report that "Mr. Murray is said to have refused to publish."

[100] Henry Crabb Robinson's diary for January 8, 1822 (Howe, *The Life of William Hazlitt*, p. 353).

predicted that this number of *The Liberal* "will probably be more generally acceptable than the first; for though it possesses nothing of caustic satire that can be compared with the *Vision of Judgment*, it possesses at the same time nothing calculated to provoke so many enemies."[101] There were, of course, exceptions. Theodore Hook, writing in *John Bull*, described *The Liberal* as "that mass of blasphemy and sedition."[102] *The British Critic* for March returned to the old charges that "an English peer vends blasphemy and sedition to buy bread for London beggars."[103] And in April, *The Monthly Censor* carried a review of both the first and second numbers of *The Liberal*, which in contents and mood was reminiscent of some of the more vitriolic articles on the first number of *The Liberal*.[104] Otherwise, the reviews of the second number were restrained in the violence of their comment, attributing the apparently improved character of the periodical to various causes.

The writer for *St. James's Chronicle* found "manifest proofs, in its mitigated immorality, as compared with former Numbers [*sic*], that the public censure has produced its proper effect."[105] *The London Literary Gazette* was apparently not so optimistic as this, for, although it recognized that the new *Liberal* was "free from those atrocities against feeling, morals and religion, which previously excited so general an abhorrence," it seems to have

---

[101] *The Morning Chronicle*, January 2, 1823, p. 3. On January 9, this paper carried an article, "The Scotch Character," in which slight mention was made of "a rather *illiberal* character of the Scotch attributed to Mr. Hazlitt in the Second Number of *The Liberal*" (p. 3).

[102] "The Loves of the Angels," *John Bull*, No. 109 (January 12, 1823), p. 14.

[103] "Werner, a Tragedy," *The British Critic*, N.S. XIX (1823), 243. This was founded in 1793 and was one of the most determined defenders of the Crown and the Establishment during fifty years of independent existence.

[104] "The Liberal or 'Verse and Prose from the South,' No. I and II," *The Monthly Censor*, II (1823), 452-56. This journal was started in 1822 by Charles Rivington, who was at the time associated with *The British Critic*. It ceased to exist in mid-1823.

[105] "The Liberal, Number II," *St. James's Chronicle*, No. 10,164 (December 31 to January 2, 1823), p. 2.

emphasized that this number was "more dull, if possible of a baser literary quality." The periodical was "in reality but a collection of papers too long for its ally the Examiner newspaper."[106] *The Edinburgh Magazine* for January found "Heaven and Earth" unworthy though "less exceptionable and odious than the 'Vision of Judgment,' " and on various grounds it condemned the other pieces, particularly "On the Scotch Character," pointing to them as evidence as to "how much they [the writers] are to be *pitied*, and how thoroughly they deserve to be despised."[107] *The Imperial Magazine*, which had devoted more than three columns to the supposed evils of the first number, offered in its February number only part of a paragraph to the second number. The new *Liberal* was "exempt from any atrocious outrage upon morals or religion," the commentator remarked, "but its literary characteristics are, if possible, of a meaner quality than those belonging to the former."[108] *The Gentleman's Magazine* was at this same time largely eclectic. It condemned nearly all of the articles as unreliable or unintelligible; it found "some signs of contrition," much as *St. James's Chronicle* had done; and it reiterated the suggestion of the *Gazette* that "the papers before us are merely rejected contributions to the *Examiner* and *Indicator*."[109]

In some instances, disapproval or contempt gave way to praise. *The Literary Museum* remarked that although "Heaven and Earth" was "the first article in station, and indeed in interest," it was not the first in merit; although the reviewer found Byron almost totally disappointing, he could look with some favor upon "The Giuli Tre," "Letters from Abroad," and

---

[106] "The Liberal, No. 11," *The London Literary Gazette*, No. 311 (January 4, 1823), pp. 2-5.
[107] "Oldmixon on 'The Liberal. No. II,' " *The Edinburgh Magazine*, N.S. XII (1823), 9-16.
[108] "Literary, Scientific, and Religious Gleanings," *The Imperial Magazine*, V (1823), 195.
[109] "The Liberal, No. II," *The Gentleman's Magazine*, XCIII, Part I (1823), 158-59.

"A Tale of the Passions."[110] The praise which came quite
surprisingly from *The Literary Register* was far more emphatic.
Although the reviewer disliked "The Dogs," "Les Charmettes
and Rousseau," and "The Suliotes," he could conclude that
"the sequel of this review—if we may so term it—is good." This
was particularly the case with "Heaven and Earth,"

a splendid fragment of the most splendid mind at present engaged
for our amusement and wonder in the embodying of high fictions.
Parts of it are equal to any thing the great poet has previously
written; and that is as much as to say, equal to any poetry that the
fraught brain and heart of man has ever combined in producing.[111]

The play itself received more extensive favorable comment
than the second number of *The Liberal*, principally because it
was reviewed in at least seven instances as distinct from the
periodical. Thomas Moore's *The Loves of the Angels*, written
upon the same subject as Byron's mystery, had appeared in
December, 1822,[112] and it was nearly inevitable that the reviewers should make comparisons. These, as might be expected,
favored "Heaven and Earth," toward which only two reviews
were clearly antagonistic. Theodore Hook found in Byron's
work only "affected piety" and unfulfilled promise.[113] The
critic in *The Eclectic Review* for March admitted that "Heaven
and Earth" was "better conceived than Mr. Moore's poem,"
but it was obviously the work "of an exhausted mind, and a
malignant, withering scepticism." Though it was not profane,
it struck "with Satanic boldness, at the character of the Almighty."[114] Elsewhere, there were varying degrees of approval.

---

[110] *The Literary Museum*, No. 37 (January 4, 1823), pp. 1-3.
[111] "The Liberal," *The Literary Register*, No. 27 (January 4, 1823), pp. 5-6;
No. 28 (January 11, 1823), pp. 22-23.
[112] Thomas Moore, *The Loves of the Angels* (London: Longman, Hurst, Rees,
Orme & Brown, 1822).
[113] "The Loves of the Angels," *John Bull*, No. 109 (January 12, 1823), p. 14.
[114] "The Loves of the Angels," *The Eclectic Review*, N.S. XIX (1823), 216. The
theme of Byron's satanism, treated rather lightly and not directed specifically

"Lord Byron shows his usual faults and excellencies," the critic in *The Times* observed:

He, as usual, moody, sullen, almost malignant, quarrels with all he cannot understand, intrudes with haughty insolence into the mysteries of Providence, feels himself baffled, "and finds no end in wandering mazes lost." At the same time he displays his usual energy of language, his usual mastery in handling the pathetic or the terrible—in a word his usual intellectual variety and strength.[115]

The New Monthly Magazine, which excluded "reference to any other point of view in which some of the latter productions of the noble peer have been considered by friends or enemies," observed simply that "this new poem . . . carries with it the peculiar impress of the writer's genius."[116] In January, *Blackwood's* considered "Heaven and Earth" far superior in force and characterization to the work of Thomas Moore, whose "angels talk like Opium-Eaters." If the poem were dull, it was possibly by intention, "to denote the occasional stupefaction, drowsiness, and torpidity of soul produced by the impending destruction upon the latest of the Antediluvians." The play revealed "little or nothing objectionable in it, either as to theological orthodoxy, or general human feeling," and it was generally "not unworthy of Byron—might have been published by Murray" without fear of the Constitutional Association.[117]

---

at "Heaven and Earth," appears in a colored engraving "A Noble Poet—Scratching up his Ideas," supposedly "*Pubd Jany* 1, 1823 *by J. Johnston* 98 *Cheapside.*" In the print, Byron is sitting at his window in Venice with a devil on his shoulder, writing on a page of *Il Liberale*, and about him on the floor are *separate* volumes entitled "Don Juan," "Vision of Judg[ment]," "Liberal," and "Heaven and Earth." See Dorothy M. George, *Catalogue of the Political and Personal Satires Preserved in the Department of Prints and Drawings in the British Museum, 1820-1827* (London, 1952), p. 352; and for a reproduction of the print, see *Keats-Shelley Memorial Bulletin*, VII (1956), 27.

[115] "Lord Byron and Thomas More," *The Times*, No. 11,759 (January 3, 1823), p. 3. For the source of the quotation used, see *Paradise Lost*, II, 561.

[116] "Heaven and Earth; A Mystery," *The New Monthly Magazine*, VII ([*Original Papers*] 1823), 353-58.

[117] "Heaven and Earth, A Mystery," *Blackwood's*, XIII (1823), 72-77.

Francis Jeffrey, who was obviously careful to mention nothing of *The Liberal* in his review of the play in *The Edinburgh Review*, proposed that "Heaven and Earth," "with whatever crudeness or defects it is chargeable, certainly has more poetry and music in it than any of his dramatic writings since Manfred."[118] And finally, *The Monthly Magazine* of February acclaimed "Heaven and Earth" as unsurpassed "in sublimity, in force, and in pathos" by Byron's other writings. It was a work "conceived in the best style of the greatest masters . . . not unworthy of Dante."[119]

Toward the close of its review of "Heaven and Earth," *Blackwood's* compared the second number of *The Liberal* to "a lion with a fine shagged, king-like head, a lean body, hungered hips, and a tawdry tail—Byron—Hazlitt—Hunt." The reviewer remarked that he had now shown the head, and he promised "Carcase, hips, and tail by and bye." As in the case of the first number of *The Liberal*, *Blackwood's* waited. Then in March, "The Candid, No. II" appeared, supposedly by the writer of the first such article, who was surprised that *Blackwood's* had published that earlier piece; he was now moved by duty to continue his work as long as his "fellow-labourers in Italy persevere in their exertions to improve and enlighten the world by continuing The Liberal." Many of his general re-

---

[118] "Moore's 'Loves of the Angels' and Byron's 'Heaven and Earth,' " *The Edinburgh Review*, XXXVIII (1823), 27-48. James A. Grieg (*Francis Jeffrey of the Edinburgh Review* [Edinburgh, 1948], p. 135) has identified the review as Jeffrey's. It was reprinted in part in "The Banquet," *The Kaleidoscope*, No. 152 (May 27, 1823), p. 384. In "The Spirit of the Age" Hazlitt agreed:

> We prefer it even to *Manfred*. *Manfred* is merely himself, with a fancy drapery on: but in the dramatic fragment published in the *Liberal*, the space between Heaven and Earth, the stage on which his characters have to pass to and fro, seems to fill his Lordship's imagination; and the Deluge, which he has so finely described, may be said to have drowned all his own idle humours (*Works*, XI, 74).

[119] "News from Parnassus. No. XXII. The Loves of the Angels, a Poem; by Thomas Moore.—Heaven and Earth, a Mystery," *The Monthly Magazine*, LV (1823), 35-39.

marks concerned the nature of the coalition behind *The Liberal*, and, although they reveal how Hazlitt's participation in the second number offered substance for this sort of personal criticism, they were more original in method than in content. "The parable of the spar and the blocks" is an example. Here, the writer proposed that if a log and a block of stone were bound together, the fate of both would depend upon the outcome of the struggle between "the buoyant power of the log" and "the bathic tendency of the block." But if another block were added, "all three go down together." He would not insist on the application of this to "such a spar as Byron" and "two such blocks as Hunt and Hazlitt; but it is hazardous, and at best an unprofitable experiment, to try how many such blocks it can float with." It is true, he conceded, that "if the blocks are but laid upon the spar," it might be able "to spill them, and right again," but after the spar had been "for a length of time water-logged, it will never again stand so well up from the water as it did before." The writer of "The Candid" was greatly concerned with specific articles in *The Liberal*, none of which he liked. *Blackwood's* had given unwarranted praise to "Heaven and Earth," he insisted. "The Giuli Tre" would cause Casti to "regard a translator with more horror than a creditor." And "the very title of *Letters from Abroad*" suggested to him, as it apparently had to the parodist in *The London Liberal*, "a self-complacency in the writer at finding himself really and truly out of London, and actually beyond the sea."[120]

Despite some cleverness, "The Candid, No. II" seems to have been far less inspired than some of the earlier *Blackwood's* articles. The second number of *The Liberal* simply offered very little that was challenging to the writers of *Blackwood's*, and the reaction to this number was so much more moderate than

---

[120] "The Candid, No. II," *Blackwood's*, XIII (1823), 263-75.

that following the first *Liberal* that even in various reviews the writers found very little on which to comment. Only one article in the second number of *The Liberal* seemed to draw their fire, and that, William Hazlitt's second, was answered by another appearing also in the March number of *Blackwood's*, "On the Scotch Character—By A Flunky." This was hardly surprising, for *Blackwood's* was, among other things, the defender of the Scotch; more to the point, however, Hazlitt had compared the writers of *Blackwood's* to "a troop of Yahoos."[121] Although the remarks on the Scotch and on *Blackwood's* might pass unfelt by some,[122] Hazlitt must be answered. The article was constructed upon the assumption that "Billy," the author of the characterization of the Scotch appearing in *The Liberal*, had taken as his models certain fellow servants, whose traits he universalized in his mind and writings. The method of the article, then, was simply to quote individual statements from Hazlitt's essay and then to comment upon them in terms of the prototype of the cockney which the *Blackwood's* writers juxtaposed to Hazlitt's prototype of the Scotchman: " 'The character of a blackguard sits ill upon a Scotchman for want of use;' but on a Cockney it sits well from constant practice." It is the opening of the article, however, which is most memorable, for it indicates the nature of what is to follow and in itself is one of the outstanding examples of the personal abuse hurled at the writers of *The Liberal*:

Lord Byron being a somewhat whimsical nobleman, has lately hired two or three Cockneys as menial servants. They are to do his dirty work, for which they are to receive his cast-off clothes,

---

[121] *The Liberal*, I, 375.

[122] Margaret Oliphant (*Annals of a Publishing House: William Blackwood and His Sons* [2 vols.; Edinburgh and London, 1897] I, 274-75) quoted a letter written during 1823 by John Wilson to William Blackwood that reveals quite clearly the almost unlimited anger of Wilson over Hunt's remarks in *The Liberal* which were supposedly directed toward the *Blackwood's* writers. The reaction to Hazlitt's comments would in all likelihood be similar.

and, we believe, twenty pounds per annum. They look about after the manner of pimps and purveyors; and as it is according to human nature to feel uppish on preferment, these flunkies occasionally enact high life below stairs, and waltz away with washer-women and bar-maids, and used-up kept-mistresses. There is no great harm in that, for the kitchen and the servants' hall must be allowed their privileges; and, among a free people, there ought to be no inquisition into the flirtation of the pantry and the coal-cellar. But when the gentlemen of the livery and the shoulder-knot become authors, and deal in National Characteristics, curiosity is excited to know how they spell; and, besides, such interest is felt by every body in all his Lordship's concerns, that it is extended even to the mental qualifications of his body-servants, his gentlemen, and his gentlemen's gentlemen.[123]

"News from Paddy," which appeared in the April *Blackwood's* was a distinct anticlimax. Concerned to some extent with Byron's "Cockneyisms," it added little to the criticism already before the public. Only in its remarks upon Mary Shelley's association with *The Liberal*, which parallel those in *The Monthly Censor* of this same month,[124] does this article reveal any suggestion of originality. "A precious trio these 'Giuli Three' . . . the *tenore* of his Lordship, the *basso* of Leigh, and the *soprano* of a female voice, scarce indeed distinguishable in pouring forth the rough notes of Jacobinism," Paddy remarked. "One should think, that a female breast, just chastised by a sad

---

[123] "On the Scotch Character—By A Flunky," *Blackwood's*, XIII (1823), 365-67. The reference to "washer-women" was made with recollection of the forty-fourth essay in the Round Table series, "Portraits of a Washerwoman," *The Examiner*, No. 455 (September 15, 1816), pp. 587-89.

[124] "Since the death of Shelly [*sic*], a poor creature, whose best excuse for the direct and desperate irreligion of his scribbling, was his probable insanity, the *filling up* is supplied by Leigh Hunt, cockney and patriot, and by some two or three women who having begun their education under philosopher *Godwin*, completed it under Atheist *Shelly*" ("The Liberal or 'Verse and Prose from the South,' No. I and II," *The Monthly Censor*, II [1823], 454-55). The writer doubtless was referring both to Mary Shelley and to Claire Clairmont, the latter of whom had utterly no connection with *The Liberal*.

calamity, might find other modes of consolation than in feeble railing against kings and gods."[125]

Since the third number of *The Liberal* was to appear before the end of April, 1823, this closed the British criticism of the second number. In the United States, there was apparently no critical comment upon this number, even like that which *The Albion* had offered upon the basis of the remarks in *The London Literary Gazette* concerning the first number of *The Liberal*. In April, *The North American Review* carried a rather full discussion of Thomas Moore's *Loves of the Angels*, but "Heaven and Earth" was never mentioned.[126] In May, *The Museum of Foreign Literature and Science* reprinted Byron's mystery. Although the editor neglected to mention the source of "Heaven and Earth," he did observe, "We do not, ourselves, entertain so high an opinion of the Mystery, as some of the British reviewers; but it certainly bears the stamp of the author's genius."[127]

The decline in critical attention probably served both as a partial cause and as a reflection of public apathy. The comment preceding and immediately following the appearance of the first *Liberal* stimulated curiosity, and three thousand copies were soon sold.[128] Although the indictment of John Hunt served to call further attention to *The Liberal*—if this is what were needed apart from the intrinsic characteristics of the journal— there were only one thousand more copies sold by late February, 1823: of 7,000 printed, some as either the second issue or the second edition of the first number, 4,050 had been sold. This

---

[125] "News from Paddy," *Blackwood's*, XIII (1823), 397-99.

[126] "The Loves of the Angels," *The North American Review*, XVI (1823), 352-65. This periodical was founded in Boston in 1815 as a monthly, but by the end of 1818 it had become a quarterly.

[127] *The Museum of Foreign Literature and Science*, II (1823), 410-31. This has been described as the principal American eclectic from 1822, when it was founded in Philadelphia, to 1842, when it ceased to be published.

[128] Leigh Hunt wrote John Hunt on December 26, 1822, "Nothing has been told us, certainly, since the news of the first sale of 3000" (the Pierpont Morgan Library).

yielded £777.16.0, from which the costs, £400, were deducted, leaving as profits, £377.16.0.[129] Of this, Leigh Hunt received £291.15.0.[130]

§ *iii*

By February, it had become quite clear that, despite the wider variety of writers and the more even literary achievement represented in the second number of *The Liberal*, public interest had declined, and the present number would not have even the success of the first. The ultimate result could probably have been foretold by nearly everyone connected with *The Liberal*. Somewhat later, contemporary biographers were to give reasons for what was happening in the winter of 1823,[131]

---

[129] Unpublished letter from John Hunt to Leigh Hunt, February 25, 1823 (British Museum MS. ADD. 38108, ff. 257-58). "In the present statement," John wrote, "the charge for publishing is not put down, as I must consult with one or two publishers before I can ascertain what is customary under the circumstances, but that will make little difference in the present amount." John did not include in this account any mention of receipts from other publishers for the advertisements which had appeared in the back pages of the first number of *The Liberal*, but possibly this was by separate arrangement with them and would be included in his charges as publisher of *The Liberal*. Nor is there any indication that he charged *The Liberal* for the postage used in connection with publication and distribution of the periodical, as Leigh Hunt had suggested in November (Gates, "Letter," p. 15); but, again, this could figure in a general publisher's price.

[130] Unpublished letter from John Hunt to Leigh Hunt, September 19, 1823 (British Museum MS. ADD. 38108, f. 308). In this letter, John referred to an account of June 1, 1823, which has not been located.

[131] Sir Cosmo Gordon ("The Life and Genius of Lord Byron," *The Pamphleteer*, XXIV [1824], 204) believed that "the spirit of the times had put an end to the love of violent political writing, or . . . the pure gold of Byron was mixed with too much of the miry clay of inferior men." The following year, Alexander Kilgour (*Anecdotes*, p. 48) argued that *The Liberal* "was so insufferably dull that the public threw it up in utter disgust." George Clinton (*Memoirs of the Life and Writings of Lord Byron* [London, 1826], p. 640) believed that the "contents were by no means calculated to satisfy the expectations that had been raised." John Galt (*The Life of Lord Byron* [Philadelphia, 1830], p. 190) blamed "the antipathy formed and fostered against it before it appeared." Thomas Medwin (*The Life of Shelley*, p. 385) assumed simply that "there must have been something 'rotten' indeed in the Liberal not to be saved" by Shelley's translation and Byron's "The Vision of Judgment." And in 1858, Thomas Love Peacock ("Memoir of Shelley," *The Works of Thomas Love Peacock*, VIII, 125-26) blamed the choice of a title for the

but at this time John Hunt found the situation difficult to understand. The second number of *The Liberal* could not be surpassed in literary merit, he believed, and "the Poem of *Heaven and Earth* is one of the finest in the English language, for sublimity, passion, pathos." He would admit that "there have been many things working against the sale," but it was also significant that *The Liberal* had been "largely advertised and every facility afforded to the booksellers." Nevertheless, of 6,000 copies of the second number, 2,700 had been sold and 3,300 remained. "If only the number *sold* were printed, (say 3000) there would yet be a profit of between, I imagine, 2 and 300 £ on that number," John observed, "but the great expence of paper & print makes all the difference." The sales had yielded only £518.8.0 against the cost of £560.2.0, so that there remained a balance of £41.14.0 against the second number of *The Liberal*.[132] By June, 1824, this had become a deficit of £58.14.0.[133]

Since the Hunts had succeeded with the first number of *The Liberal* and for the second had acquired paid writers to give variety to the periodical, it is possible that they could have continued to publish *The Liberal* beyond a fourth number; to

---

failure of *The Liberal*: "A literary periodical should have a neutral name, and leave its character to be developed in its progress. A journal might be preeminently on one side or the other, either aristocratical or democratical in its tone; but to call it the 'Aristocrat' or the 'Democrat' would be fatal to it."

[132] Unpublished letter from John Hunt to Leigh Hunt, February 25, 1823 (British Museum MS. ADD. 38108, ff. 257-58). John reported a sale of the first number amounting to £777.16.0, but actually the sale of 4,050 copies at 5s. each would yield £1,012.10.0; or, since some of the copies were bound with the second number as Volume One selling for 10/6, the sale would bring slightly more. Similarly, 2,700 copies of the second number sold at 5s. each would yield £675 rather than £518.8.0 as reported. Presumably, the difference in the amounts in both instances can be attributed to discounts or commissions for booksellers.

[133] Unpublished letter from John Hunt to Leigh Hunt, June 6, 1824 (British Museum MS. ADD. 38108, f. 323). Some copies of the second number must have been sold between February, 1823, and June, 1824; the increase in the balance against *The Liberal* might have arisen from John's addition of his publishing costs.

do this, it would be necessary to show at least a slight profit at this crucial time, after the appearance of the second number. But in this, they failed, and their failure—added to Byron's growing dissatisfaction, external pressures from all sides, and the burden of prosecution—foretold the collapse of the periodical.

VI

The Third Number and the
Inevitable Decision

§ *i*

THE FINANCIAL FAILURE OF THE SECOND NUMBER OBVIOUSLY
protracted the dependence of *The Liberal* upon Byron's will to
continue with the project. The pressure exerted by his friends
remained crucial. "I am most anxious to know that you mean
to emerge out of the *Liberal*," Thomas Moore wrote to Byron
at this time. He did not, he said, wish "to urge any thing so
much against Hunt's interest," which he would assist "in every
possible way but this." However, continuation of this literary
association would not do. "I would give him (if he would accept
of it) the profits of the same works, published separately—but
I would *not* mix myself up in this way with others. I would *not*
become a partner in this sort of miscellaneous '*pot au feu,*'
where the bad flavour of one ingredient is sure to taint all the
rest."[1] Byron showed the letter to Leigh Hunt,[2] as Moore had
anticipated,[3] and then replied on February 20. The "present

---

[1] Moore to Byron, undated (Byron, *L. & J.*, VI, 167).

[2] The assumption that Byron showed the letter to Leigh Hunt is based upon
Byron's past practice and upon the fact that Hazlitt was familiar with the remark
that Moore made about the "taint" in *The Liberal* (Hazlitt, "Notes of a Journey
through France and Italy," *Works*, X, 246). Moore might have circulated his
remark, but it appears more probable that Hazlitt knew of it because Leigh Hunt
reported it to him, directly or indirectly.

[3] Moore, *Byron*, II, 397.

situation" with Hunt, which actually involved but slight association, "arose from Shelley's unexpected wreck." It had
allowed him no alternative, Byron insisted. "You would not
have had me leave him in the street, would you?"

Moore's suggestion about separate publication of Byron's
work offered no solution, Byron remarked, for "it would
humiliate him [Hunt]—that his writings should be supposed to
be dead weight!"[4] Yet in a week, on February 27, Byron was
writing to Douglas Kinnaird concerning "The Age of Bronze"—
originally intended for *The Liberal*[5]—and matters more fundamental. He first instructed Kinnaird that the poem was "to be
published *alone* and *immediately*, and on *no* account to go into
'the *Liberal*.'" Somewhat later, he added that he wished
Kinnaird to advise John Hunt "that as long as I thought 'the
Liberal' could be of service to him and to his brother, I was
happy to conduce to it, though I *opposed* it from the beginning,
knowing how it would end, but that as it answers little to them,
and is highly injurious to me in every way, I wish to retire
from it."[6]

However, Douglas Kinnaird had already acted on his own.
On February 25, John Hunt had written to Leigh: "On
Monday week [February 10 or 17] I received a note from Mr.
Kinnaird, stating that Lord Byron had written to say that the
Age of Bronze was to be published by itself, and that the 3rd No.
of the *Liberal* was not to appear. . . . Proceedings with the *Liberal*
were, of course, stopped, and on Friday [February 21] I sent off
to Lord B. a rough proof in slips of his Poem." The situation
had remained static because Kinnaird had left London for a
week, so that now John was simply awaiting further information concerning Byron's intentions. Meanwhile, he suggested
that unless the situation should change again, Leigh might

---

[4] Byron to Moore, February 20, 1823 (*L. & J.*, VI, 167-68).
[5] Byron to Leigh Hunt, January 10, 1823 (*Ibid.*, VI, 160-61).
[6] Byron to Kinnaird, February 27, 1823 (Marchand, *Byron*, III, 1053).

consider "the employment of your pen in a publication which might be made a companion to the *Examiner* under the title of 'The Literary Examiner' to be published every week. . . . The contents should be limited to Reviews of books and Essays and you might resume the *Indicator* in it."[7] At this time John apparently decided that, since the future of *The Liberal* was at best indefinite, it would be wise to sell the first two numbers together, bound as Volume One, whenever possible, and presumably for this reason he suppressed the advertisements of the second number of *The Liberal* from February 16 through March 23, 1823.[8] The letter which Byron wrote John on March 5, after sending the corrected proof of "The Age of Bronze" to Douglas Kinnaird, did nothing to encourage John. The proof was "full . . . of the worst kind of printer's blunders," and the poem itself was to "be published alone—and by whom I know not, as I leave these things to Mr. K.ᵈ"[9]

But on March 10, Leigh Hunt received John's letter of February 25 and immediately took it to Byron, who wrote to John. "I do not know what Mr. Kinnaird intended by desiring the stoppage of *The Liberal*, which is no more in his power than in mine." Kinnaird had been instructed, Byron explained, merely to report what Byron had already mentioned to Leigh, "that, my assistance neither appearing essential to the publication nor advantageous to you or your brother, and at the same time exciting great disapprobation amongst my friends and connections in England, I craved permission to withdraw." Byron was obviously unable to understand one aspect of the situation: "Mr. Kd. *could* not have received my letter to this effect till long after the date of your letter to your brother this

---

[7] Unpublished letter from John Hunt to Leigh Hunt, February 25, 1823 (British Museum MS. ADD. 38108, f. 257).

[8] The suppression of advertisements beginning on February 16 suggests that when John wrote that he had received Kinnaird's letter "Monday week," he meant February 10 rather than February 17.

[9] Byron to John Hunt, May 5, 1823 (*L. & J.*, VI, 169-70).

day received."[10] In about two weeks, John apparently resumed preparations for the third number of *The Liberal*, which he announced in *The Examiner* of March 30 as appearing "in the course of April."[11]

The incident reveals the degree to which Byron's London friends remained concerned over his association with the Hunts. More important, however, it shows how acutely Byron had come to feel the pressure of these friends and of the press, especially since it was now quite apparent that *The Liberal* was not successful. Trelawny later referred to "the cuckoo note, 'I told you so,' sung by his friends, and the loud crowing of enemies," and, like others, Trelawny recognized Byron's desire to withdraw from *The Liberal*.[12] "I can perceive that he wishes Mr. Hunt and his family away," Lady Blessington observed, and her opinion was quite harsh: "It appears to me that Byron is a person who, without reflection, would form engagements which, when condemned by his friends or advisers, he would gladly get out of without considering the means, or, at least, without reflecting on the humiliation such a desertion must inflict on the persons he had associated with him."[13]

Byron himself continued to insist upon the distinction between his withdrawal from *The Liberal* and the actual termination of the periodical. "As to Hunt, I prefer *not* having turned him to starve in the streets to any personal honour which might have accrued from some genuine philanthropy," he emphasized to Moore. "I really act upon principle in this matter, for we have nothing much in common." Hunt seemed "incapable or unwilling to do any thing further for himself," and Byron wanted to "furnish him with the means in comfort" to return to England. There, he could "continue his Journal, or Journals, with his brother." Byron claimed that he himself could offer

[10] Byron to John Hunt, March 10, 1823 (*Ibid.*, VI, 171).
[11] *The Examiner*, No. 792 (March 30, 1823), p. 224.
[12] Trelawny, *Recollections*, p. 104.
[13] Blessington, *A Journal of Conversations with Lord Byron*, p. 100.

nothing else, "for I take it that I am as low in popularity and bookselling as any writer can be. At least, so my friends assure me. . . . This they attribute to Hunt; but they are wrong—it must be, partly at least, owing to myself."[14]

In his letters to John Hunt in which he sought release from the association with *The Liberal*, Byron emphasized his unpopularity. "The work, even by your own account, is unsuccessful, and I am not at all sure that this failure does not spring much more from *me* than any other connection of the work," he wrote on March 10.[15] A week later, his ideas were confusing. He recalled for John the plan which had been proposed in September, "to have made a kind of literary appendix to the *Examiner*." The alternative had been tried and had failed, he continued, "and it appears that the two pieces of my contribution have precipitated that failure more than any other. It was a pity to print such a quantity, especially as you might have been aware of my general unpopularity, and the universal run of the period against my productions. . . ." He was implying perhaps that if he did not drop out, his contributions hereafter would be slight. On the other hand, "the Journal, if continued (as I see no reason why it should not be), will find much more efficacious assistance in the present and other contributors than in myself." In all this, despite his previous instructions to Kinnaird, Byron for the moment appeared to lack sufficient resolution to make the final break, at least without some encouragement from John Hunt. "I will not, however, quit *The Liberal* without mature consideration," he promised, "though I feel persuaded that it would be for your advantage that I should do so."[16]

The decision seemed to be inevitable. In April, Leigh Hunt, who still could not imagine *The Liberal* without Byron, wrote

---

[14] Byron to Moore, April 2, 1823 (*L. & J.*, VI, 182-83).
[15] Byron to John Hunt, March 10, 1823 (*Ibid.*, VI, 171).
[16] Byron to John Hunt, March 17, 1823 (*Ibid.*, VI, 172-73).

Elizabeth Kent that he doubted that Byron would "be long able to withstand the malicious and envious endeavours which pretended friends as well as enemies make to hinder him from going on with the Liberal." In this event, Hunt would "resume the Indicator, or set up some other help to *The Examiner* of my own." Perhaps this would be a better course, since Byron had "hurt his own cause with the public by his weakness and inconsistency." Although Hunt professed some hope that he might cause Byron "to encourage all the better part of his nature to continuance and victory,"[17] he wrote to Byron at this time with complete frankness: "the failure of *The Liberal*, if it has failed, is no doubt partly owing to its having contained, from your pen, *none* but articles of a certain character, however meritorious in themselves, and to a certain want of superinduced cordiality towards it on your part, which you unfortunately allowed to escape to the public."[18] There was some uncertainty at Genoa concerning John Hunt's intentions for the third number.[19] Although this was soon to be relieved,[20] there was probably no real belief hereafter in the survival of *The Liberal*.

§ *ii*

Early in January, Leigh Hunt thought that he had abundant copy for the third number of *The Liberal*,[21] but he continued to work. "*Don't fag* yourself too much—but take care of your

---

[17] Leigh Hunt to Elizabeth Kent, April 7, 1823 (Brewer, *Library*, II, 126).

[18] Leigh Hunt to Byron, April 7, 1823 (Blunden, *Leigh Hunt and His Circle*, pp. 183-84).

[19] Mary Shelley to Byron, undated (*Letters*, I, 221).

[20] Though John Hunt wrote to Byron on April 1 concerning plans for the third number of *The Liberal*, he replied favorably to Byron's suggestion of March 17 that in place of the periodical there might be a literary supplement to *The Examiner* (Marchand, *Byron*, III, 1054). This, after all, had been John's own suggestion to Leigh on February 25.

[21] Unpublished letter from Leigh Hunt to Henry Hunt, January 9, 1823 (courtesy of the Pierpont Morgan Library). The indefinite nature of Leigh Hunt's knowledge of the contents of the third number of *The Liberal* appears from Mary's remark to Trelawny on May 10: "It has little in it we expected" (*Letters*, I, 226).

health," Byron advised him a week later. "You can [rest?] a little on your oars—[and le]t your home friends pull a little for the present."[22] Nevertheless, of the sixteen pieces that were to appear in the next number, nine were by Leigh Hunt. In "The Advertisement to the Second Volume" he commented upon the adverse reaction to *The Liberal* and attempted to refute the charges brought forth because of "The Vision of Judgment."[23] The third of the "Letters from Abroad" was a general discussion of Italian music and poetry,[24] in which Hunt inserted the original text and his own translation of two more of Alfieri's poems, one referred to as "a satire of his on money-getting"[25] and the other entitled "To Genoa."[26] The essay took the form of a letter which Leigh Hunt actually sent to Vincent Novello, the musician,[27] in early March, 1823. In a

---

[22] Unpublished letter from Byron to Leigh Hunt, January 16, 1823 (courtesy of the University of Texas Library. Professor Willis W. Pratt very kindly made the transcription for me).

[23] *The Liberal*, II, [v]-viii. Charles Brown attributed the "Advertisement" to Leigh Hunt (Dilke, p. 10). Internal evidence clearly supports the attribution, for the author remarked concerning "The Vision of Judgment," "We confess that had we seen a copy of it in Italy, before it went to press (for we had none by us) we should have taken more pains to explain one or two expressions with regard to that Prince" (*The Liberal*, II, vi).

[24] *The Liberal*, II, 47-65. This was reprinted in part in the chapter "Italy in General," *Autobiography*, pp. 393-99.

[25] The source was Alfieri's twelfth satire, "Il Commercio," *Opere Posthume di Vittorio Alfieri* (13 vols.; London, 1814), III, 86-92.

[26] The source was Number 77 of the "Sonetti," *Le Opere di Vittorio Alfieri*, XI, 181. This was reprinted in *The Poetical Works of Leigh Hunt* (1857, ed. Thornton Hunt, 1860).

[27] Novello was an admirer of Hunt's work in *The Liberal*, especially that concerned with Italian subjects. At approximately this time, on March 3, he was writing to Hunt: "By this time, I hope, the 3rd No. of the Liberal is very far advanced: I quite long to see it. By the way I have to thank you for the very great enjoyment I derived from reading the 'Letter from Pisa' in the first No.—Your description of the 'Campo Santo' was so very vivid, that I could fancy I had the very spot before me—or that I was reading an account of some place that I had seen before, and with which I was perfectly familiar." He concluded his comment with the hope that there would "soon be some further translations from Ariosto in the Liberal, as well as others from some of the Italian poets who are comparatively unknown in England. I was particularly delighted with the Giuli Tre which is a capital piece of fun" (British Museum MS. ADD. 38108, f. 259).

corner, apart from the main body of this somewhat contrived work, Hunt gave the instructions that he wished Novello to follow: "My dear Novello, How do you do? specially after this long, poking letter? When you have read it, be good enough to dispatch it off to my brother for the Liberal. The signature, of course, is not to appear, any more than this private, pleasantest bit of all."[28]

Hunt's poem "The Book of Beginnings" contains fifty-five stanzas, to which he appended extensive notes; the body of the work consists of translations of the openings of several Italian poems.[29] Leigh Hunt's other six contributions were to become all but one of the Minor Pieces found toward the end of this number.[30] "To a Spider Running Across a Room" is a verse satire in which Hunt compared the "poisonous rascal" to contemporary critics and writers.[31] Another verse satire,

---

[28] Unpublished portion of the letter from Leigh Hunt to Vincent Novello; postmarked, "FPO/MR.22/1823" (courtesy of the Leigh Hunt Collection of the State University of Iowa Library).

[29] *The Liberal*, II, 97-135. In the notes to the poem, Hunt indicated his sources. He offered the original and translation for the opening of Ariosto's *Orlando Furioso*, the "Exordium" of Francesco Berni's version of Matteo Boiardo's *L'Orlando Innamorato*, and Nicollo Forteguerri's *Ricciardetto* (I, i). In the *Autobiography* (p. 351), Hunt was to admit authorship of this work, Later, in 1823, he quoted his own translation of the opening of *Orlando Furioso* as an example of work superior to that of John Hoole and of William Stewart Rose in their translations ("Table Talk," *The Literary Examiner*, No. 6 [August 9, 1823], p. 96). "The Book of Beginnings" was not reprinted before the Milford edition of Hunt's *Poetical Works* (1923). Amusingly, R. C. Dallas (*Recollections of the Life of Lord Byron* [London, 1824], pp. 296-97) attributed "The Book of Beginnings" to Byron; though indirect, the attribution, occurring in the last paragraphs that Dallas wrote before his death, plays a signficant part in presenting what is the inescapable theme of Dallas' book, that had Byron kept himself under Dallas' editorial guidance, the level of quality and morality in Byron's poetry would have remained high.

[30] *The Liberal*, II, 177-92.

[31] Hunt (*Lord Byron*, p. 62) admitted authorship of this poem. In the Preface to *Ultra-Crepidarius* (1823), he remarked, "The following *jeu d'esprit* is the 'stick' which is mentioned in the third number of the Liberal, as having been cut for Mr. Gifford's special use" (*Poetical Works*, ed. Milford, p. 711). He referred to the following couplet in "To a Spider Running Across a Room": "Have I, these five years, spared the dog a stick, / Cut for his special use, and reasonable thick" (lines 70-71).

"Southeogony, or the Birth of the Laureat," tells of Jove's description of a creature so strange that no goddess except Vanity—called Honour on earth—could imagine him, so that she was chosen to give birth to him—Southey.[32] "Lines of Madame D'Houtetot," a translation of her poem "Aimer," celebrates the endurance of love into old age.[33] "Talari Innamorati" is the story of Mercury's shoes falling in love with Venus' feet.[34] "Rhymes to the Eye, by a Deaf Gentleman" is simply an attempt at humor which is based upon the distortion in certain spelling pronunciations, and "The Monarchs, An Ode for Congress" is an obvious, satirical verse about the Congress of Vienna.[35]

John Hunt had had Byron's "The Blues, A Literary Eclogue" since the summer of 1822. In March, Byron was sending "a corrected proof" through Leigh Hunt, which John could use "for some ensuing number of the journal." He preferred, however, that at this time John include the translation from Pulci in *The Liberal* instead of "The Blues," which would "only tend further to indispose a portion of your readers."[36] John seems to

---

[32] Internal evidence, particularly the style, supports Hunt's authorship. The work was clearly not Byron's, as the title might at first suggest, and it has never been attributed to him. In *Ultra-Crepidarius*, Hunt used a similar method for an attack on William Gifford, who was here described as developing from one of Mercury's shoes. It is possible that when Hunt took up this poem again in 1823, he found suggestions for the "Southeogony."

[33] Hippolyte Buffenoir, *La Comtesse d'Houtetot, Une Amie de J.-J. Rousseau* (Paris, 1901), p. 68. Hunt's translation was reprinted as "Love and Age" in *The Poetical Works of Leigh Hunt* (1844, 1857, ed. Thornton Hunt, 1860).

[34] Evidence for Leigh Hunt's authorship appears in a letter from John Hunter of Craigcrook to Thornton Hunt, May 2, 1860, in which Hunter expostulated with Thornton for not including "Talari Innamorati" in the 1860 edition of *Poetical Works* (Luther A. Brewer, *Some Letters from My Leigh Hunt Portfolios* [Cedar Rapids, Iowa, 1929], pp. 64-65).

[35] Milford (*The Poetical Works of Leigh Hunt*, p. 748) attributed both of these pieces to Leigh Hunt. Evidence of style supports him.

[36] Byron to John Hunt, March 17, 1823 (*L. & J.*, VI, 172). The proof could have been one which Byron might have received from Murray after September 20, 1821, when he advised Murray not to send a proof (*Ibid.*, V, 369), for he would not have returned such a proof to Murray. On the other hand, John Hunt might have struck off a proof after he received a copy of the work in the summer of 1822.

have disliked the idea of using a translation as Byron's major contribution to the third number, for he reserved the "Morgante Maggiore" for later use and planned to include "The Blues" in the forthcoming number of *The Liberal*.[37] There was in addition "The Island," a poetic narrative of the *Bounty* mutiny and the lives of the mutineers on Tahiti. Byron wrote this specifically for *The Liberal*[38] in January and early February, 1823.[39] But Leigh Hunt rather perceptibly "thought little of a great deal of it," and Byron decided to publish it separately. He told Leigh that the poem was too long for *The Liberal*, and also Byron himself wished "to see how the public still likes him out of the *Liberal*."[40] John Hunt published "The Island" separately on June 26, 1823, at three shillings per copy, and presumably the public answered Byron's question, for John was advertising the third edition of "The Island" at the time of the publication of the fourth number of *The Liberal* in late July.

Shelley's only work to appear in the third number of the periodical was the short poem "Lines to a Critic,"[41] which he had written in 1817.[42] The theme of the poem—the substitution of hatred of "want of truth and love" in man for hatred of man himself—afforded Leigh Hunt the opportunity to write a note to the poem, which was reminiscent of his defense of Shelley in the Preface to the first number of *The Liberal*. "In these 'Lines to a Critic,' the Reverend Calumniator, or Calum-

---

[37] *The Liberal*, II, [1]-21.

[38] Leigh Hunt to Elizabeth Kent, April 7, 1823 (Brewer, *Library*, II, 127).

[39] Byron to Leigh Hunt, January 25, 1823 (*L. & J.*, VI, 164). See *Poetry*, V, 582.

[40] Leigh Hunt to Elizabeth Kent, April 7, 1823 (Brewer, *Library*, II, 127). The tone of this letter suggests that Leigh Hunt did not strongly oppose Byron's plans to withdraw "The Island," but it seems unlikely that Hunt first rejected "The Island" and "another poem," perhaps "The Age of Bronze," in the way that he later suggested (*Lord Byron*, p. 62).

[41] *The Liberal*, II, 187-88. This short poem was the only work among the Minor Pieces which was not by Leigh Hunt.

[42] Mary Shelley gave the date of composition when she reprinted the poem (*Posthumous Poems*, p. 186).

niators, will see what sort of an answer *Mr. Shelley* would have given them," Hunt remarked with an ironically vindictive awareness of the appropriateness of the poem to the situation. "Let the reader, when he has finished them [i.e., the "Lines"], say which is the better Christian,—the 'religious' reviver of bitter and repeated calumnies upon one who differs with him in opinion, or the 'profane' philanthropist who can answer in such a spirit?"

The other contributions made in Italy were, of course, from Charles Brown and Mary Shelley. In November, as we have seen, Brown gave Leigh Hunt "Shakespear's Fools," a delightful and informal appreciation of Shakespeare's fools—Olivia's, Benedick, Touchstone, and Lear's—with at least mention of "the skull of a fifth."[43] Mary's "Madame D'Houtetot," an extremely sympathetic account of John Jacques Rousseau's love for the woman who would be his friend but the mistress of Jean Francois de St. Lambert,[44] reveals an assimilation of knowledge about Rousseau which came with Mary's rather extensive reading of his works and letters, and certainly conversation about his ideas, over a period from 1815 to 1822.[45]

Leigh Hunt's "home friends" did indeed "pull a little," as Byron had hoped. "We have two articles from Mr. Hazlitt ('My first Acquaintance with Poets'—and a set of 'Maxims') and Mr. Hogg is to let us have one soon," John reported in his letter of February 25, adding that "Mr. Patmore, a friend of Mr. Hazlitt, is also desirous of contributing."[46] The origins of "My First Acquaintance with Poets" were in 1817, when Hazlitt had written a letter signed "Semper Ego Auditor" to *The Examiner*, complaining of that newspaper's recent mention

---

[43] *The Liberal*, II, 85-95. Brown, of course, indicated that the essay was his (Dilke, p. 10), as did his son in the "Memoir" (Rollins, *The Keats Circle*, I, lix).

[44] *The Liberal*, II, 67-83. Brown attributed this to Mary (Dilke, p. 10).

[45] *Mary Shelley's Journal*, pp. 48, 90, 128, 166-68.

[46] Unpublished letter from John Hunt to Leigh Hunt, February 25, 1823 (British Museum MS. ADD. 38108, f. 257).

of a lay sermon by Coleridge.[47] "From reading your account of the Lay Sermon, I began to suspect that my notions formerly must have been little better than a deception," Hazlitt remarked, "that my faith in Mr. Coleridge's great powers must have been a vision of my youth, that like other such visions must pass away from me." In the second and third paragraphs of the body of this letter, Hazlitt settled into a discussion of his complaint, but in the first he recollected, as a kind of introduction to the real purpose of the letter, his own earliest experience hearing Coleridge speak, and this was the germ of "My First Acquaintance with Poets,"[48] which he wrote in 1822.[49] It appeared in *The Liberal* with the initials "W. H." as signature.[50] The "Maxims," however, passed from John Hunt's possession and was published anonymously somewhat later in 1823 by W. Simpkin and R. Marshall, as *Characteristics in the Manner of Rochefoucault's Maxims.*[51]

The third number of *The Liberal* was to carry Thomas Jefferson Hogg's "Apuleius," an evaluation of the second-century student of religion and the author of *The Golden Ass*, who, like Hogg himself, was by profession a lawyer and only by avocation a writer.[52] It is possible that John Hunt did not have this essay when he wrote, "Mr. Hogg is to let us have one soon." Hogg

---

[47] "Mr. Coleridge professes in his Lay Sermon to have discovered a new faculty, by which he can divine the future. This is lucky for himself and his friends, who seem to have lost all recollection of the past" ("Of Actors and Acting," *The Examiner*, No. 471 [January 5, 1817], pp. 8-10).

[48] *Ibid.*, No. 472 (January 12, 1817), pp. 28-29. With some variation, this first paragraph in the letter came to be the third paragraph in the essay, that which begins, "It was in January, 1798, that I rose one morning before daylight, to walk ten miles in the mud, and went to hear this celebrated person preach."

[49] Howe, *The Life of William Hazlitt*, p. 355.

[50] *The Liberal*, II, 23-46. The essay was attributed to Hazlitt by Brown (Dilke, p. 10), Leigh Hunt (*Lord Byron*, pp. 63-64), and W. Carew Hazlitt (*Memoirs of William Hazlitt*, II, 73). It was republished by his son William Hazlitt (*Literary Remains*, II, 359-96; and *Winterslow* [London, 1850], pp. 1-34).

[51] Hazlitt, *Works*, IX, 164.

[52] *The Liberal*, II, 151-76. Charles Brown attributed "Apuleius" to Hogg (Dilke, p. 10).

had written "Apuleius" for *The London Magazine* after Hazlitt had made arrangements, probably in March or April, 1821,[53] for both Leigh Hunt and Hogg to submit articles, but the essay was not published, possibly because it was misplaced in May, 1821, when *The London Magazine* passed from Robert Baldwin to the firm of Taylor and Hessey.[54] In early 1822, when Hogg knew that Shelley intended to start a periodical, he discussed the essay, but he seems to have believed that the work was irretrievable, for he did not suggest that Shelley plan to publish it. "I do not remember any thing about it now, but then I thought it not bad," he told Shelley and then added his own version of what had occurred: "the then editor of the magazine called Hunt, in some book which nobody reads, a 'Jack-of-the-Green,' or some such name . . . whereupon our schemes for making the human race wise and happy were given up, and degenerate man left to go to the devil."[55] If this account has truth in it, it is difficult to understand why Hogg would not have recovered his manuscript at the time that he and Hunt withdrew as contributors to *The London Magazine*; but he did not, and the matter rested until late October, when Leigh Hunt recollected the essay and through John requested that Hazlitt inquire of *The London Magazine* concerning it. "Tell Hogg of our endeavours to get it," he added, "and at all events, ask him if he will resume his intention, for us, of writing upon the subject he mentioned to me."[56] He did not specify the nature of the subject, but it is highly possible that he meant Demosthenes, on whom Hogg was to write and submit an article toward the summer of 1823. And perhaps in February, John really referred to this rather than to the essay "Apuleius."

The contribution which Peter George Patmore wished to

[53] Howe, *The Life of William Hazlitt*, p. 322.

[54] Leigh Hunt to John Hunt, October 26, 1822 (Brewer, *Library*, II, 156). See Howe, *The Life of William Hazlitt*, p. 326.

[55] Hogg to Shelley, January 29, 1822 (*S. & M.*, II, 736-37).

[56] Leigh Hunt to John Hunt, October 26, 1822 (Brewer, *Library*, II, 156).

make never appeared. Probably on the basis of John's remark that Patmore wished to contribute, Leigh Hunt said that he believed that Patmore was the author of "A Sunday's Fete at St. Cloud,"[57] which appeared in the third number of *The Liberal*,[58] and apparently Leigh's belief became the basis for others' attributing the article to Patmore.[59] It is more likely that, as Professor Blunden has suggested, Horace Smith wrote "A Sunday's Fete at St. Cloud."[60] Smith had protested, "I shall not contribute a line, even were I requested, which I have never been."[61] However, his protestations were not unswerving, and in this case might have arisen from the report in the March number of *Blackwood's* that "the author of 'Amarynthus, the Nympholet' . . . will be one of the contributors."[62] And more than likely, Horace Smith was moved by some resentment at not being asked to participate in the periodical by those to whom he felt some literary attachment and whom he had certainly assisted on various occasions. Smith's claim rather than Patmore's finds support in internal evidence, particularly

[57] Leigh Hunt to Elizabeth Kent, May 22, 1823 (Stout, "Studies Toward a Biography of Leigh Hunt," p. 461).

[58] *The Liberal*, II, 137-50.

[59] Admittedly on the basis of Leigh Hunt's belief, first Stout (p. 461) and then Landré (*Leigh Hunt*, I, 154) attributed the essay to Patmore. In the unsigned obituary of Peter George Patmore in January, 1856, *The Gentleman's Magazine* (N.S. XLV [1856], 206) reported simply, "He was a contributor to 'The Liberal.'" S. Austin Allibone (*A Critical Dictionary of English Literature* [3 vols.; Philadelphia, 1858-71], II, 1523) used this as the basis for a similar remark, which in turn became the source for Thomas Seccombe's statement, "Patmore was also a frequent contributor to the 'Liberal'" (*The Dictionary of National Biography* [21 vols.; London, 1917], XV, 478). However, in Coventry Patmore's *Memoirs* ([2 vols.; London, 1900], I, 7), *The Liberal* does not appear in the list of periodicals for which Peter George Patmore had written. This proves nothing, of course, since we cannot argue categorically on the basis of such an omission as this. In at least one instance, the article, reprinted as "A Fête at St. Cloud," was attributed to William Hazlitt (*The Talisman; or, Bouquet of Literature and The Fine Arts*, ed. Z. M. Watts [London, 1831], pp. 100-13).

[60] Blunden, *Leigh Hunt and His Circle*, p. 81.

[61] Horace Smith to Cyrus Redding, 1822 (A. H. Beavan, *James and Horatio Smith* [London, 1899], p. 164).

[62] "London Chit-Chat," *Blackwood's*, XI (1822), 331.

the rather amoral tone, the subjective reaction to externals, and the light, familiar style of the description of the holiday of the less-than-middle-class Parisians.[63] It is probable, then, that it was Horace Smith who described himself as "an Englishman . . . writing under a foreign sky."[64]

§ *iii*

John Hunt's rather vague suggestion in February that there should be fewer copies of *The Liberal* received Byron's support. "Perhaps also, you should, for the present, reduce the number printed to two thousand, and raise it gradually if necessary," Byron proposed in anticipation of the third number.[65] In reply, John suggested three thousand.[66] Available materials leave unanswered many questions about the technical and financial aspects of the third and fourth numbers of *The Liberal*; however, since sales probably remained at best static, it seems hardly possible that by June, 1824, the third number would have made a profit of £2.11.6, and the fourth number, £14.6.4[67] if John had not ordered a significant reduction in the number of copies printed. Presumably, he continued to pay the writers other than Byron and Leigh Hunt,[68] but he doubtless cut costs

---

[63] The somewhat digressive course of the essay and the sympathetic treatment suggest that it could form a companion piece to Smith's essay "The Cemetery of Père La Chaise, at Paris" (*Gaieties and Gravities*, I, 136-54). Patmore was far more objective, far more concerned with the externals of appearance or experience than Smith or the writer of "A Sunday's Fete at St. Cloud." See Patmore's *Letters on England by Victoire, Count de Soligny, Translated from the Original MSS.* (2 vols.; London, 1823).

[64] *The Liberal*, II, 140.

[65] Byron to John Hunt, March 17, 1823 (*L. & J.*, VI, 173).

[66] John Hunt to Byron, April 1, 1823 (Marchand, *Byron*, III, 1054).

[67] Unpublished letter from John Hunt to Leigh Hunt, June 6, 1824 (British Museum MS. ADD. 38108, f. 323).

[68] Mary Shelley indicated in two incompletely dated letters to Byron that she expected to be paid for her contribution to the third number (*Letters*, I, 217, 221). According to John's account of June 6, 1824, Mary received £60 from him in December, 1823, but this could have been paid in connection with Shelley's *Posthumous Poems*, published by the Hunts in 1824.

wherever he could, and advertising offered the principal possibility. After the announcement of March 30, *The Examiner* continued to carry notices of the forthcoming *Liberal*,[69] but there was not to be a review or summary immediately prior to publication, as there had been for each of the first two numbers. On April 27, the Hunts reprinted "The Monarchs—An Ode for Congress" simply as "From the Liberal, No. III,"[70] and part of "To a Spider" appeared in *The Examiner* of May 25, 1823.[71] During the month of May, advertisements appeared intermittently in *The Morning Chronicle*, but this seems to have been the extent of the commercial notice which the third number of *The Liberal* received.

The work contained exactly two hundred pages bound in the increasingly familiar dull, red-brown paper cover, on the back of which in this instance was the announcement, "The Fourth Number of the Liberal will appear on the 1st of July." The title page for Volume the Second opens the number, with the imprint of C. H. Reynell on the verso. A page of Contents[72] with verso blank, the "Advertisement to the Second Volume" ([v]-viii), and the text ([1]-192) follow. It is probable that, despite Byron's warning,[73] John Hunt mailed a copy of the number to Leigh on April 25.[74] And at the latest, the work

---

[69] On April 6, the work was advertised with "The Age of Bronze." On April 13, it was announced as "in a few days," and on April 20 as "on Wednesday next [April 23]."

[70] *The Examiner*, No. 796 (April 27, 1823), p. 283.

[71] *Ibid.*, No. 800 (May 25, 1823), p. 346.

[72] In the Contents, the essay "Apuleius" was listed for page 141, whereas it actually opens on page 151. Otherwise, the list is accurate: "Advertisement to the Second Volume," v; "The Blues, a Literary Eclogue," p. 1; "My First Acquaintance with Poets," p. 23; "Letters from Abroad. No. III.—Italy," p. 47; "Madame d'Houtetot," p. 67; "Shakespear's Fools," p. 85; "The Book of Beginnings," p. 97; "A Sunday's Fete at St. Cloud," p. 137; Minor Pieces: "To a Spider," p. 177; "Southeogony," p. 180; "Lines of Madame d'Houtetot," p. 183; "Talari Innamorati," p. 183; "Rhymes to the Eye, by a Deaf Gentleman," p. 186; "Lines to a Critic," p. 187; "The Monarch [*sic*], an Ode for Congress," p. 188.

[73] Byron to John Hunt, March 17, 1823 (*L. & J.*, VI, 174).

[74] In the account in the unpublished letter of June 6, 1824, John Hunt listed

appeared early Saturday morning, April 26, for the first reviews
were published that day.

In its issue of April 24 to 26, *St. James's Chronicle* reprinted
part of "The Book of Beginnings," *"From the Third Number of*
The Liberal *published this day,"*[75] and, in the next issue, part of
"A Sunday's Fete at St. Cloud."[76] *St. James's* carried nothing
further concerning the work. All of the other newspapers and
magazines which in any way noticed the third number of *The
Liberal* offered reviews. These were limited both in number and
in the variety of the comment, particularly with respect to
Byron's relation with *The Liberal* and the general inferiority of
"The Blues." "My First Acquaintance with Poets" and
"Apuleius" received both praise and abuse.

"Every succeeding number of the 'Liberal' has less of Lord
Byron and more of Leigh Hunt in it," *The Literary Chronicle*
observed on April 26. "We do not know that the moral or
political character of the work suffers by this, but it is certainly
a serious injury to its literary reputation." The history of the
periodical was quite simple and would do much to explain its
present state:

The first number of the "Liberal" was of Italian manufacture,
and chiefly, if not entirely, consisted of the productions of Lord
Byron, Bysshe Shelley, and Leigh Hunt. In the second, the aid of
Mr. Hazlitt was called in, to make up for the deficiencies of the
first two members of the literary co-partnership. Of No. III, we
speak hesitatingly, as to its authorship, but there certainly is not
a line in it worthy of Lord Byron, and not much worthy of Leigh
Hunt.

"My First Acquaintance with Poets" was impressive, but "The

£2.10 as "charges for shipping of two packets & a box to Genoa" on April 25,
1823 (British Museum MS. ADD. 38108, f. 323). A copy of the third number
had reached Albaro by May 10, when Mary wrote to Trelawny (Mary Shelley,
Letters, I, 226).

  [75] *St. James's Chronicle*, No. 10,212 (April 24 to 26, 1823), p. 2.
  [76] *Ibid.*, No. 10,213 (April 27 to 29, 1823), p. 2.

Blues," which the reviewer did not attribute to Byron, was merely a "silly production," of which "the author aims at wit, but invariably misses the mark."[77]

The Literary Museum of the same day was far kinder to *The Liberal* than it had been in its two previous reviews, for it had "forsworn any meddling with politics," and from a literary point of view had to describe this number as "a work of unusual interest." It ignored all of the Minor Pieces and a number of major ones. Six months before, it had attributed Hunt's "Rhyme and Reason" to Byron, and now it assigned "The Blues" to Leigh Hunt, "with a strong mixture of Byronism." "The Book of Beginnings" was, unfortunately, also by Leigh Hunt, but of this the reviewer would say little because "so many attempts have been lately made to run down Leigh Hunt," whose good works "more than excuse this instance of trifling." "My First Acquaintance with Poets" was "a beautiful sketch of self-biography," but the reviewer found at "the heart's core of the volume, the essay on *Apuleius*," which he emphatically argued, was the work of William Hazlitt:

It has all his originality of thinking, all his force of expression, and all his abominable dogmatism, as if nobody could be right but himself. One would be almost tempted to believe that he had just read Apuleius for the first time, and in the pleasure arising from a fresh acquaintance had burst out into all this prodigality of praise.[78]

The article in *The Literary Museum* hardly set the pattern for those reviews which followed the day of publication. *The London Literary Gazette* for May 3, in a critique as contemptuous as it was brief, argued that the present number of *The Liberal* was "destitute of the only contributions which (poor as they were) excited curiosity, viz. the contributions of Lord Byron." On the whole, *The Liberal* was "one of the most wearisome

---

[77] "The Liberal," *The Literary Chronicle and Weekly Review*, No. 206 (April 26, 1823), pp. 257-59.

[78] *The Literary Museum*, No. 53 (April 26, 1823), pp. 257-59.

periodicals which we have lately seen, and far below the standard of the leading Monthly Magazines," as certain articles would clearly illustrate. "The Blues" was one of these, "as vapid a performance as can well be imagined," and "a still more silly piece of egotistical vanity and self-importance, entitled 'My First Acquaintance with the [*sic*] Poets,' " was another. "Who 'My' is," the reviewer added, "and the long rigmarole about his first meeting with Coleridge and Wordsworth, however interesting to himself, cannot by possibility, interest another person in Britain."[79]

The Literary Register of the same day remarked, "We are sick of this trash, and so we should think must be most of our readers." It took up the suggestion that Leigh Hunt was the author of "The Blues," in a manner which would have been most irritating to Byron: "Where can the animals who write this trash have been bred, to fancy that ladies drink bumpers of Madeira at luncheon?" The reviewer suggested that " 'the Book of Beginnings,' written in the manner of Byron, [was] by one of Mr. Leigh Hunt's children." But otherwise, he added little to the criticism of the third number, except to point out that if Coleridge's nose was, as Hazlitt described it, "the rudder of his face," and if his eyes "were like the sea," then "before Coleridge could attempt to *steer*, he must put his nose *into his own eye*."[80] On the following day, May 4, *John Bull* quoted in part the remarks in *The Literary Register*, commenting, "This *critique* is tolerably good as far as it goes. But why did the *registering* Critic stop here?" There were to be added to the charges against the third number of *The Liberal* forced images, misused language, affected sentiment, and hypocrisy. The work was typical, however, of the writers of *The Liberal*, who "have

[79] "The Liberal. No. III," *The London Literary Gazette*, No. 328 (May 3, 1823), p. 275.

[80] "The Liberal," *The Literary Register*, No. 44 (May 3, 1823), pp. 273-75. For the passages in "The Blues"—probably satirical by intention—and "My First Acquaintance with Poets" to which he referred, see *The Liberal*, II, 13, 27.

arrived at that point—so much envied by the writers of the Book of Beginnings,—we mean their termination."[81]

Only two of the monthlies noticed *The Liberal* this time. *The Edinburgh Magazine* for May abused "Apuleius," defended "My First Acquaintance with Poets" for its characterization of Coleridge, and pointed out that "The Blues" was at least "very smooth, current, harmless drivelling." In its entirety this number of *The Liberal* revealed "infinitely less of talent and blackguardism" than its predecessors; it was hardly worth the five shillings asked for it. The *Edinburgh* saw no reason, therefore, to plan to review subsequent numbers, at least "till Lord Byron shall again . . . degrade himself."[82] In the "Noctes Ambrosianæ" appearing in the May number of *Blackwood's*, Odoherty rejoiced in his belief that Byron had left *The Liberal*:

I only wonder what the deuce it can have been, that made him countenance them even for the little time he did. His articles were libellous sometimes, (these fellows, by the way, can no more libel, than a tailor can ride) but they had no connection with, or resemblance to the sort of trash the Cockneys stuffed them in the heart of—The last Number contains *not one line* of Byron's.—Thank God! he has seen his error, and kicked them out.[83]

In England, there were apparently no piracies at this time, possibly because certain booksellers and printers, like the critics and in fact like much of the public, believed that there was little of any kind of value in this number. In the United States, *The Museum of Foreign Literature and Science* of July, 1823, reprinted the "Advertisement to the Second Volume" followed by

---

[81] *John Bull*, No. 125 (May 4, 1823), pp. 141-42.

[82] "Notes on 'The Liberal.—No. III,' " *The Edinburgh Magazine*, N.S. XII (1823), 614-16.

[83] "Noctes Ambrosianæ. No. VIII," *Blackwood's*, XIII (1823), 607. In the eighth of the "Letters of Timothy Tickler, Esq.," appearing in August, there was a brief reference to Hazlitt, "who, in the penult number of the Liberal, favoured us with all those charming particulars about the old Unitarian preacher his father, and his own first introduction to Mr Coleridge" (*Ibid.*, XIV [1823], 224).

"Rhymes to the Eye,"[84] but this seems to have been the extent of piracy and indeed of American notice.

Yet Byron liked the third number of *The Liberal*, or at least he said he did. "L. B. is better pleased with it than any other," Mary told Trelawny,[85] and perhaps for the moment those who wanted *The Liberal* to continue felt some slight hope. This was to be short-lived. On May 22, Leigh Hunt was writing to Elizabeth Kent that in all probability *The Liberal* would cease to exist after the fourth number.[86] Byron was withdrawing, and Leigh Hunt was thinking of starting another work, independent of *The Liberal*, so that he might have a means of support after the termination of *The Liberal*. It is not difficult to imagine the spirit with which he faced the preparation of the fourth number.

---

[84] *The Museum of Foreign Literature and Science*, III (1823), 43-45.

[85] Mary to Trelawny, May 10, 1823 (*Letters*, I, 226).

[86] Leigh Hunt to Elizabeth Kent, May 22, 1823 (Stout, "Studies Toward a Biography of Leigh Hunt," pp. 195-96).

VII

The Final Number

§ *i*

EARLY IN APRIL, BYRON INVITED EDWARD BLAQUIERE, THE
representative of the newly formed Greek Committee in London, to visit him on his way to the Morea.[1] According to
Trelawny, who first wrote Blaquiere of Byron's interest in
Greek independence, Blaquiere arrived with Byron's credentials
as a member of the Greek Committee.[2] This was the first
positive step of many which finally led to Byron's departure
for Greece in July, 1823. It is clearly pointless to attempt to
determine with precision the relation between Byron's desire
to dissociate himself from *The Liberal* and his decision to go to
Greece. Undoubtedly, much of it was hardly conscious, but at
least there was a definite relation. Aside from the promise of
satisfying a sincere desire to aid the Greek people, the decision
to depart for Greece offered Byron a very real solution to what
was becoming a pointless, intolerable situation, and it gave him
a clear, specific means of satisfying what appeared to be his
growing restlessness. His earlier notions of going to South
America or the United States without any clear purpose had
not held such promise. He had become, he said later, "weary
of the monotonous life I had led in Italy for several years;

---

[1] Byron to Blaquiere, April 5, 1823 (*L. & J.*, VI, 185-86). Blaquiere returned
to England later in the year, but he visited Greece again in 1824, arriving after
Byron's death. From this experience, he wrote *Narrative of a Second Visit to Greece,
Including Facts Connected with the Last Days of Lord Byron* (London, 1825).

[2] Trelawny, *Records of Shelley, Byron, and the Author*, pp. 183-84.

sickened with pleasure; more tired of scribbling than the public, perhaps is of reading my lucubrations," and he turned to Greece to find the activity that he desired.[3] His prolonged delays in moving indicate that in actuality Byron was not fascinated with activity so much as with the *idea* of activity, but the Greek project would satisfy this, just as the kind of life he was leading at Genoa clearly would not.[4] This was not unrelated to that "desire for rehabilitation in the eyes of his fellow-countrymen" to which the Marchesa Origo has attributed Byron's work with the Carbonari in Italy as well as his venture to Greece.[5] Perhaps he had hoped, rather unreasonably it now would seem, that *The Liberal* might help to bring this, but the reviews of the journal gave very convincing evidence that it was achieving the exact opposite, and Byron was soon aware of what he later called the "continual declamation against the Liberal from all parties."[6] It was this to which Mary Shelley referred eight years after Byron's death, as she tried to explain the relation between his motivations and reactions in the spring of 1823:

The opposition he met concerning the Liberal made him defy the world in D. Juan—Then it made him despise the Liberal itself so that when he wrote expressly for it, he wrote tamely—as is the case with The Island—But, in the end, this war gave him a disgust to Authorship—and he hurried to Greece to get a new name as a man of action—having arrived at the highest praise as a poet.[7]

---

[3] Julius Millingen, *Memoirs of the Affairs of Greece, with Various Anecdotes Relating to Lord Byron and an Account of His Last Illness and Death* (London, 1831), pp. 6-7. Count Pietro Gamba (*A Narrative of Lord Byron's Last Journey to Greece* [London, 1825], p. 3) reported that Byron "frequently said, that the public must be tired of his compositions, and that he was certainly more so."

[4] Trelawny (*Recollections*, p. 104) recalled that in his preparations to go to Greece, Byron "exhausted himself in planning, projecting, beginning, wishing, intending, postponing, regretting, and doing nothing."

[5] Origo, p. 17.

[6] Unpublished letter from Byron to Mary Shelley, June 24, 1823 (courtesy of the Pierpont Morgan Library).

[7] Mary Shelley to John Murray, June 8, 1832 (*Letters*, II, 61).

§ *ii*

At this time, Leigh Hunt, who doubted the basic sincerity behind Byron's commitments to the Greeks,[8] was preparing for the publication of a new journal. The first of twenty-six numbers of *The Literary Examiner* appeared in London on Saturday, July 5, 1823, and the last was to be published on Saturday, December 27, 1823.[9] The abundant literary comment in the work included reviews of *Don Juan*, VI-XIV, published by the Hunts,[10] and of Leigh Hunt's own *Ultra-Crepidarius*.[11] He praised the manner in which Shelley had translated the Walpurgisnacht scene from *Faust* "in a version that appears in the first number of *The Liberal*,"[12] and he devoted more than half of one issue to a preliminary review of the fourth number of *The Liberal*.[13]

While the new work obviously served to advertise *The Liberal*, it also diverted energies and probably literary materials from the fourth number. Although nine pieces by Leigh Hunt were to appear in this number, they covered fewer pages than did his works in any previous number.[14] "Letters from Abroad.

---

[8] Leigh Hunt to Elizabeth Kent, June 30, 1823 (Brewer, *Library*, II, 128).

[9] "The / Literary Examiner / Consisting of / The Indicator, / A Review of Books, / and / Miscellaneous Pieces in Prose and Verse. / London: / Printed for H. L. Hunt, Tavistock Street. / 1823." Each number consisted of sixteen pages. Leigh Hunt explained in the last number that he was discontinuing the work because "ill health and other circumstances" prevented him from writing the "Indicator," for which the journal had been established. However, it is significant that on September 19, 1823, after twelve numbers had appeared, John reported to Leigh that "the *Literary Examiner* does not at present quite pay its charges, though it rises gradually" (British Museum MS. ADD. 38108, f. 307).

[10] *The Literary Examiner*, No. 1 (July 5, 1823), pp. 6-12; No. 2 (July 12), pp. 23-29; No. 5 (August 2), pp. 65-68; No. 6 (August 9), pp. 81-85; No. 7 (August 16), pp. 105-10; No. 8 (August 23), pp. 120-23; No. 19 (November 8), pp. 289-94; No. 20 (November 15), pp. 305-9; No. 21 (November 22), pp. 321-25; No. 22 (November 29), pp. 337-41.

[11] *Ibid.*, No. 24 (December 13, 1823), pp. 368-72.

[12] "Faust, A Drama, by Goethe. Translated by Lord Francis Leveson Gower," *Ibid.*, No. 3 (July 19, 1823), p. 43.

[13] "The Liberal, No. IV," *Ibid.*, No. 4 (July 26, 1823), pp. 49-58.

[14] See Appendix III.

Letter IV," somewhat shorter than those of the series which preceded it, is a description of the natural phenomena and of the dialect of the people in the vicinity of Genoa.[15] Hunt wrote "The Choice"[16] in the spring or very early summer of 1823.[17] He admittedly modelled it on John Pomfret's poem although the particular aspects of the life described are clearly as Hunt imagined them:

> My study should not be, as Pomfret's was,
> Down in the garden; 'tis an awkward place
> In winter; and in summer I prefer
> To write my verses in the open air,
> Stretched on the grass, under the yellow trees,
> With a few books about me, and the bees.[18]

"The First Canto of the Squire's Tale of Chaucer, Modernized" is a translation which is at once free in its use of language but somewhat restricted by the mechanics of the verse.[19] "Mahmoud,"[20] perhaps the best remembered and certainly one of the more skillful of the verses which Leigh Hunt contributed to *The Liberal*, was based upon an account given by Barthélemy d'Herbelot in *La Bibliothèque Orientale*.[21] It tells the story of a fourth-century king who destroys a debauched fiend despite

---

[15] *The Liberal*, II, 251-64. Brown identified this as Hunt's work (Dilke, p. 10), and Hunt himself reprinted part of the description in the chapter entitled "Italy in General" in his *Autobiography* (pp. 388-93).

[16] *The Liberal*, II, 265-79. Hunt wrote, "The next article in sequence is a poem entitled *The Choice*, which will be immediately and appropriately assigned to the author of 'Letters from Abroad' " ("The Liberal, No. IV," *The Literary Examiner*, No. 4 [July 26, 1823], p. 53).

[17] In the last line of the poem, Hunt referred to Shelley's grave "by the softened walls of Rome." On April 2, 1823, Trelawny wrote Mary that he had buried Shelley's ashes at Rome (*S. & M.*, III, 930-31).

[18] *The Liberal*, II, 269.

[19] *Ibid.*, II, 317-31. This appeared in Hunt's *Stories in Verse* (London, 1855) and *Poetical Works* (1857, 1860). The version appearing in *The Poems of Geoffrey Chaucer, Modernized* (ed. Thomas Powell [London, 1841]) was longer and more literal.

[20] *The Liberal*, II, 363-65.

[21] Barthélemy d'Herbelot de Molainville, *La Bibliothèque Orientale* (4 vols.; The Hague, 1783), II, 522-23.

his fears that the man, who is concealed by darkness, might be one of his sons. In the version of the poem which was to appear in *The Liberal*, Hunt gave the episode an obvious political interpretation by a preface to the narrative itself:

> I have just read a most amazing thing,
> A true and noble story of a king:
> And to show all men, by these presents, how
> Good kings can please a Liberal, even now
> I'll vent the warmth it gave me in a verse:
> But recollect—these kings and emperors
> Are very scarce; and when they do appear,
> Had better not have graced that drunken sphere,
> Which hurts the few whose brains can bear it best,
> And turns the unhappy heads of all the rest.
> *This* prince was worthy to have ruled a state
> Plain as his heart, and by its freedom great:
> But stripped of their gilt stuff, at what would t'others rate?

In reprinting the poem, Hunt fortunately decided to omit these lines.[22] From d'Herbelot's book,[23] Hunt also took the eight lines which he translated and entitled "A Blessed Spot":

> Hamadan is my native place;
>   And I must say, in praise of it,
> It merits, for its ugly face,
>   What every body says of it.
>
> It's children equal it's [*sic*] old men
>   In vices and avidity;
> And they reflect the babes again
>   In exquisite stupidity.[24]

---

[22] *The Poetical Works of Leigh Hunt* (1832, 1844, 1857, ed. Thornton Hunt, 1860).

[23] d'Herbelot, *La Bibliothèque Orientale*, II, 116.

[24] *The Liberal*, II, 370. Hunt (*Lord Byron*, p. 62) included both "Mahmoud" and this verse among those which he "would save . . . from oblivion." The verse appeared in *The Poetical Works* (1832, ed. Thornton Hunt, 1860).

Leigh Hunt also translated two short, rather trivial verses of Alfieri, under the titles "Dialogue from Alfieri; Between a Chair in Italy and a Gentleman from England"[25] and "Dialogue Between Alfieri and his Florentine Laundress, Nera Colomboli,"[26] and an anonymous song of three short stanzas with a refrain as "The Venetian Fisherman."[27] And finally, he made a poetic translation of Jean de la Fontaine's "Le Different. De Beaux-Yeux et de Belle-Bouche,"[28] a debate ending in compromise, which appeared in *The Liberal* as "Mouth Versus Eyes."[29]

Byron's sole contribution to the fourth number of *The Liberal* was his translation of the first canto of Luigi Pulci's *Il Morgante Maggiore*, which John Hunt had had since the summer of 1822. This tells the story of Orlando's banishment from the court of Charlemagne and his subsequent destruction of two of three Saracen giants who have been molesting a solitary abbey, and of the conversion to Christianity of the third, Morgante, who becomes Orlando's comrade-in-arms. Pulci's obvious satire of monastic life and Byron's intentional translation "word for word, and verse for verse"[30] perhaps discouraged Murray from publishing the poem as much as his own notion that Pulci was an indecent writer.[31] Byron wrote an "Advertisement" to the

---

[25] *The Liberal*, II, 367-68. The source of this was Number 14 of the "Epigrammi," entitled "Dialogo fra una seggiola e chi in sta su" (*Le Opere di Vittorio Alfieri*, XII, 40). Hunt's translation was reprinted in *The Poetical Works* (1857, ed. Thornton Hunt, 1860) with the title "English Courtship."

[26] *The Liberal*, II, 369-70. The source was Number 14 of Alfieri's "Rime," entitled "Dialogo fra l'Autore e Nera Colomboli Fiorentina" (*Opere Postume di Vittorio Alfieri*, XI, 60). It was republished in *Poetical Works* (1857, 1860).

[27] *The Liberal*, II, 366 [printed "336"]. H. S. Milford (*The Poetical Works of Leigh Hunt*, p. 49) identified this as Leigh Hunt's work. Evidence of style supports him.

[28] *Oeuvres de La Fontaine*, ed. C. A. Walckanaer (6 vols.; Paris, 1827), VI, 166-70.

[29] *The Liberal*, II, 371-77. The last three of these pages contain the French text. The translation was reprinted in *The Poetical Works* (1860).

[30] Byron to Moore, June 9, 1820 (*L. & J.*, V, 42).

[31] On March 29, 1820, Byron replied to Murray's charge that Pulci was indecent (*Ibid.*, IV, 426-27).

translation, in which he defended Pulci against the charge of "irreligion." Regarding the nature of the translation and the literary merits of his work, however, he was unrelenting and insisted that Murray should print the work without alteration or omission.[32] From the beginning, he expressed his desire that the original Italian appear beside his translation.[33] Later, after John Hunt had acquired the poem, Byron repeated his wish.[34] But it seems clear that John procrastinated, preferring at various times "The Blues," "The Age of Bronze," or "The Island" as material for *The Liberal*. By the early summer of 1823, the Pulci was the only work by Byron still available for the magazine; John printed the "Advertisement," the translation, and following this the Italian text "in small character" as Byron had requested.[35]

Leigh Hunt had nothing by Shelley. Mary gave him her essay "Giovanni Villani,"[36] a general introductory discussion of the historian of the thirteenth and fourteenth centuries, which she might have written as early as the spring of 1821 when she apparently finished reading Villani's *Historia Fiorentine*.[37] In April, Charles Brown, who was still in Pisa, sent his third article for *The Liberal*.[38] This was the somewhat rambling essay "Letter-Writing," in which he pointed to the amusing faults and inconsistencies in the letters of groups as diverse as merchants

---

[32] Byron to Murray, April 23 and May 8, 1820 (*Ibid.*, V, 17, 21).

[33] Byron to Murray, February 28, 1820 (*Ibid.*, IV, 412-13).

[34] Byron and Leigh Hunt to Henry Hunt, undated (Gates, "Letter," p. 14).

[35] *The Liberal*, II, 193-249. The "Advertisement" appears on pp. 193-95, the translation on pp. 195-224, and Pulci's text on pp. 225-49. Leigh Hunt announced Byron's authorship of both the "Advertisement" and the translation in *The Literary Examiner* (No. 4 [July 26, 1823], p. 49).

[36] *The Liberal*, II, 281-97 [printed as "197"]. Brown (Dilke, p. 10) and Elizabeth Nitchie (*Mary Shelley*, p. 208) have both attributed this work to Mary.

[37] Mary reported reading Villani on various days in September, October, November, and December, 1820, and in January, April, and May, 1821 (*Journal*, pp. 138-42, 145, 152-53).

[38] Brown to Thomas Richards, April 30, 1823 (*Some Letters and Miscellanea of Charles Brown*, p. 23).

and chambermaids, and to the satisfaction accompanying letters from friends and, for those in a foreign land, letters from home.[39] In London, William Hazlitt contributed "Pulpit Oratory—Dr. Chalmers and Mr. Irving"[40] and "Arguing in a Circle."[41] The first was a comparison between the two Scottish preachers, Dr. Thomas Chalmers[42] of St. John's in Glasgow and Edward Irving[43] of the New Caledonian Chapel in London, from which the emerging impression of both is unfavorable. To this was appended "Mr. Irving, the Quack Preacher," a merciless portrait of "the half-saint, half-savage."[44] "Arguing in a Circle" was an article on political apostasy, of which Edmund Burke became for Hazlitt the outstanding example, although Southey "and some of his associates of the *Lake School*" would more than adequately illustrate Hazlitt's remarks.

In at least one instance, the Hunts appear to have failed to use available material. Thomas Jefferson Hogg sent John Hunt his article "Demosthenes,"[45] for which John possibly had been waiting since February. However, Hogg noticed that the essay

---

[39] *The Liberal*, II, 333-43. Brown, of course, indicated that this was his own (Dilke, p. 10).

[40] *Ibid.*, II, 299-313. Brown assigned "Pulpit Oratory" to Hazlitt (Dilke, p. 10), as did W. Carew Hazlitt (*Memoirs of William Hazlitt*, II, 73).

[41] *Ibid.*, II, 345-61. Charles Brown was uncertain about this essay (Dilke, p. 10), but William Hazlitt, the writer's son, reprinted "Arguing in a Circle" in *The Round Table* (London, 1841).

[42] Thomas Chalmers (1780-1847) became well known for his preaching at Glasgow. He was Professor of Moral Philosophy at St. Andrew's (1823-28) and Professor of Theology at Edinburgh (1828-43). He led the withdrawal of 470 ministers of the Church of Scotland to form the Evangelical Free Church of Scotland (1843).

[43] Edward Irving (1792-1834) was Chalmers' assistant, but in 1822 he came to the New Caledonian Chapel, where he became famous as a preacher. He built a new church in Regent Square, from which he was expelled in 1832 for accepting pentecostal doctrines. His followers were known as Irvingites.

[44] *The Liberal*, II, 313-16. A note in brackets preceded this short piece: "*The following has also lost its way to us. We take it in as a foundling, but without adopting all its sentiments.*"

[45] Hogg might have read Demosthenes on many occasions, but on December 4, 1820, at least, Peacock wrote Shelley that he and Hogg were "now reading Demosthenes" (*Thomas Love Peacock Letters*, p. 90).

was not mentioned in a list of the contents of the fourth number of *The Liberal* which appeared in *The Examiner*. "I have written to John Hunt to learn the wherefore &c.," he told Jane Williams. "I suppose he has lost, or mislaid, the MS., or forgotten it, or something whimsical. They are strange *unreliable* people these Hunts."[46] By August 25, John Hunt had answered Hogg's letter, to which Hogg now replied "somewhat in the nature of a gentle hint," which he requested Jane to read before she sealed the letter and sent it to John.[47] The nature of the hint is not difficult to surmise.

§ *iii*

As materials were accumulating and the Hunts were preparing for publication of the fourth number of *The Liberal*, affairs at Genoa were moving into their final stage. It had become clear that whatever respect Byron and Hunt might once have entertained for each other had disappeared. Byron supposedly told Charles Barry, his banker at Genoa,[48] that "he was very anxious to get rid of the Hunt connection."[49] Although Byron had seemed willing in April to help the Hunts to return to England, he was probably less inclined to do so now because he knew that he himself was to break the connection by his departure for Greece. Leigh Hunt was working, of course, and

---

[46] *After Shelley: The Letters of Thomas Jefferson Hogg to Jane Williams*, ed. Sylva Norman (London, 1934), p. 24. The letter was simply dated "Saturday morning," and the editor has conjectured that it was written in the autumn of 1823; however, since Hogg mentioned that he "saw in last Sunday's Examiner an advertisement of the Liberal No. 4," and since the letter of August 25 mentioned above would seem to have been written after this, the date would be late July or early August. The first such notice as that which Hogg described appeared in *The Examiner*, No. 809 (July 27, 1823), p. 495. This letter might, then, have been written Saturday, August 2, 1823.

[47] Thomas Jefferson Hogg to Jane Williams, August 25, 1823 (films of the Abinger Collection of Shelley materials, courtesy of Duke University Library).

[48] Charles F. Barry of Webb and Company, Genoa.

[49] John Cam Hobhouse's diary for October 3, 1826 (*Recollections*, III, 153). Hobhouse and Barry discussed Byron during dinner.

Marianne Hunt was expecting her seventh child. Mary Shelley intended to remain until after the birth of the child and then to depart for England. On June 9, 1823, the child, Vincent, was born. Leigh Hunt, aware that he and his family would soon be alone at Albaro, decided to move to Florence where he might enjoy the company of Englishmen, better climate, and reduced living expenses. He wrote to Byron requesting £50 for the journey and asking incidentally to be "exonerated" from the £250 which Byron had advanced for the voyage out from England.[50] However, Hunt had to be content with the £30[51] which Byron arranged through Charles Barry to send him.[52]

When Charles Brown wrote that Byron had not "confined his ill conduct to H. alone, but he has shown himself unfeeling and unjust to others,"[53] he was probably thinking of Mary Shelley. Byron had become closely associated in Mary's mind with the memory of Shelley. She had recollections of the "nightly conversations of Diodati" in 1816 and of the more complicated relationship of the last years. "When Albè speaks and Shelley does not answer," Mary wrote in one memorable passage, "it is as thunder without rain."[54] In the early months of her widowhood, Mary turned to Byron for the help that no other was able to give her. "Lord Byron is very kind to me & comes with the Guiccioli to see me often," she wrote in August,[55] and the affirmation continued into May of the following year.[56]

---

[50] Leigh Hunt to Byron, dated "July" (Marchand, *Byron*, III, 1082).

[51] On July 13, the day on which Byron embarked, Leigh Hunt sent a final plea for £50, which did not reach Byron (Nicolson, pp. 33-34).

[52] In a letter of July 16, Barry wrote to Byron, "I have sent Giraud to Hunt to ask him in what money he wishes to receive the 30 £ & it will be paid to him this Evening" (Marchand, *Byron*, III, 1086).

[53] Brown to Thomas Richards, October 27, 1823 (*Some Letters and Miscellanea of Charles Brown*, p. 42).

[54] Mary Shelley for October 19, 1822 (*Journal*, p. 184).

[55] Mary to Maria Gisborne, August 15, 1822 (*Letters*, I, 185).

[56] Mary to Maria Gisborne, ca. August 27, 1822, September 17, 1822, May 2, 1823 (*Ibid.*, I, 188, 195, 224).

Byron offered to be her banker "till this state of things is cleared up,"[57] and gave her copying to do for him. In October, she called upon him for the first time, for assistance in her efforts to obtain provision for her son Percy Florence and herself from Sir Timothy Shelley, and Byron acted at once, in what she described as "the kindest and fullest manner."[58] He wrote to his solicitor, John Hanson,[59] and finally, on January 7, 1823, to Sir Timothy himself.[60] Mary was pleased, especially for the sake of Percy Florence, that Byron offered to meet the expenses of a comfortable journey back to England.[61] However, when Mary informed Byron on June 10, the day following the birth of Vincent Hunt, that she was ready to depart, Byron wished to make arrangements through Leigh Hunt, and then, she reported, "gave such an air of unwillingness" during his conference with Hunt that Hunt was provoked to mention that Byron had never paid Shelley £1000 after he lost a wager with Shelley.[62] Later, Leigh Hunt wrote to Byron on Mary's behalf,[63] and supposedly received a brief reply. Shelley's name had been "unnecessarily introduced," Byron said, and Mrs. Shelley had no claim upon him. As for Hunt, Byron added, he "had only to regret that he had ever communicated so much with him, as he had thereby lost not only his money but his

---

[57] Byron to Mary, October 6, 1822 (*L. & J.*, VI, 120).

[58] Mary Shelley to Jane Williams, undated (*Letters*, I, 208).

[59] Byron to Hanson, October 23, 1822 (*L. & J.*, VI, 127-28).

[60] Mary Shelley, *Letters*, I, 215-16 n. Sir Timothy replied on February 6, refusing help to Mary but offering to give provision for Percy Florence "if he shall be placed with a person I shall approve." Mary was naturally indignant at the proposal.

[61] Mary to Maria Gisborne, May 6, 1823 (*Ibid.*, I, 224).

[62] Mary to Jane Williams, July, 1823 (*Ibid.*, I, 229). Late in 1821, Byron offered to bet Shelley that Lady Noel, Byron's mother-in-law, would outlive Sir Timothy Shelley. Shelley accepted the wager for £1000. Lady Noel died in January, 1822, but Byron did not suggest payment.

[63] Hunt to Byron, July, 1823 (Mary Shelley, *Letters*, I, 229 n.). The letter, quoted in part here, is the same in which Hunt asked for travelling expenses to Florence and forgiveness of the £250 (Marchand, *Byron*, III, 1082). It is hardly surprising that Byron considered Hunt's estimate excessive.

character."[64] Although the report of this letter might not be literally accurate, it probably conveys the spirit of the letter which Leigh Hunt showed to Mary. He told her at the same time—according to Teresa Guiccioli—"that Byron had often spoken of the insufferable tediousness of her visits, and had said that he did not mind supplying her with money, but wished he need never see her again."[65] Although Mary wrote to Trelawny for aid,[66] she sent a letter to Byron on July 13, expressing the desire "to settle this pecuniary matter first," then to see his embarkation the next day.[67]

However, Byron embarked with Trelawny on July 13 and could not have received the letter. Although calm forced the ship back on the following day, Byron soon boarded the ship again and on July 16 sailed toward Leghorn without seeing Mary.[68] A week later, on July 23, he began the voyage toward Cephalonia, leaving Italy forever.[69] Two days later, Mary Shelley began her month's journey to London. Leigh Hunt and his son Thornton accompanied her for the first twenty miles, and then turned back toward Genoa.[70] In London, five days later, the fourth number of *The Liberal* was to make its appearance.

§ *iv*

On July 27, *The Examiner* announced, "On Thursday [actually Wednesday] next, July 30, price 5 s., The Liberal,

---

[64] Hobhouse's diary for October 3, 1826 (*Recollections*, III, 153). Hobhouse's source was Charles Barry.

[65] Teresa Guiccioli, "Vie de Byron" (Origo, p. 330).

[66] As reported by Mary to Jane Williams in July (*Letters*, I, 230). Trelawny replied on July 12, "Will you tell me what sum you want, as I am settling my affairs?" (*Letters of Edward John Trelawny*, ed. H. Buxton Forman [London, 1910], p. 67. Mary reported to Jane Williams on July 23, that if Byron "were mean, Trelawny more than balanced the moral account" (*Letters*, I, 231).

[67] Mary Shelley, *Letters*, I, 230-31.

[68] Mary to Jane Williams, July 23, 1823 (*Ibid.*, I, 231).

[69] Trelawny, *Recollections*, pp. 119-21.

[70] Mary to Jane Williams, July 30, 1823 (*Letters*, I, 236). Mary wrote Leigh Hunt on September 9 that she had arrived in London August 25 (*Ibid.*, I, 258).

No. IV."[71] After publication of *The Liberal*, both *The Literary Examiner*[72] and *The Examiner*[73] reprinted excerpts. Otherwise, advertisement of *The Liberal* was confined to Leigh Hunt's preliminary notice of the fourth number appearing in *The Literary Examiner* of July 26, 1823. "We cannot possibly do any thing which falls in more with the plan and spirit of this publication, than to accompany a slight account of it with a few brief specimens of its contents," Leigh remarked at the opening of his comments. There were exceptions to the objectivity which he apparently intended, and these leave a somewhat unfortunate impression since they occurred chiefly in the discussion of his own contributions to *The Liberal*. The information conveyed in the fourth of the "Letters from Abroad" was that which could be "acquired by organs of a refined and peculiar construction alone," the poem "The Choice" was "impressively elegant," and the translation of "The Squire's Tale" was "executed with a fine feeling of the old genuine Chaucerian manner of story-telling." In conclusion, Leigh Hunt observed that this number of *The Liberal*, "for originality and variety, possesses considerable claims to general favour."[74]

The fourth number of *The Liberal* appeared as promised on

---

[71] *The Examiner*, No. 809 (July 27, 1823), p. 495. Following this, there was a list of the contents of the fourth number of *The Liberal*. The advertisement was repeated the two following weeks, announcing *The Liberal* as "Just published" (*The Examiner*, No. 810 [August 3], p. 511; No. 811 [August 10], p. 527).

[72] "Character of Burke" [from "Arguing in a Circle"] and "A Blessed Spot," *The Literary Examiner*, No. 5 (August 2, 1823), pp. 76-78, 80.

[73] "Dialogue from Alfieri, Between a Chair in Italy and a Gentleman from England," *The Examiner*, No. 810 (August 3, 1823), p. 507; "Apostates" [from "Arguing in a Circle"], "Letter-Writers," and "Mouth versus Eyes," No. 811 (August 10, 1823), pp. 519, 521.

[74] "The Liberal, No. IV," *The Literary Examiner*, No. 4 (July 26, 1823), pp. 49-58. It is possible, of course, that Leigh Hunt did not write this article, but it does not seem probable. First, Leigh knew in June what the contents of the fourth *Liberal* would be; secondly, he wrote the literary criticism for *The Examiner*, and it seems unlikely that John or Henry Hunt would have written this type of article; finally, the style is characteristic of the work of Leigh Hunt.

July 30, 1823. There were less than two hundred pages,[75] including two pages of advertisements of works published by John Hunt.[76] The number and nature of printer's errors at least suggest that John Hunt had attempted both to save on costs in his order to Reynell, the printer, and to save time in checking proofs.[77]

With several exceptions, the publication of *The Liberal* now passed unnoticed. *St. James's Chronicle* again made an excerpt, this time from "Lord Byron's contribution . . . a literary curiosity in the shape of a Translation of Pulci's *Morgante Maggiore*."[78] Although *The Literary Museum* clearly disapproved of "Mr. Irving, the Quack Preacher" and found the number "disfigured with all the affectation and bad taste of cockneyism," it could report that there were "many beautiful and many

---

[75] On the cover, the only change not already noted is that of John Hunt's address, from "22, Old Bond Street" to "38, Tavistock Street." The text covers pp. [193]-377; following p. 377, the verso is blank; "Contents of No. IV" follows this, on the verso of which is Reynell's name and address, followed in turn by two pages of advertisements. Only one error occurs on the Contents page: "On Letter-writing" [*sic*] was listed for "323," whereas it actually occurs on p. 333. The contents of this number were as follows: "Morgante Maggiore," p. 193; "Letters from Abroad. Letter IV," p. 251; "The Choice," p. 265; "Giovanni Villani," p. 281; "Pulpit Oratory," p. 299; "The First Canto of the Squire's Tale of Chaucer, Modernized," p. 317; "Letter-Writing," p. 333; "Arguing in a Circle," p. 345; Minor Pieces: "Mahmoud," p. 363; "The Venetian Fisherman," p. 366; "Dialogue from Alfieri; Between a Chair in Italy and a Gentleman from England," p. 367; "Dialogue Between Alfieri and his Florentine Laundress, Nera Colomboli," p. 369; "A Blessed Spot," p. 370; "Mouth Versus Eyes," p. 371.

[76] It is worth noting the titles which appeared in these advertisements of works published by Hunt: *Don Juan* (VI-VIII); *The Island* (3rd ed.); *The Age of Bronze*; *Liber Amoris*; Thomas Landseer's *Twenty Engravings of Lions, Tigers, Panthers, and Leopards*; *The Liberal*, No. 3; *The Liberal*, Volume the First; *The Literary Examiner*, Nos. 1-4.

[77] Signature U, which includes eleven pages of "Giovanni Villani," one blank page, and four pages of "Pulpit Oratory," should have been numbered 287-302, but it was given numbers 187-202. On the last page of "Giovanni Villani," the heading appears for "Letters from Abroad." Elsewhere there is an error in pagination, "336" instead of "366." These are not serious errors, and they can in fact be easily explained; however, failure to detect them suggests a superficial inspection of the work.

[78] *St. James's Chronicle*, No. 10,255 (July 31 to August 2, 1823), p. 2.

entertaining passages."[79] On August 3, *John Bull* merely denied that Byron's translation revealed either the humor or the simplicity that characterizes Pulci's original, but it promised to "give The Liberal its fair portion of notice next week."[80] However, those who might have expected this review were to be disappointed. *Blackwood's* made only two comments, both in articles appearing in its August issue. Hazlitt's unfavorable description of Edward Irving in "Mr. Irving, the Quack Preacher" was indefensible, the writer argued somewhat speciously, for *The Edinburgh Review*, which was "supported . . . by the same people as the Liberal," had condemned the use of description of this nature in the conservative press.[81] In "Noctes Ambrosianæ," Christopher North gave a lecture upon Hunt's poem "The Choice," in which he particularly ridiculed Hunt's claims to love nature: "His grounds!—Leigh Hunt's grounds!—A gentleman of landed property!—A Surrey freeholder!"[82] In the United States, the only notice was given by *The Museum of Foreign Literature and Science*, which reprinted much of "Pulpit Oratory" in October, 1823.[83]

On August 31, *John Bull* proclaimed, "Byron has discarded Hunt, who exclaims bitterly against his Lordship." The statement was based upon rumor, and in at least one instance it repeated a completely false report: "The widow of the wretched Shelley is compassionated by her father-in-law, who, it is said, relieves Byron of the charge of keeping a whole family."[84] Such a statement as this is significant only because it indicates that there was very little surprise at the announcement in *The Examiner* of October 31 which definitely put an end to *The Liberal*:

---

[79] "The Liberal, No. IV," *The Literary Museum*, No. 67 (August 2, 1823), pp. 486-88.

[80] *John Bull*, No. 138 (August 3, 1823), p. 245.

[81] "Letters of Timothy Tickler, Esq., No. VIII," *Blackwood's*, XIV (1823), 230.

[82] "Noctes Ambrosianæ, No. XI," *Ibid.*, XIV (1823), 243.

[83] *The Museum of Foreign Literature and Science*, III (1823), 356-63.

[84] *John Bull*, No. 142 (August 31, 1823), p. 280.

The Liberal.—We understand that this work is discontinued, and that the lately-published number, the *Fourth*, is the last. It is now collected in two octavo Volumes, forming certainly one of the most curious and interesting Miscellanies ever published. It contains three original poems, one prose article, and one poetical translation, by Lord Byron; the Translation of the May-day Night Scene in Goethe's Faust, by the late Mr. Shelley (reckoned by his admirers one of his happiest efforts); and a great number of pieces by many eminent periodical writers. We are enabled to state, that most of the hands engaged in the *Liberal* now contribute to the *Literary Examiner*.[85]

The announcement elicited comment of course. "Four Numbers only have sufficed to satisfy the curiosity of the public, and to decide their vote," dogmatized *The Gentleman's Magazine* in September.[86] Three months later, *The British Critic*, which had been rephrasing the old charge that Byron's association with the Hunts had seriously injured his abilities,[87] now proclaimed the beginnings of a regenerative process on the part of Byron: "his first step has been to leave the Liberal to die a natural death, like Herod, of its own inherent loathsomeness."[88] On the whole, however, those who commented tended to develop some of the possibilities which the situation offered. At one point the September *Blackwood's* lamented, "All is up now; all the fine dreams of floating are over. . . . I could joke, but the situation of these fellows is really almost too sore to be a fit subject of jocular reflection."[89] Elsewhere in the same issue, the facetiousness disappeared, and the attack was as scathing as anything which *Blackwood's* had levelled at *The Liberal* when it had seemed to constitute a threat:

---

[85] "Newspaper Chat," *The Examiner*, No. 814 (August 31, 1823), p. 569.

[86] *The Gentleman's Magazine*, XCIII, Part II (1823), 256.

[87] "The Island," "*Don Juan*, Cantos VI, VII, VIII," *The Brtiish Critic*, XX (1823), 16-22, 178-88.

[88] "Don Juan, Cantos XII, XIII, XIV," *Ibid.*, XX (1823), 663.

[89] "Letters of Timothy Tickler, Esq., No. X," *Blackwood's*, XIV (1823), 314.

All that was necessary for their work was a slight smattering of erroneous information, as much cleverness as belongs to a second-rate bagman, the liveliness of an under-waiter in a suburban tavern, the grace of a street-walker, not yet utterly battered, the philosophy of an itinerant lecturer on Reform, the eloquence of an unemployed barrister's clerk, the wit of an editor of the fiftieth Incarnation of Joe [*sic*], the manners of a run-away London tailor's apprentice, and the morals of a retired bagnio-keeper, ruralizing beyond East-end.—Yet in all these qualifications have they been found wanting; and unable to pick up a dishonest subsistence, they are now starving on unpaid small-beer, and parsnips taken on tick.[90]

And in the twelfth "Noctes Ambrosianæ," which appeared the following month, Timothy Tickler read a poem, of which slightly more than one stanza was significant:

> They'll say—I sha'nt believe 'em—but they'll say,
>   That Leigh's become what once he most abhorred.
> Has thrown his independence all away,
>   And dubb'd himself toad-eater to a lord;
> And though, of course, you'll hit as hard as they,
>   I fear you'll find it difficult to ward
> Their poison'd arrows off—you'd best come back,
> Before the Cockney kingdom goes to wrack.
>
> The Examiner's grown dull as well as dirty,
>   The Indicator's sick, the Liberal dead—
> I hear its readers were some six-and-thirty;
>   But really 'twas too stupid to be read.[91]

Perhaps the most successful of these obituaries of *The Liberal* was "The Cockney's Letter," which Theodore Hook wrote and published in *John Bull* on September 28. The work supposedly came from "a cockney gentleman late in the train of Lord Byron, but now discarded," who was writing with frank

---

[90] "The General Question, No. I," *Ibid.*, XIV (1823), 332.
[91] "Noctes Ambrosianæ, No. XII," *Ibid.*, XIV (1823), 488.

astonishment that "notwithstanding all the strong articles in our last Liberal Magazine, neither Government nor people has made a stir; England is still a monarchy, and not even a single change in the ministry has been effected!" He was largely concerned, however, with his own quarrel with Byron, "the only subject of conversation now in England." It arose chiefly from Byron's resentment because "some time ago, seeing him in conversation with the Earl of ——, at the end of the Strada di ——, I hopped down the street, and just to shew the intimacy that subsisted between us, slapped him on the back with a 'Ha! Byron, my boy!' " Further difficulties arose because the writer included himself in the "Satanic School" with Byron, who assured him that he was merely cockney. And finally, the situation became quite apparent one day, the writer continued, because he was able to be alone in Byron's study, where he fumbled through Byron's papers and books until he located *Rimini*, "thinking to find it full of notes" but discovering instead that it was "not even half cut open." On the last cut leaf, a verse appeared: "O! Crimini, Crimini! / What a nimini pimini / Story of Rimini." Yet the "Cockney" remained always hopeful and closed his letter with a promise: "No. V. of our Liberal Magazine shortly. Let tyrants tremble!"[92] But the spirit of this article itself and the humor with which Hook treated the subject in the usually stern *John Bull* indicate clearly enough that editors and critics, if not tyrants perhaps, no longer felt the need to tremble.

---

[92] "The Cockney's Letter," *John Bull*, No. 146 (September 28, 1823), p. 309. In the United States, this was reprinted in the second volume of *The Albion* (No. 29 [January 3, 1824], p. 227).

VIII

Aftermath: 1823-28

§ i

IN AUGUST, LEIGH HUNT TOOK HIS FAMILY TO FLORENCE, WHERE they lived first in the Piazza Sante Croce and then at Maiano, a village about two miles away. In time, Hunt became part of the circle of Englishmen which included Charles Armitage Brown, Walter Savage Landor, and Seymour Kirkup, the artist.[1] He continued to write for *The Literary Examiner*, of course, until it ceased to exist. In December, 1823, John Hunt published *Ultra-Crepidarius*, Leigh's satire upon William Gifford, but this also failed,[2] and the financial situation of Leigh Hunt and his family remained crucial.

On June 1, 1823, John Hunt allowed Leigh credit amounting to £291.15.0 from the profits of the first number of *The Liberal*, but previous debts consumed £257.8.11, so that only £34.6.1 remained.[3] He did not indicate the following year how much he accredited to Leigh from the very slight profits of the third and fourth numbers, but it would make little difference, for on January 1, 1824, the debt that Leigh owed John stood at £1790.19.10.[4] By their arrangement, Leigh was responsible for

---

[1] Hunt, *Autobiography*, pp. 368-74.

[2] In an unpublished letter of June 6, 1824, John Hunt reported to Leigh that there was a loss amounting to £14.15.7 on five hundred copies of *Ultra-Crepidarius* (British Museum MS. ADD. 38108, f. 323).

[3] Unpublished letter from John Hunt to Leigh Hunt, September 19, 1823 (British Museum MS. ADD. 38108, f. 308).

[4] Unpublished letter from John Hunt to Leigh Hunt, June 6, 1824 (*Ibid.*, f. 324).

the unsold copies of *The Liberal,* of which John had served merely as publisher. John attempted to dispose of as many of these as possible in the sets of bound volumes advertised at one guinea each.[5] "The *Liberal* volumes may or may not turn to some account," John wrote Leigh in September, 1823. By June he was less uncertain, for there remained 8,285 single numbers, which should have brought £2071. John allowed Leigh £300 for these, explaining his calculations in language so direct and reasonable that it gives a kind of dramatic emphasis to the failure of Leigh Hunt's Italian venture:

The expected sale of the work in sets, after its periodical discontinuance, altogether failed. Scarcely a single set has been sold since the accts. transmitted to Italy were made up—& not 25 copies in all of odd nos.

The sale of 1000 complete sets to the *American* booksellers is negociating. They cannot be expected to give a farthing *more* than they could print for—the price *asked* is therefore only　　　　　　　　　　　　　　　　　　　　　　200

A large number must be sold for waste paper, because they will not form sets; & it is thought best to dispose of the remainder gradually by auction, &c., which in some years may return　　　　　　　　　　　　　　　　　　　　100
　　　　　　　　　　　　　　　　　　　　　　　　　　　　———
　　　　　　　　　　　　　　　　　　　　　　　　　　£300.[6]

Leigh Hunt made claim to part ownership in *The Examiner,* which John rejected on the basis of Leigh's voluntary withdrawal to avoid prosecution in 1821. The breach opened in this way became wider. Although there was at one time an arrangement between them by which Leigh should receive both payment for contributions to *The Examiner* and an annuity

---

[5] *The Examiner,* September 7, 14, November 2, 1823. The advertisement appeared in the back pages of other Hunt publications at this time.

[6] Unpublished letter from John Hunt to Leigh Hunt, June 6, 1824 (British Museum MS. ADD. 38108, f. 324).

of £100 because of his part in founding the newspaper, negotiations were reopened and did not terminate until Leigh made an arrangement with the publisher Henry Colburn to write for *The New Monthly Magazine*.[7] This led at length to the composition and publication of *Lord Byron and Some of His Contemporaries*.

§ *ii*

On Thursday, January 15, 1824, after various delays, the Crown brought John Hunt to trial in the Court of King's Bench before Lord Chief Justice Abbott[8] and a Special Jury.[9] John Adolphus of the Constitutional Association spoke for the prosecution, and James Scarlett was counsel for the defense. Adolphus briefly reviewed the history of the first number of *The Liberal*, "a production sent forth by those whom distance made valiant, and indifferent to character, regardless of consequences; and who, from a spirit of malice, were capable of outraging all feeling and ransacking even the very grave to obtain food for their malignity." In this work, he continued, appeared "The Vision of Judgment," from which he quoted what would seem to be the most obvious instances of impiety. He was sorry to find that the author was "degraded to a level with the basest reptiles." Adolphus asked that the passages on which the accusation rested be read, but Scarlett insisted that the entire poem be read, to which the Chief Justice agreed. During the reading of those lines in which Byron described Southey's offer to write the life of Satan, there was "great merriment in Court."

---

[7] See Blunden, *Leigh Hunt and His Circle*, pp. 203 ff.; Landré, *Leigh Hunt*, I, 158 ff.

[8] Charles Abbott (1762-1832), who became the First Baron Tenterden, was made Lord Chief Justice in 1818.

[9] The account is based upon that in *The Times* (No. 12,085 [January 16, 1824], pp. 2-4), which shows substantial agreement, even in details, with all other reports of the trial which I have examined.

In his plea for the defense, James Scarlett pointed to the fantastic nature of the present prosecution. There was an immunity against public opinion attaching itself to the person and being of a king while he was living, Scarlett conceded, but this could hardly pass into the grave. What would become of history? Nevertheless, he would consent to a verdict of guilty if it could be shown that the criticism of George III could injure the happiness of George IV, as the indictment charged. This, however, was ambiguous, he observed, for praise of a deceased king might cause comparison harmful to the present King, which would therefore be criminal. Scarlett accepted certain of the charges which Byron made against George III, but it was the right of the poet and the function of the historian that concerned him, rather than the content of the particular charges found in "The Vision of Judgment." Unless the Jury

were prepared to say that no man should speak of the political character of a deceased monarch without being subject to prosecution, they could not pronounce a verdict against the defendant. If they were prepared to do so, they would set an example most fatal to the constitution, would put a stop to literature, to freedom of opinion, and to the truth of history; and these he besought them well to consider.

The Lord Chief Justice in his charge pointed to instances of impiety and to implications against the character of George III in "The Vision of Judgment," but he regarded the question before the jury as twofold: "First, therefore, they would examine whether the tendency of the poem was to taint, disgrace, and vilify the fame of the late King; and secondly, whether it was calculated to disturb and disquiet the mind of the present King, and to bring him into public scandal and disgrace." The jury retired for approximately half an hour and then "returned with a verdict of *Guilty* against the defendant."

The reaction of the press was immediate. *St. James's Chronicle* disapproved in principle of the Constitutional Association, but it hastened to point out that in this particular case the group deserved public gratitude, for "the art of printing has never been disgraced by a fouler, colder, more false, or more malignant libel than the 'Vision of Judgment.' "[10] *Bell's Weekly Messenger* considered the conviction of the defendant "to be, in effect, a verdict against Lord Byron," whose works "have long been banished from all good and decent society."[11]

However, some members of the conservative press, from which similar remarks might have been expected, merely summarized the proceedings.[12] These had certainly not come to regard *The Liberal*, particularly "The Vision of Judgment," with greater moderation than they had shown during the preceding fourteen months, but they tacitly disapproved of the part which the Constitutional Association had played in the prosecution.[13] Others were less tacit. "The trial in the King's Bench yesterday shews in the most satisfactory manner what may be done under the Libel Law of England," *The Morning Chronicle* remarked on January 16, pointing to what seemed to be the essence of the case, "the liberty to pronounce an opinion, and not the quality of that opinion." Much of the fault lay with the system of Special Juries,[14] which *The Chronicle* attacked the following day.[15] *The Times* was content on January 16 to

---

[10] *St. James's Chronicle*, No. 10,327 (January 15 to January 17, 1824), p. 4.

[11] *Bell's Weekly Messenger*, No. 1,451 (January 18, 1824), p. 20. Begun on May 1, 1796, by John Bell, bookseller to the Prince of Wales, this newspaper took no political stand at first, but later it moved to a generally conservative position. It carried no comment upon *The Liberal*.

[12] "Court of King's Bench, Jan. 15. 'The Vision of Judgment.'—The King v. Hunt," *The Courier*, No. 10,043 (January 16, 1824), pp. 3-4; *John Bull*, No. 162 (January 18, 1824), p. 26; "Domestic Occurrences," *The Gentleman's Magazine*, XCIV, Part I (1824), 78.

[13] On February 9, 1824, Mary Shelley wrote Leigh Hunt that "the Court itself seems displeased with the officiousness of the prosecutors" (*Letters*, I, 286).

[14] *The Morning Chronicle*, January 16, 1824, pp. 1-3.

[15] *Ibid.*, January 17, 1824, p. 2.

summarize the proceedings, but by the next day it seemed necessary to take a position because "contemporary prints are at work, applauding to the skies, or reprobating with equal warmth, the verdict of the Jury." The position of *The Times* was moderate. "The truth, as in most cases, will be found to lie in the middle," it remarked. The poem itself deserved oblivion, but, by prosecuting the publisher of the poem, the leaders of the Constitutional Association "have more than republished it. With what advantage to the memory of the deceased, or to the repose of the living, or to the happiness of the State, we know not."[16] *The Examiner* of January 18 summarized the proceedings with surprisingly brief comment. The conviction set a precedent, it said, which "threatens to destroy every thing like manly and spirited expression of opinion respecting Monarchs, and directly attacks the invaluable privilege of history to speak unreservedly of all deceased Kings."[17]

The following week, *The Examiner* argued that the position taken by the Lord Chief Justice in his charge to the jury was untenable unless he were prepared to maintain that "a Monarch, whose name is inseparably connected with all these disgraceful recollections, may not be safely called *a bad King* during his Successor's reign."[18] *The Political Register* blamed Scarlett for failing to develop the possibilities which the case offered. He quibbled about the law of libel, William Cobbett asserted, when he actually should have demonstrated to the jury that George III had a "*bad reign.*"[19] *The Monthly Magazine* for February pointed to both the absurdity and the danger of the situation. The real offense was Southey's "servile produc-

---

[16] *The Times*, No. 12,086 (January 17, 1824), p. 2.

[17] "Trial of the Publisher of the 'Vision of Judgment,'" *The Examiner*, No. 833 (January 18, 1824), 33-41.

[18] "Trial of the Publisher of the 'Vision of Judgment.' Further Observations: Addressed to Chief Justice Abbott," *Ibid.*, No. 834 (January 25, 1824), pp. 49-51.

[19] "To Lawyer Scarlett," *The Political Register*, XLIX, No. 4 (January 24, 1824), 192-237.

tion," while Byron's only crime was to rescue Southey's poem "from the oblivion to which it otherwise was destined." But for "the ghosts of the Constitutional Association . . . still prowling the earth like Milton's evil genius," there would have been no further ado, "for it is not to be supposed that any rational person was seriously moved in his opinions by the rhymes and points of either party." Despite this, the Constitutional Association succeeded, endangering the liberty of history and biography while they were doing it. "For our parts," the *Monthly* concluded, "we are at once concerned at the degradation of the mind which produced the original poem, at the notice with which Lord Byron honoured it, at the doctrines of the judge, and at the decision of this *special* jury."[20]

Five months after his conviction, on June 19, 1824, John Hunt was sentenced to pay a fine of £100. In the opinion of *The Examiner*, "the *sentence* can only be considered as expressing the feeling of the Court, that such an indictment should never have been brought at all; for the punishment, however vexatious to an innocent man, does not bear any proportion to the pretended flagrancy of the offence."[21] Although various journals reported the sentence, there was no further comment upon the Hunt case. After learning of the conviction, Byron had expressed his intention to pay John Hunt's fine,[22] but Byron had been dead for two months on the day that John received sentence. John maintained some hope that the executors of Byron's estate would reimburse him for the fine.[23] Despite Byron's support of John and the seemingly sincere desire to pay the fine, it is likely that the executors did nothing to fulfil this intention.

---

[20] "Literary and Miscellaneous Intelligence," *The Monthly Magazine*, LXII (1824), 67-76.

[21] *The Examiner*, No. 855 (June 20, 1824), 392.

[22] Byron to Kinnaird, March 13, 1824 (*Corr.*, II, 290).

[23] Mary Shelley to Leigh Hunt, July 29, 1824 (*Letters*, I, 301).

§ *iii*

With John Hunt's payment of his fine, the episode of *The Liberal* closed. It now belonged to the biographers, who were, as might be expected, extremely active following the death of Byron. But they soon began to minimize the episode, and on occasion they used false or inadequate information.[24] In *Lord Byron and Some of His Contemporaries*, which Henry Colburn published in 1828,[25] Leigh Hunt gave the episode a central position. Although his report of fact and incident was generally accurate, the connotations of the work were damning. The book itself revealed clearly the intensity of Leigh Hunt's reaction to his experience with *The Liberal*, which is as significant a part of the truth relating to the episode as the facts which he set forth. Criticism of *Lord Byron* was abundant, but it was largely directed toward the justification of the actions of Byron or of Hunt at the expense of the other, and it was built upon well known facts or widely accepted rumor. Those conservative journals which had most violently opposed *The Liberal* tended at this time to support Byron. A few others, such as *The Morning Chronicle*, took the side of Leigh Hunt. In one instance, a periodical which had ignored *The Liberal* at the time of its existence now commented upon it. "We remember to have seen some numbers of the 'Liberal,' " *The Monthly Review* remarked. "A more silly, a more vulgar, a more unentertaining, or at the same time, a more ostentatious work never dishonoured our literature."[26]

The excitement over Leigh Hunt's book soon subsided, and interest in the episode diminished. It was to break forth again

---

[24] "Three numbers of 'The Liberal' were published" ("Lord Byron," *The Annual Biography and Obituary*, IX [1825], 293).

[25] Colburn published a second, "cheaper edition" the same year.

[26] "Lord Byron and Some of His Contemporaries," *The Monthly Review*, VII (1828), 309-10. This work, which existed from 1749 to 1845, offered accounts and summaries of new works as they appeared. Its politics was Whig.

for a short period following the publication of Thomas Moore's edition of *The Letters and Journals of Lord Byron* in 1830. However, fresh comment upon *The Liberal* was restricted almost entirely to the remarks of those who presented new materials concerning it, and in general the biographers of Byron, Shelley, and Hunt gave it perfunctory mention. The story of the work, many seemed to feel, constituted an unfortunate episode of literary history, whether it was told from a biographical or from a critical point of view.[27]

In a few instances, the biographers have attempted to determine and explain the reasons for the failure of *The Liberal*. Too frequently they have isolated one cause and have tended thereby to become partisans of either Byron or Hunt. This has been unfortunate, for although the causes of failure, both circumstantial and personal, seem obvious, they should not be simplified. Since the human element was extensive, the causes cannot be analyzed with seemingly scientific precision. The problem arising from the geographical situation was probably insurmountable, at least in terms of other conditions. Shelley's death appears to have destroyed all possibility that Byron and Hunt could work in anything like harmony. Byron frequently lacked the truly serious attitude toward the publication that was necessary; other matters were constantly coming forth to exclude *The Liberal* from its share of his attention.[28] Hunt was unable to consider his relationship with Byron in the humorous light that the situation sometimes required; however trivial or irritating *The Liberal* might seem to Byron, the journey from the familiarity of London and the establishment of the magazine were supposed to become for Leigh Hunt the fulfillment of his hopes for financial security and of his dreams about Italy.

---

[27] White's opinion was as unusual as it was emphatic when he described *The Liberal* as a work of "four excellent issues" (*Shelley*, II, 387).

[28] Cline (p. 79) has remarked, "With Byron any matter that he was concerned over was likely to remain uppermost in his mind until another came along to drive it out."

But Byron could hardly have sympathized with this, just as Leigh Hunt would not have understood the complicated forces which were at work upon Byron. Among these was the sensitivity to public and private criticism, which obviously increased at the time that Hunt was becoming progressively more aware of possible indications that Byron resented Hunt's dependence upon him. A survey of these conditions, bound together as they came to be, suggests that the real question does not concern the causes of the failure of *The Liberal* but the reason that any of the participants thought that it could succeed.

From the critical point of view, many who have mentioned *The Liberal* have noticed that certainly after the death of Shelley there was no clear conception as to the direction that the periodical was to follow. It appeared without having an appeal to any single group. In some instances, such as certain passages in "Letters from Abroad," the writing was too personal for general interest. In other cases, such as several of Hazlitt's essays, though the writing was excellent, the content would antagonize more in one group than it would attract from another. Partly on the basis of weaknesses such as these, it seems, the articles in *The Liberal* have as a group been held in slight esteem. There was some bad writing on the part of Byron and often worse writing by Leigh Hunt, but the contributions of others, some of whom have not been so well remembered, frequently reveal strong merit. Certainly some of the pieces deserve in their own way to rank with those two which are probably best remembered, "The Vision of Judgment" and "My First Acquaintance with Poets." But if articles of Hogg and Brown and the one contribution of Horace Smith have been deprived of this position, the cause lies partly in the fact that their authors had not established, in other writings, reputations as extensive as those which posterity has preserved for Byron, the Shelleys, Hunt, and Hazlitt. The literary achievement of *The Liberal*, therefore, despite obvious and frequently painful shortcomings, is not to be dismissed in the manner of many who have dealt with the work. It approaches and possibly equals the specialized but profound historical importance of *The Liberal*, a point of brief juncture in the careers of this varied group of literary figures in the early nineteenth century.

Appendices

I

The Illiberal

The Illiberal[1] is a pamphlet of twenty pages, of which the only known copy is in the British Museum. The title page with verso blank is followed by two pages of Preface and Dramatis Personae. The text covers sixteen pages ([5]-20). The author of the pamphlet used asterisks for his footnotes. The three numbered notes are my own. The brackets appearing in the original text are printed here as parentheses.

THE
ILLIBERAL!
VERSE AND PROSE FROM THE
NORTH!!

"Let such forego the Poet's sacred name,
"Who wreck their brains for lucre, not for fame:
"Low may they sink to merited contempt,
"And scorn remunerate the mean attempt!
"Such be their meed, such still the just reward,
"Of prostituted Muse and hireling Bard."   Byron[2]

DEDICATED
TO
MY LORD BYRON
IN THE SOUTH!!

N. B. TO BE CONTINUED OCCASIONALLY!! VIS. AS A SUPPLE-
MENT TO EACH NUMBER OF THE LIBERAL.

London: Printed by G. Morgan, 25, Fleet-street;
Published by T. Holt, 1, Catharine-street, Strand;
and Sold by C. Chapple, Pall-Mall, Chappel, Royal
Exchange; and all other Booksellers.

(PRICE SIXPENCE.)

---

[1] Reprinted through the courtesy of the British Museum, which provided a microfilm.
[2] "English Bards and Scotch Reviewers," ll. 177-82.

PREFACE.

"We are not going to usher in our Publication with any pomp of Prospectus. We mean to be very pleasant and ingenious, of course; but decline proving it before-hand by a long common-place."

Vide Preface to the Liberal.

Hinc canere incipiam.—VIRG.

Hence I shall begin to sing—and, in imitation of a great Original, I shall, ere I prose it, invoke the Deities of *The Liberal!*

INVOCATION.

O! eruditest Lanterns of the South,
Who wield the goose-quill gliding o'er demy;
And O! ye little lights and nursing dames,
Who by permission of a noble Lord,
Have chang'd the *Coral* for the *Poet's Pen*,
And mingled triple-puny Epigrams,
With his new-invented *Liberal*-ities;
And particularly thou, O! Byron,
Whose seat amongst the Poets once was fixed,
I seek protection for my *Supplement.**

* IMITATION

Vos, clarissima mundi,
Lumina, labentem coelo quae ducitis annum:
Liber et alma Ceres, vestro si munere tellus
Chaoniam pingui glandem mutavit arista,
Poculaquè inventis Acheloia miscult uvis:
Tuque adeo, quem mox quae sint habitura, deorum
Concilia incertum est, ... Caesar.

VIRG. GEORG. I.

PREFACE.

To the Public I beg to apologize for intruding myself upon their notice; but, as the Authors of the *Liberal* promised in the outset to be "pleasant and ingenious," if they have failed in that particular, (and I confess I can find neither *pleasantry nor ingenuity in Number One!*) fancy I wrote the *Illiberal* to supply the defect, and chide me accordingly.

N.B. Since writing the above, I have been vastly struck with the following passage in the Preface to the *Liberal*, which passage is in itself quite Unique. "But the least we can do is to let these people see that we know them, and warn them how they assail us."

Now, as I am but a *weak body*, and cannot stand much buffeting; in case you should find me out, and thereby *"know"* me, you won't *"assail"* me, will you? If you do, I'll go to Bow-street and get a warrant to apprehend you, depend upon it!

DRAMATIS PERSONÆ.

Lord B——N	*The Magnus Apollo.*
Mr. H——T	*Versifier.*
THE LITTLE AITCHES	*. Imported from the Land of Cockney, as Assistant Scribblers to the Liberal.*

GHOST OF PERCY B. SHELLY. [*sic*]

CONGE	*Valet to Lord B.*
and	
PIZETTE	*Housekeeper to Lord B.*

THE
ILLIBERAL!!
VERSE AND PROSE FROM THE NORTH!

ACT I.   SCENE I.

Scene at Pisa, in Lord B.'s Study.—Enter Lord B.
LORD B. (Solus. Takes up a Pen and Writes.)

LINES ON THE PAST.

How have I spent the moments of my life!
I have deserted *Home, Friends, Child,* and *Wife,*
(Oh! melancholy retrospective view,)
They've felt some pain, and I have felt some too:
Besides, I fear I've been some people's ruin,
By writing that immoral work, *Don Juan!*
I do repent . . . .

> (*Interrupted by a smart rap at the door. Enter Mr. H.*

LORD B. Curse it, H——, you've spoiled the best thought I ever had in my life.

MR. H. Indeed, my Lord, I'm sorry I should have intruded so unfortunately; but, as the second Number of the "Liberal" must be thought on, I have a Sonnet in my hand, I flatter myself will be no mean acquisition to it.

LORD B. I was writing an article myself, at the moment you entered, which I intended to place at the head of it; however, let's hear your Sonnet.

MR. H. (*After hemming two or three times, reads.*)

SONNET.

From Hampstead I have look'd upon St. Paul,
> When Sol shone bright,
> O! pleasing sight,
To view the glittering of the *Cross and Ball.*

LORD B. (Interrupting him.)—'Zblood, H—— this will never do—too puerile, man, too puerile; besides, Hampstead!—stale, stale!

MR. H. I beg your Lordship's pardon; but, if you will hear me out, I am convinced you will alter your opinion.

LORD B. Well, well—read on!

MR. H. If your Lordship will allow me, I'll begin it again.

LORD B. (Peevishly.) Certainly, certainly.

MR. H. (*Hemming, begins to read.*)

SONNET.

> From Hampstead I have look'd upon St. Paul,
>> When Sol shone bright,
>>> O! pleasing sight,
> To see the glittering of the *Cross and Ball.*
> And though about me every thing was mum,
> Around St. Paul there was a busy hum.
> Porters and Jarvies swearing, people squalling;
> Carts, Hacks, and Stages, rattling o'er the stones;
> And when the way is stopp'd, you'll hear them bawling;
> "If you don't move your cart, I'll break your bones."
> "I shan't," he cries! . . . "O, won't you, Mr Prime,
> "Why then I'll move it for you, so here goes."
> They 'gin to quarrel, and it ends in blows: . . .
> And thus the folk in London *spent their time.*

LORD B. Ha, ha, ha! a, a, a!—Excellent!

MR. H. But, laughing aside, my Lord; what do you think of it?

LORD B. Think of it? Why that it deserves insertion in every print in Christendom, and ought to be placed at the end of the Koran!

Exit Mr. H.

LORD B. D——n the "Liberal;" I'm tired of the said partnership already; . . . but how to get out of it . . . that's the question.

(Exit

SCENE II.

Lord B.'s Study . . . Enter Lord B.

LORD B. (Sits down and takes up a pen.) Let me see, where was I when that damn'd Sonnetteer arriv'd? . . . O? I remember . . . . . "I do repent" . . . . . Confusion! Shall I never be at rest!

(*The door opens; and in walks one of the little Aitches, bowing.*)

LITTLE AITCH. May it please your Lordship, I have brought an Elegy on the Death of Lord Castlereagh, will your Lordship insert it in the next number of the "Liberal?"

LORD B. (Out of patience.) Damn your Elegies! I had enough of your three Epigrams.*

* We hope we do not wrong his Lordship in attributing these *Morceaux* to the *Nursery.*

Epigrams on Lord Castlereagh.

Oh, Castlereagh! thou art a Patriot now;
Cato died for his country, so didst thou;
He perished rather than see Rome enslaved,
Thou cut'st thy throat, that Britain may be saved.

———————

So Castlereagh has cut his throat! . . . The worst
Of this is . . . that his own was not the first.

———————

So *He* has cut his throat at last! . . . He! Who?
The man who cut his country's long ago.
                    Vide the Liberal, p. 164.

LITTLE AITCH. (Weeping at his Lordship's abruptness.) Mamma says it is very pretty, and she thought your Lordship would give it a place.

LORD B. Leave it, leave it, and I'll give it a perusal.

(*Exit Little Aitch.*

(*Lord B. takes up the paper and reads.*)

ELEGY ON THE DEATH OF
LORD CASTLEREAGH.

Lord Castlereagh is dead and gone,
    Sing doodle, doodle, doodle;
And he has left us all alone,
    Sing doodle, doodle, doodle.

When he was alive . . . oh! then,
    Sing doodle, doodle, doodle;
They say he was a naughty man,
    Sing doodle, doodle, doodle.

He made a law to keep rogues quiet,
    Sing doodle, doodle, doodle.
But now he's dead . . . we'll make *such riot*!
    Sing doodle, doodle, doodle.

LORD B. Sing doodle, doodle, doodle! Hear it, Apollo! Sing doodle, doodle, doodle; why, I suppose we must for once sing doodle, doodle, doodle; but I'll no more be badgered with partnerships. "Once bitten twice shy." No, no; enough of this.

(*Somebody knocking at the door.*

LORD B. Curse my unlucky stars; more interruption; come in.

(*Enter another little Aitch.*)

LITTLE AITCH. (Holding a paper towards his Lordship.) There's an Ode for the second Number of the "Liberal," will your Lordship please to read it?

LORD B. (In a great passion.) Who sent it?

LITTLE AITCH. (Trembling) . . . Pa' sent me with it, and told me, my Lord, that it was equal to your translation of Politian.

LORD B. My translation from Politian! Who composed it?

LITTLE AITCH. (Dropping his head.) I, and please your lordship.

LORD B. You! And what do you call it?

LITTLE AITCH. An Ode on Mamma's Lap-Dog.

LORD B. An Ode on Mamma's Lap-Dog; read it, read it; and let's out of purgatory; and if ever I get there again, I'll pay the Pope to fish me out.

LITTLE AITCH. (*Reads.*)

AN ODE ON MAMMA'S LAP-DOG.

There's dear little Phillis, she makes such a noise,
   When she bites our heels, and cries bow-wow,
   Bow-wow, bow-wow . . . Oh! look at her now;
   She's tearing Mamma's ridicule [*sic*] I vow;
O, the dear little darling, she is my delight.

Her great, great, great gand-dam [*sic*] belong'd to King Charles,
   Her great, great, great grand-pa was his too, mayhap;
   Yap, yap, yap, yap,—lie still in my lap,
   O, Phillis, she has such a musical yap,
And her breeding is quite *à la* "*je ne scais quoi.*"

Then, then I get up in the morning betimes,
   Taking my Phillis to sport on the grass;
   On the grass, on the grass—her capers surpass,
   The goats on the Alps, "or the sly little lass,"
And she makes the "*kids dance and the sheep also.*"

When she steals in the gardens, as sometimes she does,
   She runs o'er the beds of most beautiful flowers—
   The roses, the roses . . . she tears from the bowers;
   And such havoc she makes, that I'm weeping for hours,
And thus little Phillis she passes her time.[3]

LORD B. O! Lord.

(*Exeunt.*

---

[3] A parody of Leigh Hunt's translation of Politian, "The Country Maiden" (*The Liberal*, I, 162-63):

   The sweet country maiden she gets up betimes,
      Taking her kids to feed out on the grass,—
      On the grass, on the grass,—ah! the sly little lass,
      Her eyes make me follow with mine as they pass;
   I am sure they'd make day in the middle of night.

   Then she goes, the first thing, to the fountain hard by,
      Treading the turf with her fresh naked feet,—
      Naked feet, naked feet,—O so light and so sweet,
      Through the thyme and the myrtles they go so complete,
   And she makes up a lap, which she fills full of flowers.

ACT II. SCENE I.

Scene at Pisa, on the Banks of the Arno
(Moonlight.) Enter Lord B. leaning on
the Arm of Mr. H.

LORD B. Hark! there is music stealing o'er the streams; 'tis meditation's hour, for see, the moon has silvered all the scene. Methinks I now could hold communion with the dead. The spirit of a Dante, or Alfieri, or Petrarch kneeling at his Laura's tomb, would find me now a fit companion. I had a dream last night . . . . 'Tis folly to be mov'd as women are, but were it not for the shame of such confession . . . . I could say, it sits upon me as it were some Omen.

MR. H. My lord, if I am not intruding, may I ask the subject of the Vision?

LORD B. It pains me when I think upon it; and yet, 'tis always present to my mind, and creeps even through my inmost thoughts, as 'twere a serpent coiling round my brain.

MR. H. If it is painful to your lordship to relate it, I pray you to withhold it from me.

LORD B. Perhaps the communication will chace [*sic*] it from my mind; I will describe the scene; for, as a disappointed lover finds communion with a friend a melioration for a maiden's hate; so does the mind unburthening its cares find solace. But to be brief: . . . scarce had I stretched me on my nightly couch, aud [*sic*] fallen into the arms of balmy rest, when methought my room suddenly became illumined, and SHELLY [*sic*], ghastly to my view, stood by my side: he motioned me to follow. I did so . . . . instantly we

---

Then she tucks up her sleeve to wash her sweet face,
  And her hands, and her legs, and her bosom so white,—
  Her bosom so white,—with a gentle delight;
  I never beheld such a beautiful sight,
It makes the place smile, wheresoever it turns.

And sometimes she sings a rustical song,
  Which makes the kids dance, and the sheep alsò—
  The sheep also,—they hark, and they go;
  The goats with the kids, all so merrily O!
You would think they all tried to see who could dance best.

And sometimes, upon a green meadow, I've seen her
  Make little garlands of beautiful flowers,—
  O, most beautiful flowers,—which last her for hours,
  And the great ladies make them for their paramours,
But all of them learn from my sweet country lass.

And then in the evening she goes home to bed,
  Bare-footed, and loos'ning her laces and things,—
  Her laces and things,—and she laughs and she sings,
  And leaps all the banks with one of her springs;
And thus my sweet maiden she passes her time.

stood upon the verge of a lofty precipice; below was an immense lake of fire; he took me in his arms, and plunged through it. I then found myself in a hideous place; so hideous, I tremble now to think upon it. Around us there were beings, once men, but now so sceptre-like, they looked most horrible! Vipers seemed twisting round their every limb; and fiends more terrible than tongue can e'er describe, were scourging them the while. I turned me loathing from the sight. Just then my conductor bade me look around, exclaiming in a hollow voice, "Byron, this is the place of the damned, avoid it!" With that I awoke, and could sleep no more, so much it troubled me.

MR. H. 'Tis a strange phantasy, my Lord; heed it not—a mere lapse of the imagination: but it waxes late; shall we change the scene?

LORD B. We will: this phantasy still troubles me; I'm weary, sick at heart, at enmity with myself, yet scarcely know why or wherefore.

(*Exeunt.*)

SCENE II.

Lord B.'s Kitchen.——PIZETTE seated by the
Fire-side. Enter CONGE in haste, alarmed.

PIZETTE: You seem affrighted, Conge; what's the matter?

CONGE. De matre, Pizette! de matre! Oh! me vil no more come to mysel. (Throwing himself into a chair.)

PIZETTE: Why, I say, Conge, what ails you?

CONGE. Vy, Pizette, you must know, that as we [*sic*] dit come into Milor's study, vor to place de Chandelier on de table, juste as we did opene the door, vat vas in Milor's chair but de Spectre; for as he vas deade, it must be de Spectre of—vat you call him? O! Monsieur Shelle [*sic*]; it vas de Spectre of Monsieur Shelle.

PIZETTE. Are you mad, Conge? or do you know what nonsense you are talking?

CONGE. Vat! Nonsense! de Devil take me, but 'tis de ver true; begar me no wish to be de vitness de next time, minde you dat.

PIZETTE. Conge, you must surely be dreaming.

CONGE. Me telle you me no dreame! and de Spectre dit beckone to me, an pointe to de paper on de table, an telle me dat vas for Milor. O, ver vel, sait I—an ten de Spectre vas gone in von moment.

(*Their conference is interrupted by a loud knocking at the door*).

PIZETTE. Run to the door, Conge, it is my Lord waiting for entrance.

CONGE. Begar, me vil no go to de door, till me looke out of de vindow.— (Takes up a candle for that purpose;) vot dat may be de Spectre of Monsieur Shelle vant to come in again.—(Looks out of the window.) Who be dere?

Enter Lord B.

LORD B. Open the door, you blockheads! Would you keep me here all night.

CONGE. Me begge your pardon, Milor; but me tought it vas somebodie, Milor, not quite velcome, Milor.

LORD B. Open the door, you varlet!

CONGE. Me vil, directe, Milor; me vil, me vil.—(Goes to the door, and admits his Lordship.)

(Exeunt.)

SCENE III.

Lord B.'s Study . . . Enter Lord B.

LORD B. (Approaches the table, and takes up a letter.) What's here? a letter; and in Shelly's hand, too!! Do I see aright? . . possibly he may have escaped a watery grave. (Ring's [*sic*] the bell.)

Enter Conge.

CONGE. Milor!

LORD B. How came this letter into my study?

CONGE. Oh! Milor, me vil telle you all about dat letter.

LORD B. Tell me about it! tell me who brought it? [*sic*]

CONGE. It vas von Spectre, Milor!

LORD B. Spectre, fool! a spectre like yourself, I suppose, and quite as ignorant. I say, tell me who delivered it?

CONGE. (Trembling) Vy, Milor, juste as we entre your room, Milor, von Spectre . . . . . .

LORD B. Damn your Spectres! I say, how came it into my room?

CONGE. Vy, Milor, if it vas not de Spectre—I am . . .

LORD B. Get out of my sight, you dotard.

(Exit Conge.)

A letter from a Spectre! what can the fellow mean? (Looks at the superscription, agitated.) Why 'tis the hand of Shelly; 'tis strange! but thus I solve my doubts. (Breaks it open and reads.)

From Hades? (starting as he speaks,) that dream of mine comes fresh upon mind. (Begins again to read.)

> My dearest Lord, O Lord! I scarce can write,
> I have such horrid images in sight:
> You'll grieve to hear, I now am doom'd to dwell
> In deepest Hades—which is yclep'd Hell.
> By fiends tormented, and I fear, indeed,
> Unless you alter, that it is decreed,
> Bad as I'm us'd, your fate will be much worse
> Than e'er befel mule, ass, or hackney horse.
> I'll pass o'er that which me, at sea, befel,
> Because from newspapers you know it well.
> Suffice it that our boat perchance was wreck'd,
> And I with all my sins to Hades pack'd;
> You know I had but little faith in Heaven,

And, therefore, could not hope to be forgiven:
But, if you would avoid my hapless fate,
Seek, seek forgiveness, ere it be too late.
I died—and Charon took me in his boat,
To pass me o'er the *Styx*; we got afloat,
To go, I knew not where . . . . he kept his course;
His boat went downwards, though he plied no force.
There were no sculls, or other kind of action,
It seem'd as it were drawn by mere attraction,
Till we had pass'd the dark unfathom'd lake,
When I beheld what tongue can never speak.
God help me! I exclaim'd in supplication,—
It was a kind of prayer, ejaculation;
The first that ever from my lips had flown;
For, when on Earth, I never God had known.
I, too, rejected Christ, and all his works!
And had as little faith as Jews or Turks;
And thus bequeathed myself, without restriction,
"*The eternity of Hell's hot jurisdiction.*"
As we drew near, I look'd with eager sight,
And, oh! what scenes of horror did affright;
All kinds of reptiles, mingled in a mass,
Were spread upon the shore I had to pass;
And fiends of a most horrid aspect stood,
Ready to hurl me in this living flood
Of *serpents*, *vipers*, all the venom'd breed,
That swim in water, or on earth that feed.
Then Charon forced me on the horrid shore,
And yelling fiends, with castigation, bore
Me onward, howling, till at length we came
To an abyss which spouted massive flame;
Then hurl'd me in—and I endure such ill,
As, though it tortures me, will never kill!
Such is my fate, and will be of that man,
Who does reject Jehovah's mighty plan.
And 'tis permitted thus . . . that I to thee,
A *Warning* and a *Monitor* should be.

This is some trick; still, so like my dream; but, 'twould be weak, indeed, to give it credit for reality, and thus I give it to the flames. (Aiming to throw the paper into the fire as he speaks.)
Enter Ghost of Shelly.

GHOST. Forbear! rash man.
LORD B. (Starting back) Shelly!!
GHOST. Ay, Shelly! the poor deluded victim of his own conceit: one,

who must build a Heaven for himself. Behold his reward—(Unclosing a kind of shroud, and discovers a ghastly form, with serpents coiling round it,) Is not here enough to make thee tremble?

LORD B. (Groaning as he speaks.) How? tell me how to shun so dread a fate.

GHOST. Be virtuous, and walk humbly with your God! . . . . You still have time; a true repentance is received by Heaven; repent! it was to warn thee I revisited Earth; repent!!

(Ghost vanishes.)

LORD B. Repent! I will, I do repent;—but, oh! will Heaven forgive so great a sinner!!!

(Exit.)

Finis.

II

Extracts from *The London Liberal*

The following materials have been selected from *The London Liberal*[1]
both because they bear a relation to *The Liberal* and because they
are parodies, general or specific, of Byron, Shelley, and Hunt. The
first of these is "The Vision of Parnassus. By Andrew Mucklegrin,"
which was clearly written after the manner of *Don Juan* and "The
Vision of Judgment"; of this, the first sixteen stanzas, detailing
the background for the "Vision," appear here (*The London Liberal*,
pp. 24-28), with the parodist's several footnotes. The second
selection, "Invitation from a Late Bard to a Cockney Poet" (*Ibid.*,
61-62), a general parody of what seemed to be Shelley's method,
is perhaps less successful. And finally, the third, "Letters from
Abroad. Letter I.—Ostend" (*Ibid.*, 140-44), modelled upon Hunt's
more easily imitated piece in the first *Liberal*, is quoted in full.

A. FROM "THE VISION OF PARNASSUS. BY ANDREW MUCKLEGRIN."

I.

'Twas six o'clock; just one hour after dinner—
  I sometimes dine at five, sometimes at one;
For poets, if they would not wax still thinner,
  Must catch that passing blessing when they can—
My host upheld all sects that save a sinner—
  Jew, Papist, Quaker, Unitarian:
So *liberal* was his mind towards faith or schism
He'd sometimes slip down even to Atheism.

---

[1] Courtesy of the Bodleian Library, Oxford University, which provided a
microfilm of this extremely rare periodical.

II.

'Twas six o'clock—I being a poor relation
   Scarce dipp'd half through one glass of rum and water,
While he of *long-cork* took a free libation,
   Praising its flavour, telling where 'twas bought, or
Shewing the bottle's octoan crustation,
   Or snuffing the sweet scent with which 'twas fraught, or
Cursing the wine-duties, one and all
Which "he contended were *not liberal!*"

III.

For he loved liberty in all those things
   Which hinged upon the enjoyment of his senses;
Conscience and claret free!—these were the springs
   That would run wildly over consequences
In spite of morals, church, excise, or kings!—
   But when my *empty* grog-glass caught his glances,
He said that though *wine* was so good, he meant
To hold that *rum-grog was most excellent.*

IV.

I took the hint and fill'd again of course,
   Which he observing handed me a book:
"Read that," said he, " 'tis not a tittle worse
   Than what you're mixing." So I took,
And found it was "THE LIBERAL, PROSE AND VERSE."
   That book of knowledge from the south-wind shook!
Truly, thought I, my grog and this share merit;
Acid, much water, and but *little spirit.*

V.

"Read out," said he, "and let us hear the wits:
   "What say they after six months' promises?
"Deep dogs—keen cutting—home-spun cogent hits:
   "They'll wade I'll warrant—ay, up to the knees
"In blood-red ink! come, ease them of their fits.
   "I love such right, home radicals as these:
"They'll do more for *the Liberals* in a page,
"Than Carlile or his sister in an age.

VI.

"Begin 'the Vision'—that's their fighting bear—
   "And skip the preface; for it is a piece
"Cut from the warehouse of *The Examiner*—
   "Of which I'm just as tired as 'f Derby cheese—

"I'll have some *Parmesan*—Read there, Sir, there;
    " '*St. Peter sat*'—and then about '*the keys*'
"O! how I like to hit those gospel-givers,
"They're such rank enemies to us free livers."

VII.

Well, (as I got my dinner,) I read on,
    In hopes by labour to wipe out the debt;
At every verse my *liberal* friend, John,
    With claret gave his lips a wholesome whet,
Commenting ev'ry pretty point upon—
    Which came as often as he fancied fit—
And faith, he judged as well as many others,
Not even excepting Leigh Hunt's best of brothers!

VIII.

The mocking of the saint; the ribaldry
    Spew'd out upon the attributes of Heav'n;
The insults flung up at the Deity;
    By a *   *   *   *   *   *
✦   ✦   ✦   ✦   ✦   ✦   ✦

    The sneer at pure religion weakly given;—
All seem'd my listening host to tickle well,
And once he roar'd, "I'm damn'd if there's a hell."

IX.

"You're right," said I; at which he shook my hand
    And forced a glass of claret down my throat;
By which I judge he did not understand
    The real drift of my reply:—no doubt.
Yet, if my tell-tale countenance he'd scann'd,
    'Twould not have ta'en him long t' have found it out;
But he believed it a full confirmation,
A certain salvo from deserved damnation.

X.

But what, of all the verses, pleased him best,
    And made him cock more keen his curious ears,
Were those which trail their snake-slime o'er the rest
    Of our last, good, old, gray-hair'd King; the sneers
Flung o'er his hearse; his clay, thrice blest,
·   In cynic spite call'd "*rottenness of years;*"
His sacred pall "*the mockery of hell!*"
These made his *liberal* nostrils snort and swell.

XI.

I read on still (in memory of my dinners)
    Until I came to Southey*—here he gaped
And said 'twas nought but scratching 'twixt two sinners
    Of rhyme and rattle—envy badly kept
Scarce worthy weavers, much less distich-spinners.
    And wish'd it from the worthy *"Liberal"* swept.
In short, my host was disappointed fairly
To find the blasphemy had done so early.

* This alludes to the personal attack on Mr. Southey, which concludes the *"liberal" Vision of Judgment.*

XII.

"Read the next article†—said he—"no, hang it, skip,
    " 'Tis but another squabble in the trade:
"I hate to see two good men use the lip
    "When they could settle by the honest blade;
"Nor did I quite expect such womanship,
    "Such snivelling, scolding, Billingsgate tirade
"From one who could his mighty dart let fly
"At God Almighty *so courageously.*

† Entitled, "A Letter to My Grandmother's Review."

XIII.

"Skip, and let's have these pretty Florence-lovers,
    "Quite *Huntish* that, and I'll be sworn right good."
So on I labour'd, but these turtle-dovers
    Turn'd out, my host thought, not quite what they should,
A *Romeo and Juliet* in new covers,
    "And not a word," said he, " 'gainst saint or God!
"A Bow-street office business!—curse the bore!—
"O———a———o———um———:" and then began to snore.

XIV.

I still continued, but soon found the effects
    Of this narcotic prosing "from the South"
(Beg pardon, Mr. Hunt—with due respect
    I cannot help being plain—'tis downright froth.)
I would have snored, too, but for a laugh that check'd
    My leaden'd eyelids and outstretch'd my mouth,
'Twas when I read that fine parenthesis
    About‡ *Italian names, neat writing*—and all this.

‡ "How delicious it is to repeat those beautiful Italian names, when they are not merely names. We find ourselves almost unconsciously writing them in a better hand than the rest; not merely for the sake of the printer, but for the pleasure of lingering upon the sound! ! !"

XV.

Association in the mind works wonders.
　　Charles the Twelfth—who many think was mad—
Would turn his brows to clouds, his words to thunders,
　　When of that warlike chief he heard or read,
The German general Hoggeropp Foggerdunders,
　　The early favourite of his bomb-shell head.
Then why not Mr. Hunt, whose youthful glories
Were pretty penny-book Italian stories!

XVI.

My laugh was wash'd away by half a page;
　　Line came with line in ponderous succession,
Just as the night-hours follow a dull stage
　　Through heavy roads; hacks out of all condition.
But sleep dropp'd in, my labours to assuage,
　　And off I snored.—So here begins my vision,
Which, after sixteen stanzas, ought to be
A thing well worthy curiosity.

B. "INVITATION FROM A LATE BARD TO A COCKNEY POET."

　　　　Come over the sea,
　　　　Cockney, to me,
　　Mine thy cabbin, costs, and clothes,
　　　　Through the Strand, if you stroll,
　　　　A sly touch on the pole
　　Sends you where no one with good will goes.
In Fleet-street are sharks, if you quickly depart not,
There's a jail where thou art, here's no jail where thou art not.

　　　　Then come o'er the sea,
　　　　Cockney to me,
　　Come whenever a fair wind blows;
　　　　Through the Strand if you stroll,
　　　　A sly touch on the pole,
　　Sends you where no one with good will goes.

　　　　Here in Italy,
　　　　Your body is free,
　　Britain hath bars and bolts alone,
　　　　There we were nought,
　　　　Here our books will be bought,
　　Byron and blasphemy, all our own,
With no Bridge-street to blast, and no Blackwood to blow us,
With no God above, and no devil below us.

> Then come o'er the sea,
> Cockney, to me,
> Come, whenever a fair wind blows;
> Through the Strand if you stroll
> A sly touch on the pole,
> Sends you where no one with good will goes.

C. "LETTERS FROM ABROAD. LETTER I.—OSTEND."

My dear Miss Mortimer,

At last all my day-dreams are realized: I am on the Continent, surrounded with all those delightful associations amongst which fancy has been accustomed to dwell since my early youth; and all is now reality!—all those scenes on which you and I have hung with so much rapture when we used to sit up of a winter's night in Tooley-street, and steal up a piece of candle from the shop to finish a favourite novel of Newman's. My dear Miss Mortimer, I now address you from Flanders.

Ostend is a town upon the sea-shore, surrounded with ramparts and wind-mills, between which are seen, peeping up, the tops of the houses gleaming brownly in the sun. On entering the main street, which is called in French *Rue de l'Eglise,* and in Flemish *Kirk Straad,* the eye is saluted with a number of brick and stone houses on each side, the bottoms of which are shops, that expose for sale, cheese, butter, vegetables, and a vast deal of herrings, the smell of which at first reminds one of the Borough; but that idea is lost in the certainty that every step one takes is upon the actual stones of the Continent! nay, with me, the herring-odour produced a pleasing sensation, which served rather to increase the enjoyment I felt in thus, for the first time, standing upon a foreign earth, by reminding me of that period when the city of London seemed my prison-house, and when I vainly hoped to quit it for more genial climes;—by the force of contrast, I say, the smell of herrings by association made reality more real, and the pleasures of my imagination still more pleasant.

The first novelty that strikes you, after your dreams and matter-of-fact have recovered from the surprise of their introduction to one and other, is the similarity which the houses, in general, have to those you have been accustomed to look upon in England; romance refuses to look romantic, and insists upon retaining its familiar aspect. The consequence is a mixed feeling of admiration and disappointment, for we miss the *Gothic.* The houses seem as if they ought to have sympathized more with humanity, and are as cold and as hard-hearted as their materials.[2]

---

[2] In this and the following notes, I shall quote passages from Leigh Hunt's contributions to the first number of *The Liberal,* which were clearly the object of this parodist in *The London Liberal.* In the passage above, he was recalling some remarks in "Letters from Abroad. Letter I.—Pisa": "The first novelty that strikes you, after your dreams and matter-of-fact have recovered from the surprise of

But you soon find that Flanders is not England; and you are delightfully reminded by every other object that you are *absolutely abroad*. The names of the streets are painted on the corners in French; but the show-boards of the tradespeople are in Flemish or Dutch, which, I cannot help thinking, gives a more *foreign* air to the place than if they were in French,—so novel, and yet so forcibly characteristic of the olden time.

This advertisement, "*Ici on loge au pied et à cheval*," although quite French has not that degree of *dreaminess* about it (as Mr. Hunt says in his Pisan letter) that the following possesses "*Here men drinkin an Slaupin mit brood booter en cas te koop.*"

O, my dear friend, such little casual gleam upon the mirror of our understanding, makes us look round with an intensity of sensation truly our own, throws a life-light upon our early youth, and an odour about our inclinations, that bind us to the wings of sentiment; and the duskiness of hours gone by, gives us all we hoped to meet in the daydreams of fancy, and fixes us for a moment indelibly on the passage of anticipation!

The men here are like those of London, of various sizes—some tall and skinny—some short and squabby—some ill-shaped, and some extremely well-made. The women not much differing from our own, except in their costume, which is, in general, a small cottage-straw-bonnet, a monstrous great brown mantle, long dangling ear-rings, and wooden shoes. There is a prettiness about them not disagreeable, and they walk not unlike the London milk-carriers with short hasty steps. There are cocks and hens here; and the eggs are nearly the same shape and as big as those of London,—only a little sweeter. The little boys whistle as they go along;[3] you cannot walk a dozen yards without meeting a group of these chubby-faced urchins ready to answer your questions in *pure Flemish*![4] I have visited the Stadt-house, the brickery of which, though not very ancient, is not wholly without its interest, as it is at this moment the seat of the police, and has been the theatre of ecclesiastical devotions during the stay of the English army at this town. The day before yesterday I went up on the high part of the ramparts to take a view of the Continent. O Miss Mortimer, what a day that was compared with those that followed it! I had Captain DeMontford, who came over in the packet with me, arm in arm—he looking so romantic—

---

their introduction to one another, is the singular fairness and new look of houses that have been standing hundreds of years. This is owing to the Italian atmosphere. Antiquity every where refuses to look ancient; it insists upon retaining its youthfulness of aspect. The consequence at first is a mixed feeling of admiration and disappointment; for we miss the venerable. The houses seem as if they ought to have sympathized more with humanity, and were as cold and as hard-hearted as their materials" (*The Liberal*, I, 100).

[3] "Boys go about of an evening, and parties sit at their doors, singing popular airs" ("Letters from Abroad," *Ibid.*, I, 119).

[4] "Let the reader add to this scene a few boys playing about, all ready to answer your questions in pure Tuscan" ("Letters from Abroad," *Ibid.*, I, 105-6).

the time—the place—the thought—I must plunge again into my writing that I may try to forget it.[5]

Ostend has been the scene of all the pomp and circumstance of military glory, immediately preceding and subsequent to the memorable battle of Waterloo. The French voltigeurs (as the chamber-maid of our hotel informs me), were quartered here. Even in my bed-room at this moment I see before me scratched legibly on the wall, the names of several of the officers who occupied this very spot:—*"Henri de Fouchard,"*—*"Etienne Fouchong,"*—*"Pierre De Rolles,"*—and *"Gregorie Slaughenhausen."*—How delicious it is to repeat these beautiful *foreign* names when they are not merely names, and when one is *absolutely abroad*. I find myself almost unconsciously writing them in a better hand than the rest; not merely for your sake, my dear friend, but for the pleasure of lingering upon the sound.[6] One feels in these marks of what has been the essences of agreeable confusion, a consolation of saintlike sound moving amidst the streams of conception and the conglomeration of fancy. The characters appear alive—they breathe—I gaze at them with wonder. At first they look like actors in the same piece; but I *dream* and am reconciled.[7] It is curious to feel oneself sitting quietly in one of the old Flemish inns, and think of all the interests and passions that have agitated the hearts of its visitors; all the revels and quarrels that have echoed along its walls; all the heads that have looked out of its windows; all the feet that have walked in at its doors. Along the floor how many waltzes have been danced! How many pretty girls have blest their lovers! How much blood perhaps been shed! The ground-floors of many of the houses in Ostend, as in other Flemish towns, have iron bars at the windows and bolts upon their doors, evidently for security. The look is at first gloomy and *prison*-like; but, as Mr. Hunt says—*"you get used to it."*[8]

---

[5] "On the Sunday following however I went to see it, and the majestic spot in which it stands, with Mr. Shelley. Good God! what a day that was, compared with all that have followed it! I had my friend with me, arm-in-arm, after a separation of years: he was looking better than I had ever seen him—we talked of a thousand things—we anticipated a thousand pleasures———I must plunge again into my writing, that I may try to forget it" ("Letters from Abroad," *Ibid.*, I, 103).

[6] "How delicious it is to repeat these beautiful Italian names, when they are not merely names. We find ourselves almost unconsciously writing them in a better hand than the rest; not merely for the sake of the printer, but for the pleasure of lingering upon the sound" ("The Florentine Lovers," *Ibid.*, I, 53).

[7] "There is a painting for instance devoted to the celebrated anchorites or hermits of the desert. They are represented according to their several legends—reading, dying, undergoing temptations, assisted by lions, &c. At first they all look like fantastic actors in the same piece; but you dream, and are reconciled" ("Letters from Abroad," *Ibid.*, I, 113-14).

[8] "It is curious to feel oneself sitting quietly in one of the old Italian houses, and think of all the interests and passions that have agitated the hearts of so many generations of its tenants; all the revels and the quarrels that have echoed along its walls; all the guitars that have tinkled under its windows; all the scuffles that

There is an old Roman Catholic church, in which are the aisles furnished with chairs and pictures, an altar decorated with saints and wax candles, a deep loud organ and a cloaked crowd of devotionists; here I have loitered in delightful revery and enthusiastic fancy, till I believed I trod upon the chapel floor of *"Lewis's Ambrosio,"* or beneath the vaulted roof of *"the Mysteries of Udolpho."* Tender and noble Mrs. Radcliffe, be thou blessed beyond the happiness of thine own heaven! Regina Maria Roche, be thou a name to me hereafter of kindred brevity, solidity, and stableness with that of thy follower, Anne of Swansea!

About a mile from Ostend, upon the banks of the canal, is a village called *Sass*, which is the holyday resort of all classes. Here are to be seen the original of the immortal Teniers,—the broad-faced peasant, with brown and ill-made small clothes, thick horse-skin boots, and hat of flexibility, dancing to the rustic measures of a cracked and crazy violin, while the gazing groups around make his exertions go down with draughts of Dutch white beer, and shreds of dried fish. Various and incongruous are the figures which here present themselves to the eye, they are like a succession of quaint dreams of humanity upon the twilight of creation. The other day I walked out *upon the Continent*, and in my way stepped into a farm-yard, where reposing, lay a big dog not unlike our mastiff.—The animal seemed to welcome me, and instead of a surly English snarl, I was greeted by a true Flanders wag of the tail. The *Bos* invited me in *pure Flemish*, to go in; I accepted his invitation. There sat the *Vrow* and her family, consisting of nine children, boys and girls; all habited like old men and women. Every utensil of this apartment put me forcibly in mind of the old Dutch school of rustic painting—the same clumsiness of costume—the same rudeness of arrangement—the same mixture of the natural with the grotesque—the same fine old *dreamy* character, which reminds us of what we have *slept* upon in the visions of our youth—a glow of intellectual and sympathetic reasoning with humanity— a power of dipping beneath the surface of effervescence, and establishing the mind's tuition in its birth, upon the ideal wonders of eternity—a glory and concatenation of superlative and innocent recollections, by which we melt in the beauteous mists of obscure and tender affectation.

Ostend is a famous fishy, wooden-shoe town. It looks like the residence of the old Dutch peasants, and one feels as if one ought to "walk clogged." It possesses the *"groot kirk,"* rich above earthly treasures; its dykes are the dykes of Flemish duck-meat, and furnished Clobberstock with his taste for

---

have disputed its doors. Along the great halls, how many feet have hurried in alarm! how many stately beauties have drawn their quiet trains! how many huge torches have ushered magnificence up the staircases! how much blood perhaps been shed! The ground-floors of all the great houses in Pisa, as in other Italian cities, have iron bars at the windows, evidently for security in time of trouble. The look is at first very gloomy and prison-like, but you get used to it" ("Letters from Abroad," *Ibid.*, I, 101).

vegetables; here was his mind born, *and another great impulse given to the progress of philosophy and liberal opinion!!!*[9] O my dear friend, only think of MY BEING ABROAD!!!

Most truly yours and for ever,
ETHELINDA WIGGIN.

---

[9] "Pisa is a tranquil, an imposing, and even now a beautiful and stately city. It looks like the residence of an university: many parts of it seem made up of colleges; and we feel as if we ought to 'walk gowned.' It possesses the Campo Santo, rich above earthly treasure; its river is the river of Tuscan poetry, and furnished Michael Angelo with the subject of his cartoon; and it disputes with Florence the birth of Galileo. Here at all events he studied and he taught: here his mind was born, and another great impulse given to the progress of philosophy and Liberal Opinion" ("Letters from Abroad," *Ibid.*, I, 120).

III

The Individual Contributions
to *The Liberal*

In the following tables, I have attempted to reveal the relative quantity of material contributed to *The Liberal*, first in articles, then in pages. I have considered as a full page any part of a page on which appears the work of one writer if the remainder of the page is blank; otherwise, I have treated it only as one-half of a page. Regarding the first number of *The Liberal*, I have not included Leigh Hunt's introduction to Shelley's translation as a separate article, but I have counted the two pages involved, and I have not included Byron's Preface to "The Vision of Judgment," which appeared only in the second edition. In the fourth number, twenty-five pages of Pulci's original text were printed, which deceivingly increase Byron's total; Hazlitt's "Pulpit Oratory" and "Mr. Irving, the Quack Preacher" are taken as one article.

	No. I	No. II	No. III	No. IV	TOTAL
NUMBER OF ARTICLES					
Leigh Hunt	8	8	9	9	34
Byron	3	4	1	1	9
Shelley	1	1	1	—	3
Mary Shelley	—	1	1	1	3
Hazlitt	—	2	1	2	5
Hogg	—	1	1	—	2
Brown	—	1	1	1	3
Horace Smith	—	—	1	—	1

	No. I	No. II	No. III	No. IV	Total
NUMBER OF PAGES					
Leigh Hunt	102	83	77	59	321
Byron	47	43	21	57	168
Shelley	15	1	1	—	17
Mary Shelley	—	37	17	17	71
Hazlitt	—	28	24	35	87
Hogg	—	20	26	—	46
Brown	—	19	11	11	41
Horace Smith	—	—	14	—	14

IV

The Liberal and the Press

The following list includes reference to comments made in anticipation of the proposed periodical of Pisa, reviews of *The Liberal*, and remarks concerning the journal appearing in the press at the time that *The Liberal* ceased to be an active publication. It does not include reference to simple advertisements and to republication of articles originally printed in *The Liberal*. The page numbers given are those for entire reviews of *The Liberal* or, in the case of articles of more general concern, of specific references to *The Liberal*. Obviously, new items will come to light, but it is doubtful that they will significantly alter our impression of the reaction of the press to *The Liberal*.

The Albion, or British, Colonial, and Foreign Weekly Gazette.
    "The Liberal—Lord Byron," No. 27 (December 21, 1822), pp. 214-15.
The Bard.
    "Rejected Addresses . . . by L. B.," October 26, 1822, p. 11.
La Belle Assemblée, Being Bell's Court and Fashionable Magazine.
    "Lord Byron," N.S. XXVI (1822), 526-27.
    "Lord Byron," N.S. XXVIII (1823), 194.
Blackwood's Edinburgh Magazine.
    "Letter from London," XI (1822), 237.
    "London Chit-Chat," XI, 331.
    "Noctes Ambrosianæ. No. I," XI, 363-64.
    "Critique on Lord Byron," XI, 460.
    "Letter from Paddy," XI, 463.

"Cambridge Pamphlets," XI, 740-41.

"Noctes Ambrosianæ. No. VI," XII (1822), 695-709.

"Odoherty on Werner," XII, 710.

"On the Cockney School. No. VII. Hunt's Art of Love," XII, 775-81.

"Heaven and Earth, A Mystery," XIII (1823), 72-77.

"The Candid. No. I," XIII, 108-24.

"Matters of Fact," XIII, 207.

"The Candid. No. II," XIII, 263-75.

"On the Scotch Character—By a Flunky," XIII, 365-67.

"News from Paddy," XIII, 397-99.

"Noctes Ambrosianæ, No. VIII," XIII, 607.

"Letters of Timothy Tickler, Esq. No. VII. On the Last Number of the Quarterly Review," XIV (1823), 87.

"Letters of Timothy Tickler, Esq. No. VIII," XIV, 224 [printed "242"], 230.

"Noctes Ambrosianæ. No. XI," XIV, 243.

"Letters of Timothy Tickler, Esq. No. X," XIV, 314.

"The General Question. No. I," XIV, 332.

"Noctes Ambrosianæ. No. XII," XIV, 488.

The British Critic.

"The Island," XX (1823), 16-22.

"Don Juan. Cantos VI, VII, VIII," XX, 179.

"Don Juan. Cantos XII, XIII, XIV," XX, 663.

The British Luminary and Weekly Intelligencer.

"The Liberal," No. 212 (October 20, 1822), p. 754.

The British Review and London Critical Journal.

"Poems by Bernard Barton," XX (1822), 420-22.

The Council of Ten.

"On Liberality. 'The Liberal; Verse and Prose from the South.' Postscript to Lord Byron," II (1822), 149-78.

The Courier.

"The Liberal," No. 9,677 (October 26, 1822), pp. 2-3.

A Critique on "The Liberal." London: Printed for the Author by William Day, 1822.

The Eclectic Review.

"Moore's Loves of the Angels," N.S. XIX (1823), 216.

The Edinburgh Magazine, and Literary Miscellany.

"Oldmixon's Account of 'The Liberal,' " N.S. XI (1822), 561-73.

"Oldmixon on 'The Liberal. No. II,' " N.S. XII (1823), 9-16.

"Note on 'The Liberal.—No. III,' " N.S. XII, 614-16.

The Edinburgh Review.

"Moore's 'Loves of the Angels' and Byron's 'Heaven and Earth,' " XXXVIII (1823), 27-48.

The European Magazine and London Review: Illustrative of the Literature, History, Biography, Politics, Arts, Manners, and Amusements of the Age.

"Literary Intelligence," LXXXI (1822), 71.

The Examiner.

"Letters to the Readers of the Examiner. No. 1," No. 748 (May 26, 1822), pp. 329-30.

A major advertisement, No. 766 (September 29, 1822), p. 615.

Announcement of the name and contents of the first number of the new periodical, No. 767 (October 6, 1822), p. 640.

"*The Liberal: Verse and Prose from the South. To be continued occasionally. No. I*," No. 768 (October 13, 1822), pp. 648-52.

Concerning Byron's letter to Murray, No. 770 (October 27, 1822), p. 679.

"Odious Cant—George the Third and Lord Castlereagh," No. 771 (November 3, 1822), pp. 689-91.

"The Secret of Over-Acted Zeal," No. 771, p. 693.

"*The Liberal,*" No. 771, p. 697.

"Odious Cant—George the Third and Lord Castlereagh," No. 772 (November 10, 1822), pp. 705-7.

"Prosecution of The Liberal," No. 777 (December 15, 1822), pp. 789-90.

Report of the prohibition of *The Liberal* by the French government, No. 778 (December 22, 1822), p. 812.

"The Liberal. No. 11," No. 779 (December 29, 1822), pp. 818-22.

Further comment on the indictment, No. 779, p. 825.

Printing of the indictment, No. 780 (January 5, 1823), pp. 5-6.

Warning against a pirated edition of "The Vision of Judgment," No. 782 (January 19, 1823), p. 64.

"More Indictments," No. 798 (May 11, 1823), pp. 305-7.

"Newspaper Chat," No. 814 (August 31, 1823), p. 569.

The Gazette of Fashion, and Magazine of Literature, the Fine Arts, and Belles Lettres.

"Literary Notices," No. 5 (March 2, 1822), p. 83.

The Gentleman's Magazine.

"Percy Bysshe Shelley, Esq.," XCII, Part II (1822), 283.

"The *Liberal*. The New Periodical Work from Italy," XCII, Part II (1822), 348-51.

"Elegy on the Death of Percy Byssche [*sic*] Shelley. By Arthur Brooke," XCII, Part II (1822), 623.

"The *Liberal*, No. II," XCIII, Part I (1823), 158-59.

"The *London Liberal*," XCIII, Part I (1823), 159.

"The Liberal," XCIII, Part II (1823), 256.

The Imperial Magazine; or, Compendium of Religious, Moral and Philosophical Knowledge.

"Memoirs of the Living Poets of Great Britain (Byron)," IV (1822), 825.

"*The Liberal, Verse and Prose from the South,*" IV, 1139-42.

"Literary, Scientific, and Religious Gleanings," V (1823), 195.

John Bull.

Shelley's obituary, No. 87 (August 11, 1822), p. 693.

Review of the first *Liberal*, No. 98 (October 27, 1822), pp. 780-81.

"The Loves of the Angels," No. 109 (January 12, 1823), p. 14.

Review of the third *Liberal*, No. 125 (May 4, 1823), pp. 141-42.

Brief comment upon the fourth *Liberal*, No. 138 (August 3, 1823), p. 245.

"*Don Juan*. VI, VII, VIII," No. 142 (August 31, 1823), p. 280.

"The Cockney's Letter," No. 146 (September 28, 1823), p. 309.

The Literary Chronicle and Weekly Review.

"Biography," No. 169 (August 10, 1822), p. 504.

"*The Liberal. Verse and Prose from the South. Volume the First.*" No. 179 (October 19, 1822), pp. 655-58; No. 180 (October 26, 1822), pp. 675-77.

"*The Liberal. Verse and Prose from the South,*" No. 206 (April 26, 1823), pp. 257-59.

17

The Literary Examiner.

"*The Liberal, No. IV*," No. 4 (July 26, 1823), pp. 49-58.

The Literary Museum, or Records of Literature, Fine Arts, Science.

"The Liberal, No. I," No. 26 (October 19, 1822), p. 405; No. 27 (October 26, 1822), pp. 422-23.

"Lord Byron and The Liberal," No. 34 (December 14, 1822), p. 544.

"The Liberal, No. II," No. 37 (January 4, 1823), pp. 1-3.

"The Liberal, No. III," No. 53 (April 26, 1823), pp. 257-59.

"The Liberal, No. IV," No. 67 (August 2, 1823), pp. 486-88.

The Literary Register of the Fine Arts, Sciences, and Belles Lettres.

"*The Liberal: Verses [sic] and Prose from the South, To be continued occasionally.*—No. I," No. 16 (October 19, 1822), pp. 241-43; No. 17 (October 26, 1822), pp. 260-62.

"*The Liberal. Verse and Prose from the South, No. 11,*" No. 27 (January 4, 1823), pp. 5-6; No. 28 (January 11, 1823), pp. 22-23.

"*The Liberal. Verse and Prose from the South. Vol. II. No. III,*" No. 44 (May 3, 1823), pp. 273-75.

The Literary Speculum.

"The Liberal," II (1822), 422-32.

The London Liberal.

"Introduction," I (1823), 1-8.

"The Stars of Pisa," I, 9-23.

"The Vision of Parnassus. By Andrew Mucklegrin," I, 24-42.

"The Liberal 'Amenities' from the South," I, 43-60.

"Invitation from a Late Bard to a Cockney Poet," I, 61.

"Letters from Abroad. Letter I.—Ostend," I, 140-44.

The London Literary Gazette, and Journal of Belles Lettres, Arts, Science.

"The Liberal," No. 300 (October 19, 1822), pp. 655-58; No. 301 (October 26, 1822), pp. 678-79; No. 302 (November 2, 1822), pp. 693-95.

"The Liberal, No. II," No. 311 (January 4, 1823), pp. 2-5.

"The Liberal, No. III," No. 328 (May 3, 1823), p. 275.

The Monthly Censor.

"The Liberal or 'Verse and Prose from the South,' No. I and II," II (1823), 452-56.

The Monthly Magazine, and British Register.

    "Literary and Critical Proemium," LIV (1822-23), 452.

    "Literary and Philosophical Intelligence," LIV, 538.

    "The Loves of the Angels, a Poem; by Thomas Moore.— Heaven and Earth, a Mystery," LV (1823), 35-39.

The Morning Chronicle.

    Report of the move of Byron, the Hunts, and Mary Shelley to Genoa, October 14, 1822, p. 3.

    "Libel," October 25, 1822, p. 3.

    "Rhyme and Reason," October 26, 1822, p. 3.

    "Inuendos," October 29, 1822, p. 3.

    "The Liberal," January 2, 1822, p. 3.

The New European Magazine.

    "The Liberal. Verse and Prose from the South. To be continued occasionally. No. I," I (1822), 354-63.

The New Monthly Magazine and Universal Register.

    "Grimm's Ghost. Letter VII," IV ([*Original Papers*], 1822), 160-61.

    "Annus Mirabilis! or a Parthian Glance at 1822," VII ([*Original Papers*], 1823), 21, 24.

    "Heaven and Earth; A Mystery," VII, 353-58.

Paris Monthly Review of British and Continental Literature.

    "Epitaph for Robert Southey, Esq.," No. 12 (January 1823), p. 578.

St. James's Chronicle.

    "The Liberal. The New Periodical Work from Italy," No. 10,131 (October 12-15, 1822), p. 2.

    "The Liberal, Number II," No. 10,164 (December 31, 1822-January 2, 1823), p. 2.

The Times.

    "Lord Byron and Thomas Moore," No. 11,759 (January 3, 1823), p. 3.

The Windsor and Eton Express and General Advertiser.

    "Court, Fashionables, &c," January 12, 1822, p. 3.

    "Literary Notices," October 26, 1822, p. 3.

Bibliography

This list includes only those works which have made particular contributions. I have listed only by title those early nineteenth-century periodicals which carry various significant articles specified in Appendix IV.

Alfieri, Vittorio. *Le Opere*. 12 vols. Padua: Nicolo Zanon Bettoni, 1809-10.

————. *Opere Posthume*. 13 vols. London (no publisher listed), 1814.

Allibone, S. Austin. *A Critical Dictionary of English Literature and British and American Authors*. 3 vols. Philadelphia: J. B. Lippincott, 1898.

Andrews, Alexander. *The History of British Journalism, from the Foundation of the Newspaper Press in England, to the Repeal of the Stamp Act in 1855*. 2 vols. London: Bentley, 1859.

Anonymous. *The Illiberal! Verse and Prose from the North!!* London: T. Holt, n.d.

————. "The Law of Libel," *The Beacon*, No. 12 (March 24, 1821), p. 95.

————. *Life, Writings, Opinions and Times of the Right Hon. George Gordon Noel Byron, Lord Byron*. By an English Gentleman in the Greek Military Service. 3 vols. London: Matthew Iley, 1825.

————. "Lord Byron," *The Annual Biography and Obituary*, IX (1825), 254-327.

————. "Lord Byron and Some of His Contemporaries," *The Monthly Review*, VII (1828), 300-12.

The Atheneum; or, Spirit of the English Magazines.

The Athenians: Being Correspondence Between Thomas Jefferson Hogg and His Friends Thomas Love Peacock, Leigh Hunt, Percy Bysshe Shelley, and Others, ed. Walter Sidney Scott. London: Golden Cockerel Press, 1943.

Bancroft, George. "Letters and Diaries," ed. M. A. deWolfe Howe, *Scribner's Magazine*, XXXVIII (1905), 488-505.

Beavan, A. H. *James and Horatio Smith*. London: Hurst & Blackett, 1899.

Bebbington, W. G. "Charles Knight and Shelley," *Keats-Shelley Journal*, VI (1957), 75-85.

———. "The Most Remarkable Man of His Age: Byron in *The Windsor and Eton Express and General Advertiser*," *Keats-Shelley Memorial Bulletin*, VII (1956), 27-31.

Bell's Weekly Messenger.

Blessington, Marguerite, Countess of. *A Journal of Conversations with Lord Byron*. Boston: William Veazie, 1858.

Blunden, Edmund. *Leigh Hunt and His Circle: A Biography*. New York: Harper & Bros., 1930.

———. *Leigh Hunt's "Examiner" Examined, 1808-1825*. London: Cobden-Sanderson, 1928.

———. *Shelley: A Life Story*. New York: The Viking Press, 1947.

Bourne, Henry Richard Fox. *English Newspapers. Chapters in the History of Journalism*. 2 vols. London: Chatto & Windus, 1887.

Brewer, Luther A. *My Leigh Hunt Library Collected and Described*. 2 vols. Iowa City: Privately printed, 1932-38.

———. *Some Letters from My Leigh Hunt Portfolios*. Cedar Rapids, Iowa: Privately printed, 1929.

The British Review and London Critical Journal.

Brown, Charles. *Some Letters and Miscellanea*, ed. M. B. Forman. London: Oxford University Press, 1937.

Buffenoir, Hippolyte. *La Comtesse d'Houdetot, Une Amie de J.-J. Rousseau*. Paris: Calmann Lévy, 1901.

Byron, Lord. *Correspondence, Chiefly with Lady Melbourne, Mr. Hobhouse, the Hon. Douglas Kinnaird, and P. B. Shelley*, ed. John Murray. 2 vols. London: John Murray, 1922.

———. *Works: Poetry*, ed. E. H. Coleridge. 7 vols.; *Letters and Journals*, ed. R. E. Prothero. 6 vols. London: John Murray, 1898-1903.

Carlyle, Thomas. *The Love Letters of Thomas Carlyle and Jane Welsh*, ed. Alexander Carlyle. 2 vols. London: John Lane, 1908.

Casti, Giambatista. *Opere*. Brussels: Meline, 1838.

Chew, Samuel C. *Byron in England: His Fame and After-Fame.* London: John Murray, 1924.

Clarke, Charles and Mary Cowden, *Recollections of Writers.* New York: Scribner's, 1878.

Cline, C. L. *Byron, Shelley and Their Pisan Circle.* Cambridge, Massachusetts: Harvard University Press, 1952.

Clinton, George. *Memoirs of the Life and Writings of Lord Byron.* London: James Robins & Co., 1831.

[Cobbett, William] "To Lawyer Scarlett. On the Trial of Mr. John Hunt, for Printing and Publishing Lord Byron's Poem on King George the Third," *The Political Register,* XLIX, No. 4 (January 24, 1824), 192-237.

Cockburn, Lord [Henry]. *Life of Lord Jeffrey, with a Selection from His Correspondence.* 2 vols. Philadelphia: J. B. Lippincott & Co., 1856.

The Courier.

Dallas, R. C. *Recollections of the Life of Lord Byron, From the Year 1808 to the End of 1814.* London: Charles Knight, 1824.

The Dictionary of National Biography. 21 vols. London: Smith, Elder, & Co., 1917.

Dilke, Charles W. "The Liberal," *Notes and Queries,* Ser. 8, IV (1893), 10.

Doane, G. H. "Byron's Letter to the Editor of My Grandmother's Review (1819)," *Bibliographical Notes and Queries,* I (1935), 8.

Dobell, Bertram. "Shelleyana," *The Athenaeum,* No. 2,993 (March 7, 1885), p. 313.

Dowden, Edward. *The Life of Shelley.* 2 vols. London: Kegan Paul, Trench & Co., 1886.

Duncan, Robert W. "Byron and the London Literary Gazette," *Boston University Studies in English,* II (1956), 240-50.

Edgcumbe, Richard. *Byron: The Last Phase.* New York: Charles Scribner's Sons, 1909.

———. "Talks with Trelawny," *Living Age,* Ser. 5, LXX (1890), 475-82.

The Examiner.

Galt, John. *The Life of Lord Byron.* Philadelphia: E. Littell, 1830.

Gamba, Pietro. *A Narrative of Lord Byron's Last Journey to Greece.* London: John Murray, 1825.

Gates, Payson G. "A Leigh Hunt-Byron Letter," *Keats-Shelley Journal*, II (1953), 11-17.

———. "Leigh Hunt's Review of Shelley's *Posthumous Poems*," *The Papers of the Bibliographical Society of America*, XLII (1948), 1-40.

The Gentleman's Magazine.

George, M. Dorothy. *Catalogue of the Political and Personal Satires Preserved in the Department of Prints and Drawings in the British Museum, 1820-1827.* London: Printed by Order of the Trustees, 1952.

Gisborne, Maria. *Maria Gisborne and Edward E. Williams, Shelley's Friends: Their Journals and Letters*, ed. Frederick L. Jones. Norman, Oklahoma: University of Oklahoma Press, 1951.

[Gordon, Sir Cosmo] "The Life and Genius of Lord Byron," *The Pamphleteer*, XXIV (1824), 175-220.

Graham, Walter. *English Literary Periodicals.* New York: Thomas Nelson & Sons, 1930.

———. "Shelley's Debt to Leigh Hunt and the *Examiner*," *Publications of the Modern Language Association*, XL (1925), 185-92.

Grant, James. *The Newspaper Press: Its Origin—Progress—and Present Position.* 3 vols. London: Tinsley Bros., 1871.

Grieg, James A. *Francis Jeffrey of the Edinburgh Review.* Edinburgh: Oliver & Boyd, 1948.

Grylls, Rosalie Glynn. *Trelawny.* London: Constable, 1950.

Guiccioli, Teresa. *My Recollections of Lord Byron.* New York: Harper & Bros., 1869.

Haydon, Benjamin Robert. *Correspondence and Table Talk*, ed. Frederick Wordsworth Haydon. 2 vols. London: Chatto & Windus, 1876.

Hazlitt, W. Carew. *Four Generations of a Literary Family.* 2 vols. London: George Redway, 1897.

———. *The Hazlitts.* Edinburgh: Ballantyne, Hanson, & Co., 1911.

———. *Lamb and Hazlitt.* New York: Dodd, Mead & Co., 1899.

———. *Memoirs of William Hazlitt.* 2 vols. London: Richard Bentley, 1867.

Hazlitt, William. *The Collected Works*, ed. A. R. Waller and Arnold Glover. Introduction by W. E. Henley. 12 vols. London: J. M. Dent & Co., 1902-4.

——. *The Complete Works*, ed. P. P. Howe. 21 vols. London and Toronto: J. M. Dent & Sons, Ltd., 1930-34.

——. *Liber Amoris*, ed. Richard LeGallienne. London: Mathews & John Lane, 1893.

——. *Literary Remains*, ed. his Son. 2 vols. London: Saunders & Otley, 1836.

——. *The Round Table, Northcote's Conversations, Characteristics, and Miscellanea*, ed. W. Carew Hazlitt. London: G. Bell & Sons, 1903.

——. *Winterslow: Essays and Characters Written There*, ed. his Son. London: D. Bogue, 1850.

Herbelot de Molainville, Barthélemy d'. *La Bibliothèque Orientale*. 4 vols. The Hague: N. van Daalen, 1783.

Hildyard, M. Clive. *Lockhart's Literary Criticism*. Oxford: Basil Blackwell, 1931.

Hobhouse, John Cam. "Dallas's *Recollections* and Medwin's *Conversations*," *The Westminster Review*, V (1825), 3-35.

——. *Recollections of a Long Life*, ed. Lady Dorchester. 6 vols. London: John Murray, 1910-11.

Hook, Theodore. *The Life and Remains*, ed. Richard Henry Dalton Barham. 2 vols. London: Richard Bentley, 1849.

Hotson, Leslie. "Shelley's Lost Letters to Harriet," *Atlantic Monthly*, CXLV (1930), 166-77.

Howe, P. P. *The Life of William Hazlitt*. London: Hamish Hamilton, 1949.

Hunt, Leigh. *Autobiography*, ed. J. E. Morpurgo. London: Cresset Press, 1949.

——. *Correspondence*, ed. his Eldest Son. 2 vols. London: Smith, Elder & Co., 1862.

——. *Lord Byron and Some of His Contemporaries*. London: Henry Colburn, 1828.

——. "Lord Byron—Mr. Moore—and Mr. Leigh Hunt," *The Tatler*, No. 114 (January 14, 1831), p. 453.

——. *The Poetical Works*, ed. H. S. Milford. London: Oxford University Press, 1923.

——. *The Seer; or, Common-places Refreshed*. London: E. Moxon, 1840.

Hunt, Marianne. "Unpublished Diary," *Bulletin and Review of the Keats-Shelley Memorial Association*, II (1910), 69-77.

Hunt, Thornton. "A Man of Letters of the Last Generation," *Cornhill Magazine*, I (1860), 85-95.

————. "Shelley, By One Who Knew Him," *Atlantic Monthly*, XI (1863), 184-204.

Ireland, Alexander. *List of the Writings of William Hazlitt and Leigh Hunt*. London: J. R. Smith, 1868.

Irving, Edward. *For the Oracles of God. Four Orations for Judgment to Come*. Philadelphia: A. Sherman, 1824.

Jeaffreson, John Cordy. *The Real Lord Byron*. 2 vols. London: Hurst & Blackett, 1883.

John Bull.

Johnson, R. Brimley. *Shelley-Leigh Hunt: How Friendship Made History*. London: Ingpen & Grant, 1929.

Jones, Frederick L. "Mary Shelley to Maria Gisborne: New Letters, 1818-1822," *Studies in Philology*, LII (1955), 39-74.

————. "Shelley's Boat," *The Times Literary Supplement*, January 18, 1936, p. 55.

Kennedy, James. *Conversations on Religion with Lord Byron and Others*. Philadelphia: Carey & Lea, 1833.

Keynes, Geoffrey. *Bibliography of William Hazlitt*. New York: Nonesuch, 1931.

[Kilgour, Alexander] *Anecdotes of Lord Byron from Authentic Sources, with Remarks Illustrative of his Connection with the Principal Literary Characters of the Present Day*. London: Knight & Lacey, 1825.

Koszul, A. H. *La Jeunesse de Shelley*. Paris: Librairie Bloud & Cie., 1910.

Lamb, Charles. "Letter of Elia to Robert Southey, Esquire," *The London Magazine*, VIII (1823), 400-7.

Landré, Louis. *Leigh Hunt (1784-1859): Contribution à l'histoire du Romantisme anglais*. 2 vols. Paris: Societé d'Edition, 1935.

Lang, Andrew. *The Life and Letters of John Gibson Lockhart*. 2 vols. London: John C. Nimmo, 1897.

Lastri, Marco. *L'osservatore Fiorentino sugli edifizi della sua patria (per servire alla storia della medesima)*. 8 vols. Florence: Gaspero Ricci, 1821.

The Liberal: Verse and Prose from the South.

The Literary Examiner.

Lucas, E. V. *The Life of Charles Lamb.* 2 vols. London: Methuen, 1905.

Maclean, Catherine M. *Born Under Saturn: A Biography of William Hazlitt.* New York: Macmillan, 1944.

Marchand, Leslie A. *Byron: A Biography.* 3 vols. New York: Alfred A. Knopf, 1957.

―――. "Trelawny on the Death of Shelley," *Keats-Shelley Memorial Bulletin,* IV (1952), 9-34.

Marsh, George L. "Early Reviews of Shelley," *Modern Philology,* XXVII (1929), 73-95.

Marshall, Mrs. Julian. *The Life and Letters of Mary Wollstonecraft Shelley.* 2 vols. London: Richard Bentley & Son, 1889.

Marshall, William H. "The Misdating of a Letter: An Exoneration of Byron," *Notes and Queries,* N.S. IV (1957), 122-23.

Massingham, H. J. *The Friend of Shelley: A Memoir of Edward John Trelawny.* New York: D. Appleton & Co., 1930.

Mayer, S. R. Townshend. "The Liberal," *Notes and Queries,* Ser. 5, VII (1877), 388.

Mayne, Ethel Colburn. *Byron.* New York: Charles Scribner's Sons, 1924.

McCartney, Hunter Pell. "The Letters of Leigh Hunt in the Luther A. Brewer Collection: 1816-1825." Doctoral dissertation, University of Pennsylvania, 1958.

Medwin, Thomas. *Conversations of Lord Byron: Noted during a Residence with His Lordship at Pisa, in the Years 1821 and 1822.* London: Henry Colburn, second edition, 1824.

―――. *The Life of Percy Bysshe Shelley,* ed. H. B. Forman. London: Oxford University Press, 1913.

―――. *The Shelley Papers. Memoirs of Percy Bysshe Shelley.* London: Whittaker, Treacher & Co., 1833.

Miller, Barnette. *Leigh Hunt's Relations with Byron, Shelley and Keats.* New York: Columbia University Press, 1910.

Millingen, Julius. *Memoirs of the Affairs of Greece; with Various Anecdotes Relating to Lord Byron and an Account of His Last Illness and Death.* London: John Rodwell, 1831.

Moore, Thomas. *The Letters and Journals of Lord Byron, with Notices of His Life.* 2 vols. Philadelphia: Thomas Wardle, 1840.

———. *The Loves of the Angels.* London: Longman, Hurst, Rees, Orme & Brown, 1822.

———. *Memoirs, Journals, and Correspondence*, ed. Lord John Russell. 8 vols. London: Longman, Brown, Green, & Longmans, 1853-56.

The Morning Chronicle.

The Morning Herald.

The Morning Post.

Mott, Frank Luther. *A History of American Magazines, 1741-1850.* 3 vols. New York: D. Appleton Co., 1930.

Muir, H. Skey, Jr. "Byroniana," *Notes and Queries*, Ser. 6, IX (1884), 81-82.

The New Times.

Nicolson, Harold. *Byron: The Last Journey, April 1823—April 1824.* London: Constable & Co., 1948.

[Noble, James Ashcroft] "Leigh Hunt: His Life, Character, and Work," *The London Quarterly and Holburn Review*, N.S. VII (1887), 331-54.

———. "Leigh Hunt, Lord Byron, and 'The Liberal.' " Unpublished article, Manchester Public Libraries.

Norman, Sylva. *After Shelley: The Letters of Thomas Jefferson Hogg and Jane Williams.* London: Oxford University Press, 1934.

———. "Leigh Hunt, Moore, and Byron," *The Times Literary Supplement*, January 2, 1953, p. 16.

Oliphant, Margaret. *Annals of a Publishing House: William Blackwood and his Sons.* 2 vols. Edinburgh and London, 1897.

Origo, Iris. *The Last Attachment.* London: Jonathan Cape, Ltd., 1949.

Parry, William. *The Last Days of Lord Byron: with His Lordship's Opinions of Various Subjects, Particularly on the State and Prospects of Greece.* Philadelphia: H. C. Carey & I. Lea, and R. H. Small, 1825.

Patmore, P. G. *My Friends and Acquaintances.* 3 vols. London: Saunders & Otley, 1854.

Peacock, Thomas Love. *Letters to Edward Hookham and Percy B. Shelley, with Fragments of Unpublished Mss.*, ed. Richard Garnett. Boston: The Bibliophile Society, 1910.

————. *Works: The Halliford Edition*, ed. H. F. B. Brett-Smith and
C. E. Jones. 10 vols. London: Constable & Co., Ltd., 1924-34.

Peck, Walter E. *Shelley: His Life and Work*. 2 vols. London: Ernest
Benn, Ltd., 1927.

Pickering, Leslie P. *Lord Byron, Leigh Hunt and the "Liberal."* London:
Drane's Ltd., n.d.

Poliziano, Angelo Ambrogini. *Opere Volgari*. Florence: Sansoni,
1885.

Pratt, Willis. *Lord Byron and His Circle. A Calendar of Manuscripts in the
University of Texas Library*. Austin: University of Texas Press, 1947.

The Quarterly Review.

Redding, Cyrus. *Yesterday and Today*. 3 vols. London: T. Cautley
Newby, 1863.

The Republican.

Roberts, William. *Life, Letters and Opinions*, ed. Arthur Roberts.
London: Seeleys, 1850.

Robinson, Henry Crabb. *The Diary, Reminiscences, and Correspondences*,
ed. Thomas Sadler. 2 vols. Boston: Fields, Osgood & Co., 1869.

Rollins, Hyder E. *The Keats Circle: Letters and Papers, 1816-1878*.
2 vols. Cambridge, Massachusetts: Harvard University Press,
1948.

Ross, Janet. "Byron at Pisa," *The Nineteenth Century*, XXX (1891),
753-63.

Rossetti, William Michael. *Memoir of Shelley*. London: John Slark,
1886.

Ryan, M. J. "The Adventures of Lord Byron's Prefaces," *Bookman's
Journal*, XVI (1928), 419-30.

Scott, Winifred. *Jefferson Hogg*. London: Jonathan Cape, 1951.

Sharp, William. *The Life and Letters of Joseph Severn*. New York:
Charles Scribner's Sons, 1892.

Shelley, Lady Jane. *Shelley Memorials, from Authentic Sources*. London:
King, 1875.

Shelley, Mary. *Journal*, ed. Frederick L. Jones. Norman, Oklahoma:
University of Oklahoma Press, 1947.

————. *The Letters of Mary Wollstonecraft Shelley*, ed. Frederick L.
Jones, 2 vols. Norman, Oklahoma: University of Oklahoma
Press, 1944.

————. *Tales and Stories,* ed. Richard Garnett. London: W. Paterson & Co., 1891.

Shelley, Percy Bysshe. *The Complete Works,* ed. Roger Ingpen and Walter E. Peck. 10 vols. London: Ernest Benn, 1926-30.

————. *Essays, Letters from Abroad, Translations and Fragments,* ed. Mrs. Shelley. London: Edward Moxon, 1840.

————. *Poetical Works,* ed. Mrs. Shelley. 4 vols. London: Edward Moxon, 1839.

————. *Posthumous Poems,* ed. Mrs. Shelley. London: John Hunt, 1824.

————. *Relics,* ed. Richard Garnett. London: Edward Moxon, 1862.

————. *Shelley and Mary,* ed. Lady Jane Shelley. 3 vols. London: For private circulation only, 1882.

Smiles, Samuel. *A Publisher and his Friends. Memoir and Correspondence of the Late John Murray, with an Account of the Origin and Progress of the House.* 2 vols. London: John Murray, 1891.

Smith, Horatio. *Gaieties and Gravities: A Series of Essays, Comic Tales, and Fugitive Vagaries.* 2 vols. Philadelphia: Carey, Lea, 1825.

Southey, Robert. *Life and Correspondence,* ed. Charles Cuthbert Southey. 6 vols. London: Longman, Brown, Green & Longmans, 1850.

————. *Poetical Works.* 10 vols. Boston: James R. Osgood & Co., 1875.

————. *Selections from the Letters,* ed. John Wood Warter. 4 vols. London: Longman, Brown, Green, Longmans [& Roberts], 1856.

Stout, George Dumas. "Studies Toward a Biography of Leigh Hunt." Doctoral dissertation, Harvard, 1928.

Thackeray, William Makepeace. "Liberalism," *Cornhill Magazine,* V (1862), 70-83.

Tillett, Nettie S. " 'The Unholy Alliance of Pisa—' A Literary Episode," *The South Atlantic Quarterly,* XXVIII (1929), 27-44.

The Times.

Tinker, Chauncey B. " Shelley's Indian Serenade," *Yale University Library Gazette,* XXV (1950), 70-72.

Trelawny, Edward John. *Letters,* ed. H. Buxton Forman. New York: Oxford University Press, 1910.

————. *Recollections of the Last Days of Shelley and Byron*, ed. Edward Dowden. London: Humphrey Milford, 1923.

————. *Records of Shelley, Byron, and the Author.* London: Basil Montagu Pickering, 1878.

Vail, Curtis C. D. "Shelley's Translations from Goethe's *Faust*," *Symposium*, III (1949), 187-213.

Ward, W. S. "Lord Byron and 'My Grandmother's Review,' " *Modern Language Notes*, LXIV (1949), 25-29.

Warzée, André. *Essai historique et critique sur les Journaux belges. Journaux politiques.* Brussels: A. Van Dale, 1845.

[Watkins, John] *Memoirs, Historical and Critical, of the Life and Writings of the Right Honourable Lord Byron, with Anecdotes of Some of His Contemporaries.* London: Henry Colburn, 1822.

The Weekly Entertainer, and West of England Miscellany.

White, Newman Ivey. *Shelley.* 2 vols. London: Secker & Warburg, 1947.

————. *The Unextinguished Hearth: Shelley and His Contemporary Critics.* Durham, North Carolina: Duke University Press, 1938.

Wise, Thomas J. *The Ashley Catalogue.* 11 vols. London: For private circulation only, 1922-36.

————. *A Bibliography of the Writings in Verse and Prose of Lord Byron.* 2 vols. London: For private circulation only, 1932-33.

————. *A Shelley Library.* London: For private circulation only, 1924.

Wordsworth, William and Dorothy. *Letters: The Later Years*, ed. Ernest de Selincourt. 3 vols. Oxford: The Clarendon Press, 1939.

Index

Index

18